THE WEEKEND STARTS ON WEDNESDAY

THE WEEKEND

STARTS ON WEDNESDAY

True Stories of
Remarkable NASCAR Fans

By Andrew Giangola

First published in 2010 by MBI Publishing Company and Motorbooks, an imprint of MBI Publishing Company, 400 First Avenue North, Suite 300, Minneapolis, MN 55401 USA

Motorbooks titles are also available at discounts in bulk quantity for industrial or sales-promotional use. For details write to Special Sales Manager at MBI Publishing Company, 400 First Avenue North, Suite 300, Minneapolis, MN 55401 USA.

To find out more about our books, visit us online at www.motorbooks.com.

ISBN-13: 978-0-7603-3831-5

Library of Congress Cataloging-in-Publication Data

Giangola, Andrew.
  The weekend starts on Wednesday : true stories of remarkable NASCAR fans / Andrew Giangola.
    p. cm.
  ISBN 978-0-7603-3831-5 (hb w/ jkt)
  1. Stock car racing--United States. 2. Automobile racing fans--United States--Anecdotes. 3. NASCAR (Association). I. Title.
  GV1029.9.S74G515 2010
  796.72--dc22
                        2009037134

On the front cover: background by *Harry How/Getty Images*, main by *Rusty Jarrett* /Getty Images.

Back cover photos: left by *Rob Kinker/Carolyn Hastings*; center by *Mike Wright*; right *author's photo*

Editor: Chris Endres
Designer: Diana Boger
Jacket Designer: Simon Larkin

Printed in China

For anyone who's ever bought a ticket
to watch cars race around a lopsided circle.

CONTENTS

Foreword by Tony Stewart 9

Introduction: You Hungry? 11

PART I FANS FOR LIFE

A Moment in the Sun 18

The King and I 26

Decades at Darlington 36

PART II REMEMBERING DALE

The Lucky Penny Girl 42

A Purple Heart and a Titanium Leg 49

America's Anchor Finds His Slice of Heaven 56

PART III FLIRTING WITH FAME

There's Nothing Flat About Tire Man 64

Toasting a Hero 71

NASCAR's Candy Man 79

The Fathead Guy 87

Jeff Burton and the World's Fastest Grandmother 92

Friday Night Lights Lead into Saturday Night Racing 96

PART IV ALIGNED WITH THE STARS

Spencer Roy Sees the Other Side of Smoke 104

Ryan's Hope 109

A Bad Case of NASCAR Disease 115

Nursing Junior to a Championship 123

Paying It Forward 129

PART V STUPENDOUS FEATS OF OVER-THE-TOP FANDOM

The Summit of Fandom 136

Houston, We Have a Fan 143

Bob's Party Bus 148

Hearts Big and Brave 154

Always in Victory Lane...161

Moments Missed, Encased as Indelible Memories 164

The Big Apple's Biggest Fan 170

PART VI   FAMOUS FACES

Cookin' on the High Side with Mario Batali and Rachael Ray 176

Tom Cruise's *Days of Thunder*...183

No Fan Is Finer than Miss North Carolina.......................................192

Jim Cramer Is Mad About NASCAR...197

Walking to the Pacific, George Martin Sees America in NASCAR 204

Kevin Costner: Mixing Dreams with NASCAR Gasoline 209

A Black-and-White Sport Goes Technicolor.....................................214

PART VII   LADIES LOVING NASCAR

Good Vibrations 222

NASCAR is a Thing of Beauty in a Boise Salon................................227

Cold Steel, Cow Farts, and the Science of Speed 233

A NASCAR Alien in New York 240

PART VIII   CHASING A RACING DREAM

Brad Daugherty Measures His Own Success 248

This Girl Wants to Be Jeff Gordon in a Skirt 255

Gunning for the NASCAR Sprint Cup Series...

with a Little Help from His Friends.......................................261

Miss Sprint Cup 270

PART IX   I'M A FAN TOO

My Doctors Only Want to Talk NASCAR..278

Wardrobe Malfunctions 285

A Fact Check with Peter Jennings 290

Epilogue: A Matter of Life and Death 294

Afterword by Kyle Busch..296

Acknowledgments...299

Index..302

I went to Charlotte, North Carolina to a NASCAR race
and had more fun than is generally allowed unless you turn
Buddhist and get another lifetime.

—*P.J. O'Rourke*

FOREWORD

BY TONY STEWART

T his is a book for fans . . . about fans . . .
NASCAR fans!

The most loyal sports fans in America.

I don't know of anyone in the racing
industry who doesn't appreciate our fans.
They're tough. They're dedicated. They're
persevering. They're fun-loving, and they're
out-spoken. They call 'em like they see 'em.

Author photo

Sound familiar?

Imagine that—NASCAR fans in my own image. I'd put one of those
little smiley faces at the end of that last sentence if I knew where it was on
the keyboard.

When you consider the loyalty of NASCAR fans—the amount of
time and energy and money they invest in this sport—it's really amazing.
I don't know that this kind of loyalty exists in any other sport. I do know
without it, I couldn't have pursued a career that I absolutely love, and for
that I want to say thank you, to each and every NASCAR fan.

The late Bill France Jr. used to say, "NASCAR fans are the kind of
people you want with you in the foxhole. They're the kind of people who
win wars for America."

This book is about those people, everyday folks who have the same
kind of passion for racing I do. There are a few Tony Stewart fan stories
in this book, and I'm sincerely flattered to have remarkable people pulling
for me so hard. But there are stories about Dale Earnhardt fans, Jimmie
Johnson fans, Mark Martin fans, Jeff Gordon fans, Ryan Newman fans,
Matt Kenseth fans, Kasey Kahne fans, Carl Edwards fans. Kyle Busch
fans, too. There are stories about fans of all types . . . genuine, hard-working,
earnest people who like to watch us race. Thank goodness for that. This

sport would be nothing without the fan support.

I thank guys like Richard Petty and David Pearson and Bobby Allison every day for paving the way for us today. They spent a lot of time with fans. Those fans found out these guys were just ordinary folks like themselves.

Drivers really appreciated the fans in those days, and I really appreciate them today. Those loyal fans got me home many a night. They bought one of my t-shirts. And there were plenty of nights when I was running sprints and midgets when t-shirt money was all I made in a night. If you raced, you were gonna have bad nights and bad days. Same holds true today. But that's the thing about our fans. They stick with us no matter what happens.

My dad always told me when I was growing up, "Remember the people who helped you on your way up, you'll meet them again on your way down. Don't ever think you're better than anybody else. Treat folks the way you want to be treated."

Fans cheer for drivers and sometimes boo drivers, but that's okay. They have a passion for the sport no matter who their favorite driver is. They work hard all week and save their money to come see us race, whether it's NASCAR Sprint Cup Series or short-track racing at Eldora, and our sport wouldn't be where we are today without them.

When I mention loyalty and NASCAR fans, you're talking about another level of loyalty. Our fans take their loyalty to the store with them.

If they need office supplies, they're gonna buy them from Office Depot, which is one of my sponsors. Lord knows we all need deodorant, and a heck of a lot of NASCAR fans use Old Spice, my other main sponsor. Our fans buy products from the companies that support the sport, Sprint phones and Sunoco gasoline, for example. They choose Goodyear tires, eat M&Ms, and drink Coca-Cola. The list goes on and on.

This book gives some of those fans an opportunity to let other people know why they're hooked on NASCAR.

Chances are, they'll make fans out of you.

—Tony Stewart
Indianapolis, Indiana
July 2009

INTRODUCTION
YOU HUNGRY?

I sleep with the fans.

Not in the biblical sense, mind you.

At the race track, I spend nights in cozy wooden bunk beds surrounded by NASCAR fans snoring like foghorns, each well bundled in sturdy sleeping quarters bolted to the floors and walls of a retired yellow school bus. This time, it's the infield at Pocono Raceway, in the top bunk in the middle of a row of compact, efficiently constructed beds lining both sides of the converted camper. The outside of the bus is painted brown and black in ordinary house paint because someone found barely touched cans of Dutch Boy in the back of a garage, and ordinary latex exterior normally used on your three-bedroom colonial is a lot cheaper than acrylic enamel auto paint for a 1983 Ford. Inside, the twin rows of bunk beds separated by a narrow walk space make the long vehicle feel like a maternity ward for NASCAR fanatics. Except newborns don't snore like large opossums gargling Campbell's chunky soup. Though, we are undoubtedly cuter.

Black construction paper is taped over the windows to keep out the light. I roll over, and my arm yanks down the pseudo curtain. Solar energy deserves all the press it's getting, and you can see why this track is building, not too far from where I'm sweating, the world's largest solar farm powering a sports venue. The blinding 7 a.m. Pennsylvania sun magnified through a side bus window has the same effect as a young boy with a magnifying glass on a supply of ants. It fries your face and lights the inner eyelids rare-steak pink. I'd sure like to harness that sun and power an electric toothbrush right about now.

Last night, I'd met a group of tremendous fans—true salt of the earth . . . on the lip of a margarita glass. If people are the glue binding a sport, NASCAR fans are Krazy Glue, not the milky wait-all-day-for-it-to-dry stuff. NASCAR fans can create strong, lasting bonds, and they do it fast without a whiff of pretension or self-consciousness. Twelve hours ago, these guys and gals didn't know me from a hole in the wall, but we ate and drank and sang and played games involving Ping-Pong balls and bean-bags before calling it a night well past the American Medical Association's recommended bedtime. I'm now tired, still full, lubricated, unwashed, and smiling like a lottery-winning fool for getting to know the real, genuine fans, the ones market researchers call the sport's "core" followers.

In my NASCAR public relations job, I had been boasting to report-ers about these so-called "avid" fans without understanding who they are and why they're so crazy for this sport. Research points to tens of millions of devoted NASCAR fans. But using an abstract number to try to describe a major group of Americans who make stock car racing a significant part of their lives is like describing a rose by stating there are 270,000 species of flowers. Platitudes like "NASCAR is a lifestyle," "NASCAR is a community," or "NASCAR fans are the most loyal in sports" are all true but don't reveal much either. To understand NASCAR fans, you need to plumb their hearts and desires and experiences. You need to walk the track in their shoes, eat barbecue from their grills, and listen to their stories at their campfires. My bosses at NASCAR have granted me the assignment of finding and sharing those stories. So here I am looking for leads. And sleeping with the fans.

During waking hours, I've hiked through many an infield, carrying a sense of curiosity, a reporter's notebook, and a camera the size of a cigarette pack, which I'd given my wife as a birthday present after seeing the Ashton Kutcher ads then promptly filched from her so I could photograph fans. They like to be noticed, and the little lipstick-red point-and-shoot endorsed by Demi's boy toy might as well have been a crew from *ABC News* for the way it routinely drew hoots, hollers, and invitations to snap photos. But greater than any desire for fame, the fans want to share their stories. And they want to feed me. More than a few have said, "I don't care if I'm in any book. I got some good memories at this track, though. You hungry?"

In fact, that could have been this book's title: "You Hungry?" I've fielded that question over and over in the infield, the sprawling home of the friendliest and most generous fans in sports contributing to a multi-day feast of exuberance where everyone's welcome. Hiking through the smoky makeshift villages populating the track, hoping to stumble across the next incredible "you got to be kidding!" story, everybody shares their eats. A retired welder from the GM plant in Flint served me large cubes of venison. A Texas trucker offered baked alligator. I ate a hot dog cooked in an actual car engine—a Chevy 305 short-block bored from the inside and turned into a working grill. NASCAR fans make my four-foot-wide Italian grandmother look stingy with the food.

One fan, Joe Striley of Binghamton, New York, pointed me to his cooler for a helping of chicken. Under the cover was a massive collection of glazed breasts and thighs and wings jamming the box to the gills. If anyone from PETA had popped open that ice chest to be confronted by this chopped-up consortium of gooey bird, they would have had a cow, then been ashamed to have brought the cow into this world for all the suffering it would endure. I nearly swallowed a thumb polishing off a plump chicken breast slathered in Joe's homemade sauce. During the course of several NASCAR seasons wandering the campgrounds collecting fan stories, so many warm, generous, fascinating people opened their motor homes, hearts, and coolers to me.

Guys like Joe, a big Dale Sr. fan who spent $6,000 to feed other fans at Pocono simply because he loves the sport and its followers, could have had a chapter all to themselves. But this book doesn't purport to be an all-inclusive almanac of every single amazing fan. Oh, they're out there. Thousands like Joe could have been included in some way. In ways subtle or dramatic, every fan has a story. As sure as the sun comes up at a track the next race weekend and will shine hot on the face of a fan crashed out in a bus lacking real curtains, I have missed many fantastic tales. Hey, if you have a good one, give me a shout or go to our website. There's always the paperback.

I didn't use scientific procedure for selecting the NASCAR fans you're going to meet. They are simply the most noteworthy, interesting, and compelling people I've had the good fortune to come across in scouring tracks, reading newspapers and fan magazines, surfing the web, listening to satellite radio, and putting feelers out across the racing industry.

My criteria for consideration were broad, and I improvised as the project moved along. Mostly, I was looking for a special and distinctive devotion for NASCAR, allowing the stories to unfold from there. For some, like Mike Wright (page 26) and Barbie Robbins (page 123), NASCAR is an all-consuming 24/7 passion with favorite drivers never far from their thoughts. Others, such as Kevin Costner (page 209) and Tom Cruise (page 183), aren't fanatical enough to have Dale Jr. tattoos (although I didn't check) but nonetheless exhibit a keen, intelligent appreciation for the sport and have in their own ways contributed to its growth and success. Inspirational fans like Patrick Hickey (page 136) and Dr. Diandra Leslie-Pelecky (page 233) are working to better the lives of others, while true American heroes like Cpl. John Hyland (page 49), Sgt. Russ Friedman (page 71), and Lt. Col. Doug Hurley (page 143) represent the very best this country has to offer.

I suspected something before beginning to grill fans for their stories, and now I'm absolutely convinced of it: the ardent followers of NASCAR deserve their own book. Certainly, people all over the world are wildly devoted to their favorite games. Admittedly, I've never sung *futbol* songs for the home team in places like Argentina or Scotland. Nor have I sat through five full days of cricket in India. But if there were a showdown to crown the most enthusiastic and knowledgeable fans, my money is with NASCAR Nation. I'd take a random selection of people plucked from their campers at a NASCAR race against anyone from anywhere else.

By sharing the stories of a few extraordinary NASCAR fans, we celebrate all fans. It's like when one cousin gets into Harvard, the whole family feels a bit smarter. That's because NASCAR fans feel connected to one another, whether or not they've met. As Shawn Smith, a retired member of a secret elite division of the U.S. Air Force, told me, "NASCAR is the only place where I feel the same camaraderie as the military. The group of people at the track makes me proud. You can rely on them. They stick together. You don't see that in any other sport."

A word about *The Weekend Starts on Wednesday* title: Book browsers may be lulled into expecting a gonzo trip across the sweeping controlled mayhem of NASCAR event weekends. In reality, you're going to find a range of stories about people of all ages and walks of life. They take place in the fans' homes, their workplaces, and, yes, the infield, where events can turn colorfully weird near the stroke of midnight. (One fan in Michigan, Ron Murphy, walked over hot coals. "I'm a trained professional," he told me. "You learn where the ash is and not to get it between your toes.") Since I truly believe the most fervent sports fans on the planet make their temporary homes in the ramshackle villages coming to life in the campgrounds of NASCAR race tracks, the title pays homage to these folks, who arrive days before the event—coming 6, 8, 10, 12 times a year—and leave well after. The weekend does, in fact, start on Wednesday, although one fan, Norma Horner of Toledo, Ohio, pulled me aside, and lectured, "You've got it all wrong. The weekend starts on Monday!" (Norma then declared Kyle Busch must be banned from NASCAR because no one can be permitted to be cockier than her.) Norma and her husband, Jim, arrive at the track in Michigan on Monday, set up a bar in the infield, hold court for the better part of seven days, watch the race on Sunday, and leave the Monday after.

For Norma, Jim, and hundreds of thousands of others, NASCAR races represent the family vacation. The track is Disney World and the Grand Canyon and the Pyramids and the Roman Coliseum wrapped into one great trip where new friendships are made, old ones are rekindled, and a pretty good race breaks out. These hard-working families save up all year to get to the races. With a sizable commitment like that, is it any wonder fans make every effort to have the maximum amount of fun achievable without falling down?

When beginning this project two years ago, I had simplistic preconceptions of what to expect in the biggest NASCAR fans. I anticipated knee-slapping examples of over-the-top fan passion—a hearty all-star collection of face painters and tattooed exhibitionists. Make no mistake; fans go to astounding lengths to express their fandom: branding their bodies, going naked at the track save a Goodyear tire, adding rooms to their homes to hold all that NASCAR paraphernalia. But I also found something deeper, and, dare I say, full of meaning. It's silly to get metaphysical because, after all, this is a book about people who derive great joy in watching cars whiz around in circles. But hear me out an extra moment. After sleeping in their buses, watching races in their homes, spending countless hours on the phone, sitting in the grandstands, and walking campgrounds on the circuit, I'm convinced NASCAR's "core" fans are a special, different breed. At the risk of offering a laughable generalization, I want to perpetuate a new stereotype of NASCAR fans. They are, at their core, *very good people.* NASCAR fans are decent, generous, kind, charitable Americans. They like to have fun. And they want you to join the party.

The fans you are about to meet, and the drivers who inspire them, embody a fundamental goodness that makes NASCAR fans unique and NASCAR a sport worth following. But don't rely solely on my observations of a sport filled with big-hearted people. Go find out for yourself. Just buy a ticket to a race, walk the campgrounds, and count how many times you're asked, "You hungry?"

PART I
FANS FOR LIFE

The National Association for Stock Car Auto Racing (NASCAR) is downright youthful compared to its peers in other major professional sports. Major League Baseball started in 1871. The National Football League played its first game in 1920. Even the first professional hockey games trace back to the World War I era.

Comparatively, NASCAR is the new kid on the block, formed in 1948. The sport recently celebrated its 60th birthday, which means some fans who attended the first races (and took their vitamins) are still around. Over the decades, these fans have lived through triumph and tragedy while watching a small, dusty sport grow into a polished global enterprise. They carry colorful memories from a bygone era and today remain loyal to the sport to enjoy the experience that snared them in the first place—joining a roaring crowd of like-minded friends in the grandstands on a Sunday afternoon to watch "real" men in stock cars bumping and banging with no other intention than to finish first.

Let's meet a few of the "old guard" who have followed NASCAR their whole lives.

A Moment in the Sun

BEFORE THE 51ST RUNNING OF THE DAYTONA 500, 82-year-old Jack Hege was led into the "driver's meeting": a mandatory gathering of drivers and crew chiefs, attended by dignitaries as well. This fascinating pre-race meeting before NASCAR Sprint Cup Series races is unique in sports. Before battling on the track, the competitors file into a room and sit next to one another like fidgety students in the auditorium poised to bust out on the last day of school. Military heroes and the rich and famous attending the race are first recognized. The NASCAR race director then recites the rules of the road for the particular track—pit road RPMs, yellow line regulations, double-file restart pointers, and the like. The meeting that started off like the Academy Awards finishes like a local city council zoning meeting. Chapel follows.

The rookies generally sit in the front. One notable exception was when Pamela Anderson was Grand Marshal and strutted in wearing a white leather micro skirt that was a violation in the garage area, and probably the

---

Hege's ticket to the first Daytona 500, which ended in a three-way photo finish, presaging years of exciting races to come at the famed Daytona International Speedway. *NASCAR Media Group/Scott Hunter*

entire county. That was the first known driver's meeting in which veteran drivers Tony Stewart and Dale Earnhardt Jr. arrived 15 minutes early and were spotted in the front row.

Here at the Daytona 500 pre-race meeting, a wide-eyed Jack Hege was led to the V.I.P row of folding chairs facing the drivers and crew chiefs. He was next to 1983 NASCAR champion Bobby Allison. A few seats away, a grinning Tom Cruise caught the eye of his buddy Jeff Gordon and nodded in conspiratorial assent as if his *Days of Thunder* character Cole Trickle were getting ready to rumble this afternoon. Heisman Trophy winner Tim Tebow was to Jack's right. Singer Gavin DeGraw shook Jack's hand. For the son of a chicken farmer who worked 46 years in a textile factory, this sure was an unusual place to be on a Sunday morning.

While Jack Hege had attended every single Daytona 500—an astounding *51 in a row*—about this time, he'd usually be seated in the grandstands off Turn Four. Jack wasn't even sure a driver's meeting was held prior to the inaugural "Great American Race" on February 22, 1959. If there was, it surely lacked the pomp, circumstance, and boldface celebrity presence infusing with a palpable buzz the entire hangar. Yes, it's a good bet Cary Grant and Grace Kelly were not introduced alongside Lee Petty and Red Byron at that race in 1959.

Jack took his V.I.P seat after chatting with Raymond Parks, the first NASCAR championship owner from the sport's inaugural 1948 season. Parks sat stiff and upright in his seat, patiently listening and saying little. At 94 years old, his wife, Violet, now does most of the talking. Parks was the best-dressed man in the room, in a dapper suit and snazzy fedora, reminiscent of how a half-century ago the once-prominent Atlanta liquor-store merchant brought formality to a ragtag sport in financing many of its early drivers, including Byron, who raced in the 1940s and 1950s and won the first NASCAR championship. Jack Hege attended many of those races. Sixty years later, looking around the packed room, he thought, *I'm one of the few original fans left. Everyone else is gone.*

Sandwiched between big-name athletes and A-list celebrities who jetted in to Daytona, Hege's hangdog face alternated between wondrous disbelief about his role in this unexpected scene and the blunt satisfaction of being recognized for a well-deserved lifelong achievement. Adhering to Daytona 500 tradition, Mike Helton, president of NASCAR, began the meeting by announcing the dignitaries on hand.

After recognizing actor Gene Hackman, he thanked one of the sport's most loyal fans, Mr. Jack Hege, for attending every single season opener. The drivers and crew chiefs, NASCAR executives, captains of industry, Grammy-nominated singers, Heisman Trophy winners, and NFL coaches exploded in applause. Hege froze for an instant—as if the room's boisterous decibel surge had shorted his hearing aide—then smiled and nodded. Despite his outward embarrassment, Jack believed there was no more devoted NASCAR fan than he. Were any other men or women present at the birth of NASCAR still showing up and rooting for whoever was running up on the leader's tail? And now the competitors he admired were saluting one humble fan's contribution to the sport. Hearing the applause, Jack was an old man living a little boy's dream. Moments later, Tom Cruise would get an equally boisterous reception. But Jack Hege had arrived in NASCAR.

Walking slowly on sore knees toward his seat across from pit road, the same section he had occupied through the years ("because that's where the action is"), Jack recalled the no man's land infield at the Daytona International Speedway when it was new. There were no media centers, speedway clubs, or mini grocery stores. The grandstands were a mere 15 rows high. Even row three, where he sat in 1959, offered a clear view across the track. The infield was nothing but dirt and a large, rectangular lake running parallel to the long backstretch. The lake within the track was formed after millions of pounds of soil were dug out and piled high to create the track's formidable banking. The three-story banks tilted 31 degrees, as steep as dirt can be stacked before running downhill. Jack opened his eyes wide and said, "The cars running on them banks would shoot down the backstretch, come apart, and go crashing off the track. They had boats on standby in case a car went in that lake!"

Before starting his incredible Daytona 500 streak, Hege watched NASCAR races on nearby Daytona Beach. The cars ran south for two miles on A1A and took a sharp left turn through rutted sand onto the wide, level beach. They ran north on the smooth, hard-packed sand before taking another quick left onto paved A1A where the cars reached speeds of 150 miles per hour.

"There were no grandstands at the first beach races. You'd stand five or six deep and had to watch for cars coming and then run," Hege said. "There were no loudspeakers. We'd listen to the race on the radio."

Jack Hege with Juanita "Lightning" Epton, who in 1959 sold him a ticket to the Daytona 500. Hege has returned to the "Great American Race" every year since, getting his ticket from Lightning, who still works for the track. *NASCAR Media Group/Scott Hunter*

In 1958, Jack's friend Jimmy Meyers drove down to Daytona in his new two-door Chevy hardtop. Fans parked their cars on the beach, in the center of the racecourse, and watched from the grass-covered sand dunes. Before the race was over, Jimmy wanted to return to the motel. He pulled his car onto the course and gunned it ahead of the field. Instead of turning left onto A1A, Jimmy kept driving up the beach. Two drivers followed. They drove behind Jimmy for a half-mile before realizing they were off the course and turning back.

"NASCAR raced stock cars right from the dealer's lot. Jimmy had a white car, and there were no logos on the back anyway. It was easy to mistake him for a racer," Hege said.

Jack and friends from Lexington, North Carolina, would pile into a half dozen cars and drive down to Daytona Beach in one shot. Jack always had a Chevy—a '55 Bel Air that could do 110 miles per hour, a '58 Impala, a '62 Impala two-door hardtop.

Hege was in relatively good health, but he didn't want to drive to the 2009 Daytona 500, which would have been his 51st straight season opener. Though he had five race tickets, the streak appeared to be coming to an end, and it made the local newspaper. Greensboro resident Ron Collier was among dozens of fans who saw the story and contacted the paper, offering to accompany Hege. Collier met Hege at a Krispy Kreme donut shop. The two men hit it off, and Collier agreed to chauffer Jack to the race, bringing his son and friends, and keeping the streak alive.

When Jack was behind the wheel, the Daytona trip took nine hours. "You could do it in eight, but you'd get caught," he said. There was no interstate system; the caravan from Lexington took two-lane highways all the way to central Florida.

At those beach races, just about anyone who wanted to cheat Bill France and his merry band of speed demons out of eight bucks could duck onto the beach for free. Hege knew part of his ticket money went to the beloved daredevils fishtailing in front of the breaking surf. He always paid, but when his Chevy passed through the opening in a line of men Bill France paid to stand watch on the beach, two or three friends were hidden in the car's trunk. "Racing was a poor man's sport," Hege said. "Bootleggers got together and ran. People wanted to see it, but about a quarter of them didn't want to pay. And they didn't."

Up until the 1980s, Hege—and all fans—paid for the tickets with cash. NASCAR founder Bill France's wife, Annie B., who handled the track's financial matters, wouldn't accept credit. If a family couldn't pay for the tickets with cash or a money order, she reasoned, they couldn't afford it. Instead of a day at the races, the money was better meant for food and clothes. Everyone who knew Annie B. says the Speedway wouldn't exist if not for her dedication to the fans and diligently caring for the finances of a growing family business.

Each year, Hege's ticket order was taken by Juanita Epton, known to everyone as "Lightning." Juanita's husband gave her that nickname. He said he never knew when she'd strike. "Betty Jane France [wife of Bill France Jr., the second president of NASCAR] warned me if anyone came to the window and asked for 'Juanita,' be extra nice because they're from church," Lightning said. She knew Jack as "Thomas J. Hege," the name she'd enter into her ledger when he called, one of the track's first ticket renewals each year.

Jack, who never married, had extra money and time to follow NASCAR throughout the southeast. He was a regular at tracks like North Wilkesboro, Rockingham, and Martinsville. Once, on the way to the North Wilkesboro race, Jack discovered he was carrying the wrong envelope containing tickets to the Martinsville event. There was no time to turn around to retrieve the proper tickets. He proceeded ahead to the track. "The ticket manager saw I was in reservations and got me four new tickets," he said. "That's one of the reasons I enjoy going to the races. People appreciate you and treat you right."

Over the years, Hege has crossed paths with individuals of interest and note. He shook the hand of George Wallace when the Alabama governor attended the 1972 Daytona 500. Three months later, Wallace, who was running for president, was paralyzed in an assassination attempt. Hege had lunch at the Red Lobster with L. G. DeWitt, owner of Rockingham Raceway. The night that driver Tim Richmond moved his sponsorship from Folger's to Old Milwaukee, Hege found himself having a can of beer with the sensational driver with the perpetual tan outside the motel of the press conference. "Tim was a charger, the kind of driver I liked. He reminded me of Curtis Turner and Fireball Roberts. He had too many girlfriends and died of AIDS not too long after that."

With a career and life taken away too early, Richmond never won at Daytona. Even if he did, for Hege, it probably wouldn't have topped the first Daytona 500, still fresh in his mind for its three-way photo finish. "We came from the beach to this giant new track," he explained. "Everything was so new. And then after five hundred miles, there was nothing like that finish. It was so close, no one knew who won for three days. They had to look at photos to see it was Lee Petty."

Prior to each race, Jack spends a week in Daytona Beach, always at a beachfront motel. He drives up and down the coast highway, keeping an eye on the world going by his window, noting developments large and small, new palm trees planted, a burger joint he hadn't seen, motels built and destroyed. After taking all that time off, he had to work the Monday after the race. By parking a mile away from the track, he could avoid the worst traffic. He did the driving while friends slept hunched against the doors. Back in Lexington, he grabbed two hours of sleep and then went to work.

At his 51st consecutive Daytona 500, Jack Hege (center) met Raymond Parks, NASCAR's first
championship owner from the sport's inaugural 1948 season, and was joined by author Andrew
Giangola, who apparently missed the memo instructing PR guys to stand apart from the shot.
Courtesy Brad Ball

No one slept the night of the 2001 race. As Michael Waltrip surged to
the checkered flag, Hege watched a last-lap wreck putting Dale Earnhardt
Sr. into the wall. After the smoke cleared, Jack walked out to his car. On
the car radio, he heard the stunning announcement: "NASCAR has lost
Dale Earnhardt." Jack's favorite driver was gone. "We listened to the AM
radio all night long. They were going without commercials. Every station
had fans calling in, paying tribute. It was like the loss of a president."

Hege is reminded of "Senior" in today's hard chargers like Carl
Edwards, Kyle Busch, and Tony Stewart, all cut in the up-on-the-wheel,
no-holds-barred mold of the sport's earliest competitors. As Hege slowly
moved through the wall-to-wall crowds in Daytona's Fan Zone during
the 51st race, he said he missed the small-town feel of the sport and the
reckless flamboyance of yesteryear. He chuckled in the memory of driver
antics that were downright crazy. "Curtis Turner had engine trouble at
Rockingham, smoke pouring out. Did he slow down? No. He drove
the car until it exploded. He then got in his airplane and took off from

the speedway. He flew that plane under the power line going from the infield to the press box. The FAA grounded him for that."

Flamboyant wheelmen with a devil-may-care attitude weren't the only risk takers. In the early 1960s, a group from Wisconsin spent the night on Daytona Beach. Four fans slept on quilts on the sand next to their Oldsmobile convertible. When morning came, only three were left. The tide had carried one person away. "When I left the beach the night before, they had their guitars out. They were singing and dancing and drinking," Hege said.

The Daytona 500 is such a monumental event in sports, and I felt truly fortunate to spend its 51st edition with Jack Hege, the man who'd seen them all and this time was duly honored for his devotion. If Jack stays healthy, I hope he will continue to come back and share with others his personal slice of the colorful history of a sport that's come so far.

Before we said goodbye, I had one final question for Jack. I wanted to pinpoint the one particular thing that drew him to Daytona every February like a migratory bird.

Hege didn't pause at all. "Everyone wants to see and do something different, I reckon. And racing has been that. You want to see and do it all."

No one can say they've seen *everything*. But from experiencing first-hand the pioneering races on the beaches of Daytona, where fans popped from the trunks of cars, to today's events drawing 200,000 fans in person and a TV audience of millions more around the world, it's safe to say no NASCAR fan comes closer to seeing it all than Jack Hege. The smart money says, come mid-February next year, he'll be headed toward Daytona, like a migratory bird, pointed through a hard-wired instinct to where it feels right.

The King and I

MIKE WRIGHT CONSIDERS RICHARD PETTY his absolute hero in life. Aside from his dad, no one comes close. "What's great is, Richard is a hero you can literally touch," Wright said. He has asked for Petty's autograph more than one hundred times. The King has never once said, "no."

"If you want Richard Petty's autograph, and he is physically in the area, you *will* get it. I don't even ask for the autograph anymore. I'll shake his hand and take a photo. It's kind of neat that your hero knows who you are."

Wright has met the seven-time NASCAR champion countless times—at the track as a boy, then as a man who structured his trucking runs to include a pit stop at Petty's race shop in Randleman, North Carolina. Wright stopped off most Mondays to say hello and grab an autograph. "I have a gazillion of them, too many to even count, but the piece of paper is less important than a reason to ask the King about Sunday's race. Richard doesn't hear so well, and sometimes you're not having the same conversation. But that's okay. I mean, you're with the King! You're talking to history! You just learn to let him go on."

Mike Wright considers Richard Petty his absolute hero in life. He's never been denied Petty's autograph—even after asking more than 100 times. *Courtesy Mike Wright*

Before Wright was married to his wife, Karen, in 1997, he made sure to have a clear agreement on one crucial matter: he would continue to go the races—more than a dozen per year. "That was definite, everything else was negotiable," he explained.

Karen understood, and would be awed by, Mike's extraordinary passion. She became a NASCAR fan after discovering the cars weren't just numbers but driven by real personalities. She got in touch with the Petty shop and asked if the King could call his biggest fan, who was about to get married. Richard couldn't do that, she was told; he had difficulty hearing. The King couldn't speak with anyone on the phone, not even the president, if he were to call. Karen didn't tell Mike. Her fiancé would understand, and he probably knew about the King's aversion to phones, but what was the point of admitting to a failed plan?

When the Wrights checked into the hotel in Daytona Beach for their honeymoon, however, the phone in the room was blinking. An envelope was waiting at the reception desk. It was a beautiful wedding card, signed by none other than Richard Petty.

"Richard Petty is the nicest man I've ever met," Wright said. "He's been my hero since I [was] a little kid, and he's never let me down once. When I see Richard, it is literally like the rays of heaven shine down on him."

Wright was delighted to discover he and Petty share a passion for collecting Civil War memorabilia. Using a metal detector, he's found many Union and Confederate uniform medals, buttons, bullets, and shells from the battles fought in southern Virginia, most from the Siege of Petersburg, where his great-grandfather served in the Confederate army. He's presented medals dug up from that bloody 10-month battle to Petty, who displays them in the Richard Petty Museum.

Wright has made his own mini-museum—a display most noteworthy for well over 100 Petty autographs garnered over the years. It's clear none of the signatures was rushed. Each was carefully signed in elegant, looping, Palmer-method cursive script school kids were taught when penmanship counted before computers invaded the classroom. The autographs are showcased in three distinct styles. "There's 'Richard Petty #43' at the beginning of autograph sessions, then 'R. Petty #43,' and finally 'RP #43' when he gets really tired," Wright explained. "The King considers it his privilege to sign. He says every autograph is his way to say 'thank you' to each fan for letting him do what he loves."

The room has sheet metal from the famous No. 43 car, ticket stubs, programs, and other NASCAR memorabilia collected over the years, sometimes with the help of Wright's dad, who passed on a fascination with the Pettys. Jerry Wright was a fan of Lee Petty, who bought a street car for $900 and won the first Daytona 500 in 1959. At the same race two years later, Lee's car jumped the flimsy guardrail at Daytona and literally flew from the track. Lee survived the incredible crash, but he traded places with his son, who'd been serving on his dad's crew. Richard became the breadwinner for the family business as NASCAR's first "second generation" driver and the first to follow in a champion's footsteps. Winning 101 races and 2 championships in the 1960s, he'd also become the head of racing's royal family, known to all fans as simply, "The King."

When little Mike came along, father and son enthusiastically cheered on Richard Petty for the second phase of his 200 career wins. Before each race, Jerry would compile a ledger of statistics: how many laps the King had led at that track, prior races he'd won. On weekends, Mike would lie on his dad's bed for hours discussing the numbers.

Mike Wright attended his first NASCAR race in September 1968. Jerry had bought good seats, right near the flag stand at Richmond Fairgrounds Speedway. But Mike didn't see a thing from the wooden grandstands. He was in his mother's belly. "I was brought up in a racing family that's always been old school," Wright proudly stated.

On weekends, other families would go to the beach or the mountains. The Wrights, who lived about half an hour south of the track, went to the races, even with mom bountifully expectant.

The tracks, the cars, the people, the whole NASCAR fan experience was different in the late 1960s. The world beyond the sport's dusty race tracks had been bursting into color in music, fashion and especially on television. NASCAR was a few steps behind, still locked in the old black-and-white traditions. The sport was then called the NASCAR Grand National Series. (Winston would later come on the scene as NASCAR's title sponsor after cigarette ads were banned from television and racing provided the perfect marketing outlet.) If fans didn't watch a race live at the track, they likely didn't see the sport at all; a NASCAR season on network TV was still 30 years away. Many drivers got behind the wheel in short-sleeve dress shirts. "You took your shirt and a pair of britches, dumped it in starch, and that was supposed to make it fireproof," Richard Petty said. "You put on a seat belt and a helmet, but you didn't look at the safety of it." Metal guardrails like you'd see on the local highway rather than today's sturdy, high-tech, flexible barriers ringed the tracks, which didn't have today's varied concession stands and updated restroom facilities.

A tough expectant mom could get by, but the race track was no place for an infant. The Wrights waited until Mike was three years old to bring him to the races. The abundant sights and sounds infused the lad to the core. Since that day, Mike has been to more than 250 NASCAR races prior to celebrating his 40th birthday.

Wright's voice carried a pitch of wonder and delight when summoning the sights and sounds absorbed at the race track as a young boy, like hanging out on the backstretch of Richmond Fairgrounds Speedway, outside the ticket gates, where enterprising fans with little money and less fear would climb trees to watch the races. "I remember one gentleman had a cooler tied to a rope. He'd pull the rope, and up the tree came the cooler. He'd reach in for a beer, close the lid, and expertly lower the cooler halfway

Mike Wright at Richmond International Raceway for the race in September 1972. His hero Richard Petty bumped and banged with Bobby Allison before taking the checkered flag. *Courtesy Mike Wright*

to the ground. It hung there in the air, until the next refill. As a kid, I thought, man, that's ingenious."

Track president Paul Sawyer could have sent the police to shake the freeloaders from those oak trees. But he didn't, and the sight of fans perched in the leafy branches like big, exotic birds nipping canned beer was one more thing little Mike Wright filed in his mind about this marvelous sport beginning to cover him like a second skin.

Wright would later meet Sawyer after Hurricane Fran blew through in 1996. "Our camper rocked back and forth all night long. There were tents hanging in the trees the next morning. Mr. Sawyer came through the campgrounds checking to see if everyone was OK. That was some unforgettable gesture showing he cared about us."

The track, now known as Richmond International Raceway, with over 110,000 seats and no more trees to offer a free, unobstructed view, was where Wright fell in love with NASCAR. He has also been ritualistically attending the Memorial Day race in Charlotte for more than 30 years. But his personal racing Mecca, where memories are the fondest, and his gratitude the deepest, is Darlington Raceway. Since 1980, Wright hasn't missed a race at the unforgiving, egg-shaped course.

Darlington Raceway is NASCAR's Lambeau Field, a storied venue loaded with history and charm in a small market that many believe will always have a place on the schedule even if it's difficult to get to and lacks the big-city attractions of newer stops on the circuit like Las Vegas, Kansas City, and Miami. The track, built on a cotton and peanut field, took on its curious egg shape to protect a minnow farm the land owner had refused to relocate. Wright enjoys the history and lore of Darlington and will explain how the track's retaining walls, white before the race, turn black by the day's end due to a multitude of tire contact.

"This is a track you have to battle all day long; there's no riding around by anyone on any lap," he said. Because of its unique configuration—with one turn tighter, narrower, and more steeply banked, shooting cars down the straightaway like an amusement park carnival ride—Darlington gives drivers coming off that wicked turn and scraping up against the wall their inevitable "Darlington stripe."

Wright won't be denied in attending races at Darlington. One rare year when he and Karen weren't camping or RVing at the race, they stayed at the Diplomat Motel in Myrtle Beach. A bad storm came, and lightning struck the hotel. All the building's emergency sirens were blaring. People were screaming to get out as the building filled with gas. Wright ran from the hotel in his underwear, holding his race tickets and scanner. "I could go to Wal-Mart and get clothes; I couldn't get another race ticket," he explained.

Jerry, who worked with the Virginia Department of Corrections, would buy his race tickets at automobile dealerships or right at the box office. A signature family outing trumpeting the arrival of summer was waking up at 3 a.m. and heading to Charlotte for the Coca-Cola 600 race on Memorial Day weekend. "We weren't poor, but driving to Charlotte was a big deal," Wright said. "Six of us would pile into a Pontiac big as the Titanic, four hours to Charlotte, then back home after the race." He still carries the ticket stub to one of those World 600 races, now called the Coca-Cola 600—a $40 ticket on the start-finish line, 40th row.

As NASCAR barnstormed the southeastern United States, the boat-like Bonneville took Jerry and Anne Wright, Mike, his sister Susan, and their grandparents to stops in Atlanta; Bristol, Tennessee; Martinsville, Virginia; Rockingham, North Carolina; and North Wilkesboro, North Carolina. To newer NASCAR fans, places like Rockingham and North Wilkesboro are romantic-sounding names and fading images on grainy highlight reels. For Wright, the memories are clear as yesterday. After one particular race at North Wilkesboro, a frustrating traffic jam leaving the North Carolina track kept the family car hemmed in, going nowhere. Jerry had to work the next day. He wasn't going to sit patiently in a seemingly endless line of immobilized cars. Jerry jerked the wheel and pulled the Pontiac onto the grass. He drove through a creek leading into someone's back yard. He tore through the unkempt grass and blew past the house, down the gravel driveway with a cloud of dust. "Chickens were scrambling, dogs were barking, it was just a mad scene," Wright said. "I peeked out the back window and saw a shot gun pointed at the car. But before you knew it we were back on the highway, sailing home."

The races were held on Sunday, but fans didn't wear their Sunday best. "The bottom five rows in Rockingham left you covered in red mud by the end of the race," Wright said.

He was still a wide-eyed kid in 1978 at Richmond when Darrell Waltrip used his "chrome horn" to move Neil Bonnett out of the way for the win. On pit road, an incensed Bonnett, acting as proxy for thousands in the grandstands, then smashed into Waltrip, who had a reputation for being quite a loudmouth. In fact, when Steven Spielberg had made a summer blockbuster film about a large man-eating shark, the motor mouth driver was dubbed "Jaws." Waltrip was brash but backed up the entertaining bravado with a pedal-to-the-floor, "out of my way" driving style that won many races like this one. The Richmond crowd was still buzzing about his use of the chrome horn and Bonnett's showing that enough was enough by knocking into DW's DiGuard Chevy near Victory Lane. As race winner, Waltrip had to climb the steps of the grandstand and walk through the crowd to get to the press box for post-race interviews.

"Waltrip was heading up there, and fans were throwing anything not bolted down at him. Next to me, a woman who must have been 80 years old gets up and shouts, 'I hate you Darrell Waltrip!' She hurls a ham biscuit at him—hits DW right in the shoulder! The roll came apart as it hit him. You could see the ham fly out. I was about 10 years old watching this, and my eyes must have been half as big as my head."

Another time, a woman too well dressed to be walking through the gate at Martinsville was accompanied by a man in a Rusty Wallace t-shirt with big sunglasses and his cap pulled over his eyes. "I recognized Bobby Labonte right away," Wright said. "When Bobby passed me, I whispered in his ear, 'nice disguise.'"

NASCAR was a smaller, more personal sport when drivers walked among the fans in disguise and elderly ladies pelted drivers with dinner rolls. The campgrounds were more intimate. The RVs and campers weren't quite so lavish. The chasm between rich and poor, the haves and the have-nots, wasn't quite as large. It was easier to meet new people and look back 15 years later to realize you're still sending friends met at the track Virginia country hams for Christmas. The pace was slower. Fans weren't quite as busy, seemed to have fewer worries. There were no cell phones and Blackberries to chirp strange electronic tunes that interrupted warm conversations over cold beers in front of crackling wood fires. Access to the sport and its drivers was loose and informal in innocent, less guarded times. NASCAR today is bigger, faster, safer, higher-stakes, more competitive, and higher-profile. The "small fraternity" to which Wright proudly belongs has progressively grown into a larger and therefore more impersonal NASCAR Nation. The sport is no longer a secret undiscovered except by those in the South who lack big-city baseball and football teams.

NASCAR is now for all Americans. Wright realizes giving the sport to everyone meant taking part of it away from some. Westward expansion meant Rockingham and North Wilkesboro would lose their race dates. What used to be two Darlington races a year for Mike Wright—especially the marquee Labor Day race, an important end-of-summer ritual for tens of thousands of NASCAR fans—is now the lone spring event, the storied track's remaining single date on the NASCAR Sprint Cup Series schedule. After NASCAR moved its Labor Day race date to Auto Club Speedway near Los Angeles, Wright attended the last Southern 500 with a heavy heart. Following the race, when others had left for the parking lots, he sat in the stands and cried.

The sport has changed. The world has changed. Wright accepts all of that. He understands change is part of life—not a part he necessarily fully understands or always wants to embrace, but it is a constant force any American who appreciates progress learns to deal with.

"I'm a Southerner. It's no secret we're not much for new things. Yeah, I'd like to have the way it used to be with fans up in the trees and the garages open to everyone. Back in the day, after the race, they'd open the gates, and you could go right into the pits." Wright often found himself standing next to legends like to Junior Johnson, David Pearson, Bobby Allison, and, most importantly, Richard Petty. "I realize it's all gotten too big to allow that now. There'd be a riot down there. But heck, today you can be a driver's friend on Facebook or listen to their crew conversations on your Sprint phone. NASCAR has figured out how to keep the fans close to the drivers."

If the world were to end tomorrow, Mike Wright wouldn't miss the race today. He still finds himself reminiscing about the "old days," like the first race he and his dad saw on TV, the 1979 Daytona 500, the first flag-to-flag NASCAR race carried live. The heat had gone out in the Wright's house on that snowy Sunday in February, forcing his mother and sister to flee to warmer confines at their grandparents' place. The men stayed behind, glued to the TV, bundled in hats and blankets, not wanting to miss a lap. "When the King won, we were hugging one another, because we were happy and because it was so darn cold."

In those days, NASCAR was rarely on TV. Long car trips were planned to listen to the races on the radio. Thanks to the radio broadcast, the young lad was able to see just about every major attraction in the Southeast.

When Petty won at Daytona in 1977, the Wrights were on their way to Virginia Beach. When he won at Michigan in 1981, they were listening in the parking lot at historic Colonial Williamsburg. When Petty won his final race, the Wrights had the radio up loud at an I-95 truck stop on the way to Gettysburg. "My dad turned around, gripped my knee and announced, 'That's 200!'"

Wright's mom enjoyed listening on the radio and going to the track mostly because it was something the family could do together every week. Sometimes, there were surprises. At one Bristol race, she found an abandoned kitten by the dumpster of their hotel. "Mom took that cat home, and we had it 17 years," Wright said.

Jerry stopped attending races in the mid 1980s. The crowds had gotten too big, and he was physically slowing down. Mike began going on his own. During college, he and a buddy drove 10 hours in a Ford Thunderbird from North Carolina to Daytona Beach to see the annual Independence Day race. They had just enough money to cover the tickets, gas, beer, a loaf of bread, and a jar of peanut butter. After the race, they drove 10 more hours, straight home. Like the NASCAR commercial says, this is a sport where the fans drive 700 miles to watch their heroes drive 500 miles. How many would do all that driving on the same day?

"There's people who have more money and can buy more souvenirs than me, go to more races than me, but no one loves this sport more than me," Wright said.

In 1999, he took his dad back to the track at Richmond. It had been 15 years since Jerry had been to a race. Mike was walking toward the seats and noticed his dad was missing. "I looked around, and he was 50 yards back, stopped in his tracks, standing with his mouth wide open, looking at all those souvenir trailers like he was gonna pass out. The last race he'd been to, the drivers had set up card tables to sell a t-shirt, a hat, maybe a bumper sticker. You'd get one shirt, and that would be the driver's design for the whole season. Dad asked, 'Is there something special going on?' He'd never seen these huge merchandise trailers for every driver with different shirts and jackets and all the mementoes available now."

One of my fondest memories in researching this book was to sit with Wright on a clear and chilly night in the Blue Ox campground on a hill behind Bristol Motor Speedway in front of a snapping wood fire he'd built. He spoke seriously about how NASCAR has defined him as a person. He admitted to the sport's undeniably large and forceful role in his life, discussing the life-shaping aspects of the sport thoughtfully, in a tone ranging from solemn to joyful. Serious words came from the heart, a timbre of revelatory conversation that wouldn't be out of place in a church confessional.

"Racing has given me a lot in life, taught me valuable lessons about friendship and being a good person," Wright said. "I think I've experienced everything racing has had to offer over the years. Anyone who knows me knows racing is such a big part of my life. Me and racing are the same. I love the fires and the steaks and the cans of beer and the people. This is my lazy boy chair. I'm home here. When I sit and hear the 'Gentlemen, start your engines,' I forget everything. Nothing else matters. I'm a kid again. My heart starts pounding, and I can't sit still. By the second pace lap, when you can smell the fumes of the gas and the rubber coming off the tires, oh man, it is instant adrenaline. If that smell could go into my alarm clock, I'd always wake up happy."

"What if you could wake to Richard Petty's voice?" I asked.

"The King? Oh, heaven. Yeah, that's waking up in heaven."

Decades at Darlington

I N THE SPRING OF 1950, a group of teenagers out of high school were racing on the highways of Pennsylvania. One boy, Jack Hoenstine, passed his days working at a local brickyard but came alive on nights and weekends when he drove his cousin's souped-up Ford coupe at local feature race events.

"We were rippin' and tearin' it up one day on the highway when a buddy asked me, 'Did you see there's a 500-mile stock car race happening down in Darlington?'" Hoenstine said. Sure enough, his friend produced a racing magazine with a number to call. Hoenstine bought four tickets and with his buddies drove 540 miles to Darlington, South Carolina. Jack was smitten by the action on the track, but even better, afterward, the chance to

Longtime fan Jack Hoenstine hasn't missed a race at Dover International Speedway since 1969. His Darlington streak is even longer—2010 will be 59 straight years of seeing every NASCAR race at the "Lady in Black." *Courtesy Jack Hoenstine*

meet drivers like Fireball Roberts, Joe Weatherly, and LeeRoy Yarbrough. These were swashbuckling heroes you'd expect to find in a comic book. Only they were here at the track in real life, and they'd actually talk to you. Jack has since made the trip from Queen, Pennsylvania, to every NASCAR race at Darlington Raceway.

"This year [2010] will be 59 straight years attending Darlington," the 78-year-old Hoenstine said. "I just immediately got into it and loved it right away."

The rough-around-the-edges sport that grabbed Hoenstine's attention has evolved into a polished multi-billion-dollar enterprise fans follow on their mobile phones. Back in the days of rotary phones and cracking AM radio race broadcasts, Hoenstine stayed in a room at a boarding house in nearby Florence. Darlington Raceway's grandstands were uncomfortable concrete slabs. The drivers had scant protection—maybe an open-face helmet with a seat belt across their laps. Fonte Flock drove in Bermuda shorts and a t-shirt. The closest thing to a pre-race flyover was NASCAR's resident wild man Curtis Turner buzzing the crowd with his propeller airplane. Drivers would enjoy a cigarette during tire changes, which were usually performed by friends volunteering for pit duty. A few drivers would keep a thermos under the seat.

The best part was that any fan could meet these colorful characters. After the Darlington races, the gate under the flag stand would open, and fans would dash down to meet the hard-charging, hard-living drivers. "Nothing was fenced in. LeeRoy Yarbrough, Marvin Panch, and Coo Coo Marlin, Sterling's dad, would be leaning against their cars. Anyone could go strike up a conversation."

If fans missed a driver on pit road, it wasn't hard to find him elsewhere. Hoenstine ran into Fireball Roberts at a Union 76 gas station. Roberts was a popular, dashing figure. He would be known as the best driver never to win a NASCAR championship. Jack approached Fireball as he was filling the tank of his 1959 Bonneville and taking a look at the engine. "Fireball said, 'It's all OK under here,' and slammed down the hood!" Hoenstine remembered. He snuck a peak at the driver's charge card, which read "Courtesy of Union Oil Co." "That gas cost him nothing!" Hoenstine said.

On the way home to Pennsylvania, Hoenstine would stop at Richard Petty's race shop in Randleman, North Carolina, which was an inauspicious two-car garage prior to the growth of Petty Enterprises. Like many other

NASCAR fans, he posed for photos with Petty, who would always thank Jack for taking time to visit and would come to know him by name.

Joe Weatherly, a charismatic and fun-loving personality who was known to drive flat out all the time and who won back-to-back championships in 1962 and 1963, often stayed at the same motel as Hoenstine in Darlington. Known as "the Clown Prince of NASCAR," Weatherly enjoyed fraternizing with fans, explaining why he brought a mongoose to the track (he was deathly afraid of snakes), and spinning yarns of how he obtained a scar that started above his left eye, sliced through his eyelid, veered down his cheek, and disappeared into his mouth.

Hoenstine met Weatherly at the motel after the driver had wrecked during that afternoon's race. Weatherly was wearing his trademark black-and-white oxford saddle shoes, the same ones he drove with. "Joe said with his big smile, 'I'm OK, I just crashed out of the race, but everything's fine.' We talked a while that night as if we'd known each other for years. Joe said he got that scar fighting in World War II."

The true story behind the crease down his face was more tragic. It was a reminder he couldn't escape of a night as a teenager when the car Weatherly drove plowed into a tree, killing one passenger and leaving Joe and several others badly injured.

In the 1960s, the cars on the race track were nowhere near as safe as they are today. "I'm so glad they improved the cars and tracks because there was a time when we were losing a good many drivers," Hoenstine said. "Today you see crashes just as bad where the driver jumps from the car like he's coming off an amusement park ride."

As the Darlington races grew in popularity, more local motels sprouted up, drawing drivers and team owners as well as fans. In the late 1960s, Hoenstine befriended Ronnie Thomas, who wanted to enter the race but was short of money. Jack and his friends pooled the cash to buy tires and got their names on Thomas' No. 25 Chevrolet.

Hoenstine's own racing career was short-lived, ending in the early 1950s when his cousin sold the race car he was using. But Jack still found a way to get onto the track. Following a Darlington race in 1964, he and a friend stopped in Rockingham, North Carolina, to see the new raceway. "We were in my buddy's new Pontiac and noticed the gates were open. We started running laps, but a man in a suit came out and flagged us down. He turned out to be a nice gentleman. Asked us how we liked the track. Gave us his business card and said to call him if we ever needed tickets. He told us, 'Go ahead and run a few more laps, but don't wreck!'"

Hoenstine took the wheel and stood on the gas for all the Bonneville's powerful 421 engine was worth. "Coming off Turn Three, my friend reached across and grabbed onto my thigh so hard, I had black-and-blue bruises for three weeks."

Fifteen years later, on the way to Daytona, Hoenstine would take a detour through Charlotte and spot an open gate at Charlotte Motor Speedway. He ran a few laps in his Chevy Suburban, this time undetected by track management.

His attendance streak in Charlotte is almost as impressive as that for Darlington. Since attending the 1964 600-mile race, Hoenstine has also been to NASCAR's Memorial Day race, now called the Coca-Cola 600, every year. He has not missed a NASCAR race at Dover since 1969. Another incredible attendance streak at Bristol recently ended after 45 years. Hoenstine is an energetic and youthful 78 years old—you'd guess he was at least 15 years younger—but the steep inclines at Bristol Motor Speedway, a bowl-shaped track nestled in the foothills of the Appalachian Mountains in Tennessee, put too great a strain on his knees.

He attends more than a dozen races a year, flying to events in Texas, Phoenix, Las Vegas, and Michigan, and driving his motor home to Charlotte, Darlington, Bristol, Richmond, Talladega, Dover, and Pocono.

"I've been to hundreds of NASCAR races over the years, too many to even count," he said. "My sister-in-law asked me, 'My goodness, Jack, what if you saved all that money instead?' Well, I wouldn't have seen all them races, met the drivers, fans I've come to know, and had such a good time. I've always wanted to enjoy life, and NASCAR's been a big part of that."

Robert Laberge/Allsport/Getty Images

PART II
REMEMBERING DALE

To many NASCAR fans, Dale Earnhardt Sr. was simply the greatest there ever was. He embodied stock car racing. While Richard Petty will always be "The King," Earnhardt was John Wayne and Elvis wrapped into one imposing dude no driver ever wanted to see looming in his or her rearview mirror. To fans, he was larger than life but always within reach. When he won, it felt like a victory for the working man. Even those who booed the iron-headed driver known as "The Intimidator" would grant him that.

In trying to sum up Dale Earnhardt, there are the easy-to-cite statistics: the 7 championships and 76 NASCAR Sprint Cup Series wins. Finding words to describe his impact on the sport and its fans, even nine years after his passing, is impossible.

So many fans still evoke the name and memory of Dale Earnhardt. He stood at the center of their treasured racing memories. He was the reason they became NASCAR fans . . . and why they remain fans. And the legend of the driver of that imposing black No. 3 car is still helping pull in the next generation of NASCAR fans. After all, in many parts of North Carolina, especially in the small towns like his, this is how they teach kids to count: *1, 2, Earnhardt, 4.*

He was the principled son of a race car driver who once said, "I just want to drive a car like my daddy." He was tough as nails but had a heart of gold he preferred to conceal. Fans knew it was there. Maybe that's why Dale Earnhardt continues to have such a profound and lasting influence on more of those fans than you can imagine.

The Lucky Penny Girl

You CAN'T USE THEM in vending machines. On the street, few people bother to bend over and pick them up. They cost more to make than they're worth. It will surprise no one when the U.S. penny goes out of commission.

But a penny can be worth more than one cent. Sometimes, a penny can have value beyond measure, like the one brought to a NASCAR race by an extraordinary little girl whose lucky coin found its way into the sport's lore and the hearts of millions of fans.

The little girl, Wessa Miller, was born with spina bifida, a birth defect of the spine. Doctors gave her three days to live, a grim diagnosis based on dire medical facts. But there was a lot about Wessa the doctors couldn't see. X-rays, scans, and blood samples can't detect courage, determination, and faith.

Wessa fought hard and made it home, and the doctors said she'd live only 2 years. Wessa again proved them wrong. After she celebrated

Wessa Miller holding one of her lucky pennies. In 1998, when she was six, Wessa gave her best lucky coin to Dale Earnhardt Sr. "The Intimidator" secretly glued the penny to his dashboard, and after 19 unsuccessful tries he finally won the Daytona 500. *Getty Images for NASCAR*

a second birthday, the specialists called that a gift; she probably wouldn't make it to 5. Wessa had that birthday too, and the medical experts said 10 would be a miracle. When the girl who wasn't expected to make it out of the children's ICU ward was named eighth grade homecoming queen, doctors finally had the good sense to stop setting a time frame on a miracle life.

"Wessa is tough, she doesn't complain. She lives by God's good grace, that's the only way I can explain it," said her dad, Booker Miller. Twice, Wessa's wheelchair tipped over and she busted up her mouth and teeth. Wessa didn't utter a cross word. "I could have sued, but I'm not that kind of person to put blame on someone else," Booker said. "Wessa's tough. She healed up."

Booker left high school at 16 to work in a Kentucky coal mine. He spent 26 years below ground, narrowly escaping cave-ins and tasting copper from the blown-up cable for three days afterward. Consider him a credible authority on human toughness and grit.

Wessa attends church "every time the doors are open," according to Booker. In addition to her religion and family, NASCAR is Wessa's great source of comfort and joy. "She doesn't get to enjoy a lot in life, but she does get a lot of pleasure from racing."

From the time she could watch television, Wessa had been a fan of Dale Earnhardt. So when she was chosen for the Make-A-Wish program, which grants wishes for seriously ill children, the six-year-old didn't hesitate. She wanted to meet Dale Earnhardt.

Wessa's mom, Juanita, was concerned. Her precious daughter had so much vested in a man Juanita knew little about, other than his gun-slinging reputation for aggressive driving. Earnhardt was aptly nicknamed "Ironhead" and "The Intimidator." He wore the sport's black hat, unafraid to move anyone out of the way, even if it wrecked the field. His hair-trigger temper and swinging moods were difficult to predict. Who knew what he'd say to Wessa? She might wind up greatly disappointed, maybe even emotionally hurt.

"I knew Dale from the TV and was worried he'd be moody and mean to Wessa," Juanita said. Yet she wasn't going to try to sway Wessa from her dream. Juanita knew how much the driver meant to her daughter. A trip was scheduled for the family to attend the 1998 Daytona 500, where Wessa would meet her idol at a crucial race.

Earnhardt, a 7-time NASCAR champion, had won 30 races at Daytona International Speedway but never when it counted most, at the Daytona 500. He appeared to be cursed in NASCAR's marquee event. Despite winning every possible important race in all possible ways, he'd always been denied at the Great American Race. "We've lost this race just about every way you can lose it," Earnhardt said after one of his 19 unsuccessful tries. "We've been out-gassed, out-tired, out-run, out every-thinged." Once, his tire went down, and Earnhardt claimed a chicken bone cut it on the backstretch. Twice, he clearly had the best car and, after driving 499 miles, still didn't win. What Dale lacked was luck. Little Wessa Miller wanted to bring him some.

"Dale was my favorite race car driver, so I wanted to give him my lucky penny," Wessa said. "I thought it would help him win the race."

The day before the Daytona 500, the Millers waited for Dale in the garage area as he finished his final test runs. Booker was uncharacteristi-cally anxious. He heard Dale was upset with his sputtering car. There was talk the engine might have to be replaced. As the minutes ticked down before the meeting with Wessa, he wondered if Earnhardt would be tense and distant. But the Intimidator strode in wearing a wry smile. He got down on one knee, right beside Wessa's wheelchair. It was like no one else in the room existed. He spent 15 minutes with her.

"When Dale met Wessa, I saw such a different man," Juanita said. "He had a heartfelt goodness. They made a connection you could see."

"I guess Dale was a mean person on the track, but he had a soft spot big as heaven," Booker said. "He got right down to her level and had nothin' to say to nobody but Wessa. There was a real gentleness in him. He told her, 'Wessa, you can do anything you want.' He meant it. She's never forgotten that."

As Wessa reached from her wheelchair to hand over her lucky penny, the driver was hatching a plan. When the crowds dissipated and the cam-eras went away, crusty old Earnhardt rummaged around the garage for some adhesive and secretly glued the copper coin to his dashboard. "Dale had enough yellow glue smeared around to put about 100 pennies on that dash," said his crew chief Larry MacReynolds. The next day, after 19 years of heartbreak and futility, Dale Earnhardt finally won the Daytona 500.

The Millers watched an unprecedented celebration. As Earnhardt drove down pit road toward Victory Lane, hundreds of crewmen from every

In 2009, Wessa Miller, with her parents Juanita and Booker, returned to Bristol Motor Speedway, where Dale Earnhardt Sr. had hosted the family 11 years earlier. *Author photo*

team lined pit road to congratulate him, touching Dale's outstretched hand as he drove by.

Saturday's meeting with Dale had already been the best day of Wessa's life. Sunday's win slathered icing all over the cake. The family left Daytona Beach for Disney World without knowing Wessa's penny was in Dale's car. The secret didn't hold for long, and the dream trip would get even better. The next day, the news media tracked the Millers down, and NASCAR Nation learned about the "Lucky Penny Girl."

But her story didn't end there. Two months later, to say thank you, Earnhardt arranged for the family to attend the NASCAR race at Bristol. It was his turn to present a gift. With no fanfare, he gave the Millers a much-needed Chevy van for frequent trips to doctors 175 miles away. He even made sure the van was blue, Wessa's favorite color. The vehicle was a godsend for two or three weekly treks from their home in Phyllis, Kentucky, to the University of Kentucky Medical Center. The Millers have put more than 150,000 miles on the van getting to Wessa's medical appointments.

Two years later, to celebrate Wessa's ninth birthday, Juanita planned a special gift: a trip to Earnhardt's Chevy dealership for its annual open house. Mother and daughter quietly joined the back of the long line queuing for Dale's autograph. When they got to the front, Earnhardt shouted out, "Wessa!" and gave her a big hug. For the rest of the meet-and-greet, Wessa sat next to her hero, who was wearing his patented crooked smile underneath that bushy mustache that could have swept a city street clean.

That would be the last time Wessa spent time with Dale. She was at home watching the 2001 Daytona 500 when the black No. 3 car crashed in the final turn on the last lap. The announcers weren't saying much. The car was crunched against the wall. There was no sign of Dale. Wessa was crying as the family prepared for church. Juanita said she'd find out how Dale was doing after church. There, the Millers heard Dale was gone. "When we got home, I said, 'Wessa, baby, mamma's got something to tell you.'"

Wessa cried for days. She stayed away from NASCAR for a year. Gradually, the sting lessened. She reclaimed her old spot in front of the TV on Sunday afternoons and eventually became an avid fan of Dale Earnhardt Jr.

"Dale's death is something we're reminded of every day," Booker said. "He's the best there ever was. He was a big part of Wessa's life. And he still is part of her life."

Seven years after the tragic accident, Wessa would be reminded of that, and again enter the consciousness of NASCAR fans, thanks to motorsports reporter David Poole. As the 2008 season approached, Poole was preparing a 10th-anniversary story of the 1998 Daytona 500 for the *Charlotte Observer*. Other reporters were covering Earnhardt's emotional win. Poole remembered the Lucky Penny Girl. "Every reporter who's ever written a story knows the 'Where are they now?' one," he said. "The problem was, I literally didn't know where Wessa lived."

Scouring the Internet, Poole found the name "Wessa Miller" on the blog of a professional wrestler who had appeared at a middle school festival in Kentucky. With the Millers' home state revealed, Poole was able to get the family's telephone number from the Kentucky chapter of Make-A-Wish.

He and Juanita spent two and a half hours on the phone. "I walked downstairs and told my wife, Katy, if I can't write this story, take me off this job," Poole said. "I felt like a stenographer; Wessa's story wrote itself."

The article ran on the front page, and offers to help the Millers poured in. Caring for her daughter was always a daunting task for Juanita, who drives a handicapped-accessible school bus Wessa rides to school when

Wessa has become part of NASCAR lore. Here, she poses with NASCAR legend Bobby Allison.
Author photo

well enough to attend. Now Juanita also had to worry about Booker, who'd gone through emergency heart surgery.

In more than 15 years covering NASCAR, Poole had seen race fans and drivers give millions of dollars to the sport's charities. It was his time to give back. He established the Pennies for Wessa fund to assist the Millers with medical bills, travel expenses to faraway doctors, and home renovations for Wessa's special needs. A special online auction also raised funds for the family. One of the items for bid was a lunch and race shop tour with David Poole.

"You're not supposed to be part of the story," the veteran reporter and SiriusXM radio personality said. "But sometimes the story becomes part of you. Every one of us has good days and bad days. A good day for the Millers is when nothing really bad happens. The things they deal with on their good days would be a pretty bad day for anyone else. But they look at every single day as an absolute gift. If all of us thought like that it would be a much better world."

Working with the *NASCAR Angels* TV program, the NASCAR Foundation, and Motor Racing Outreach, Poole arranged to bring Wessa

Miller and her family back to Bristol Motor Speedway in 2009. Wessa was featured in a "Heart of NASCAR" segment on the show and was introduced during pre-race ceremonies, waving to the cheering crowd with the breezy confidence of a president at his inaugural parade. She also met Dale Jr., giving him a 1988 penny to match his car number, 88. Lightning didn't strike twice—Earnhardt had a tough race—but no one really expected it to.

There can only be one Lucky Penny. The coin Wessa handed to Junior's dad is the one NASCAR fans remember. It remains glued to the dashboard of the No. 3 Goodwrench Chevrolet, now on display in the RCR Racing Museum in Welcome, North Carolina.

Wessa Miller often thinks about that day, and the wondrous time spent with a hero who declared she could do anything. She'd always liked Dale because he was so tough. Now she'd be like him. Wessa had been suffering regular seizures before coming to Bristol, where Dale once brought her family. Back at that track, she didn't have a single one all weekend. When the Millers returned to Kentucky, so did the seizures. Wessa didn't complain. Dale wouldn't.

Juanita and Booker continue to live one day at a time, appreciating each as a gift to spend with a courageous daughter who defies the odds while delighting and surprising whomever she meets. Like that penny that softened even the Intimidator, they consider themselves very, very lucky.

Less than two months after arranging for the Millers to return to Bristol, David Poole died of a massive heart attack. He was 50 years old. Fans who wish to honor David or help the girl who found a place in his heart can donate directly to the Pennies for Wessa fund by visiting www.penniesforwessa.org, or by mail at Pennies for Wessa, Attention: Mike Damron, Community Trust Bank, P.O. Box 39, Mouthcard, KY 41548.

A Purple Heart and a Titanium Leg

WHEN HE WAS 17, JOHN HYLAND scored a job at the track in Charlotte. Serving corporate guests in the suites above Lowe's Motor Speedway was ideal. During breaks, he could sneak down and squeeze his face inside the retaining fence to watch the cars whiz by close enough to make your eyes water.

Once, during qualifying, John was trackside in his starched white apron. His favorite driver, Dale Earnhardt Sr., was steaming toward the first turn, where John stood alone at his private perch. The car bobbled, and Dale spun and crashed into the wall directly in front of the stunned boy. Earnhardt climbed out and disgustedly removed his helmet. If "pissed off" were a term in Webster's, this would be the accompanying picture. Dale briefly inspected his spent ride and walked over to the boy gripping the fence with white knuckles.

"How ya doin' kid?" Earnhardt asked.

"Uh, um, I'm alright," John replied. "Mr. Earnhardt, are you okay?"

Dale's mood had changed. He shrugged. "Hey, what can you do? It's just another race car."

As a U.S. Army Scout, Cpl. John Hyland scoured enemy territory for combatants planting improvised explosive devices. He was seriously injured when his Humvee ran over two antitank bombs. *Courtesy John Hyland*

NASCAR team owner Rick Hendrick read about Corporal Hyland in the newspaper. He arranged for the wounded soldier to be brought home for Christmas and gave the family a custom van and John a long overdue hero's welcome. *Author photo*

It was as bizarrely surreal as life's surreally bizarre scenes can get. The Intimidator had just totaled his car . . . then strolled over to share a private, funny moment completely divorced from the previous distressing events. From then on, Hyland was truly hooked on NASCAR.

"Looking back, I realize that's what I love about this sport," he said. "Dale could have gotten seriously hurt. He'd just wrecked his car. He comes over and starts chatting with me like he's out for a walk on a sunny day off. These drivers have so much going on, but they look you in the eye, say, 'hello kid,' sign an autograph, meet a sick kid. There are so many good people in the sport doing unnoticed, decent, nice things all the time."

Of course, Hyland had no idea that two decades later, he would wind up on the receiving end of that kindness in a significant and life-changing way.

He graduated high school and went on to other food service jobs. Eager to perform, he enrolled in the North Carolina School of Art. A teacher sensed potential, and he started singing opera. He joined the Piedmont Opera Company in the Carolinas and performed arias at the Opera Festival di Roma in Italy. He was an understudy for *Phantom of the Opera* in New York. But the opera life was a tough one. Those not named Pavarotti had better be prepared to take a second job.

Hyland returned to restaurant work in the southeast where he met a beautiful college girl. Erica and John were married and had two kids. He ran several Hooters restaurants, developing a knack for managing and motivating a gaggle of attractive, needy drama queens whose strutting in those oh-so-orange shorts typically brought each girl more than a thousand dollars a week.

At the Hooters in Washington, where seemingly all 48,000 law enforcement officers in D.C. were his customers, Hyland befriended several members of the area's police. Many men have experienced an epiphany in Hooters, but his was unique. Hyland wanted to become a cop.

He moved the brood back to Charlotte and charted a path for becoming a Charlotte police officer, starting with a private police agency. The pay was terrible, the conditions dangerous. The job offered no health insurance. He then met a veteran fresh out of the U.S. Army who extolled the virtues of a military career. At 33 years old, Hyland took the army entrance test and scored high enough to choose his path. He wanted to be a scout, an elite position performing reconnaissance and gathering intelligence on the enemy.

Corporal Hyland was deployed to Iraq. He quickly became accustomed to and craved the adrenaline rush of being part of a small kill team—three or four scouts spending a week in dangerous enemy territory seeking combatants who were planting improvised explosive devices. He and his army brothers, entrusted with each other's lives, would camp on a mountain on the Iranian border, binoculars trained on enemy soldiers crossing the border. He'd fix a laser on the target, and air force jets would swoop in and blow up the caravan. "At my age, it was a pretty cool job," he said.

On September 11, 2007, Hyland was on a scouting mission 60 miles northeast of Baghdad. He was in a Humvee sitting behind the driver, operating a sophisticated computerized tracking system and .50-caliber gun that could take off an insurgent's head from 1,200 meters away.

Even though Hyland felt like he was playing a video game, sitting behind a vivid color computer screen with a joystick in his right hand, this was no routine mission by any definition. A patrol bringing supplies to an army outpost had been attacked by Iraqi insurgents. A quick response force had been dispatched and promptly blown up. Hyland's small reconnaissance squad was called on to secure the scene. At least, that was the plan. The enemy had orchestrated a textbook setup.

The scouts were traveling over a small bridge when their vehicle ran over two antitank bombs attached to the bottom of the bridge, directly under Hyland. The massive explosion threw the Humvee's 500-pound door 20 meters. Everything behind Hyland was gone. He found himself wrapped around the vehicle's roll bar.

"What I remember was a thud," Hyland said. "I can't describe it, and hopefully no one else will ever experience that sound. It was just a massive thud. Everything got quiet. Then I heard a high, piercing ringing. I was shot up into the roll bar, holding on, and we were ambushed, shots going off all around us. The next thing I remember was a medic beside me, giving me shot after shot of morphine."

Hyland had taped a photo of his wife and two boys onto the Humvee. Lying in the middle of the Godforsaken desert, he was screaming for his buddies to get that picture. He didn't want to suffer the indignity of terrorists finding it and disrespecting his family.

To his comrades, the dazed yet howling scout looked to be fine. He had all his limbs, and his only major wounds appeared to be a banged-up, bleeding head and a fractured right leg. But on the barren ground, no one could see the soldier's serious internal injuries. Taking the brunt of a massive detonation, Hyland's insides had literally imploded. Both his heels were badly shattered. His pelvis was broken in five places and separated from his spine. Both his shoulder blades were shattered. Three lower vertebrae were fractured.

Stabilized on the battlefield by the medic, Hyland was spirited away in a Bradley. Four days later, the medic and three soldiers who rescued him were killed. In his fallen friends' memory, Hyland wears a bracelet bearing their names, which will never come off his wrist.

After a few days in Germany, he was sent to Walter Reed Army Medical Center in Washington, D.C., then Brooke Army Hospital in San Antonio. He had 33 operations, including the placement of large pins in his legs and several bolts as long as a finger to hold together his pelvis.

When the cast came off Hyland's left leg, the doctors noticed a large pressure wound on the back of his heel. They tried to clean and irrigate the infection, but it kept getting bigger. To close the stubborn wound, they applied leeches, artificial skin, even the skin from an animal. They tried everything in the book and improvised never-before-used tactics to save the soldier's lower leg. Finally, it had to be amputated.

As he recuperated in San Antonio in late 2007, Hyland's hometown paper, the *Charlotte Observer*, covered his story. The holidays were approaching, and Erica had no way to bring John home for Christmas. The family's car was broken down. They had no money to fly him to North Carolina. The reporter included the Hylands' phone number, in case anyone wanted to lend assistance. That help would come virtually before the ink dried on the newspaper.

The morning the article appeared, Rick Hendrick was walking his dog and picked up the morning paper. Normally, the NASCAR team owner thumbs right to the sports pages. But the front-page photo of John Hyland in a wheelchair with his young son in tow stopped the NASCAR team owner in his tracks. Hendrick was touched by the tragic story. "Some things are just meant to be, and this was one of them," he

At Texas Motor Speedway, Corporal Hyland climbed into a Humvee that was the same as the one in which he was attacked in Iraq. Plans are currently being made for the former opera singer to perform the national anthem at an upcoming NASCAR race. *Author photo*

The Hyland family with the van NASCAR team owner Rick Hendrick donated. Hendrick had never met Corporal Hyland, but after learning about his injuries, he instantly knew what he was giving Hyland for Christmas. *Courtesy John Hyland*

said. Hendrick saw his wife in the kitchen and said, "I know what I'm going to do for Christmas." He picked up the phone and called the Hyland residence.

"At 6:30 a.m. my mother gets a phone call, and it's Rick Hendrick," Hyland said. "He told her, 'You call John and tell him not to worry. He'll have a way home for Christmas.'"

Hendrick, who owns 80 car dealerships across the country, delivered to the hospital a new handicapped-accessible Honda Odyssey, complete with a hydraulic ramp to lift John. It was wrapped in a big red bow and full of presents. "There were toys and shirts and jackets, skateboards and bicycles," Hyland said. "My little boy was three years old. He ran and grabbed his bike and was just off to the races. I sat in my wheelchair just speechless."

When Hyland was fitted with a prosthetic leg and able to get around, Hendrick invited the wounded war hero, who now had a Purple Heart, and his family to the Coca-Cola 600 race in Charlotte, traditionally held on Memorial Day weekend. Hendrick paid for tickets, airfare, hotel, and a driver and at-track guide. Hyland landed in Charlotte and was greeted with the true homecoming he never had. "I came into the terminal, and the whole airport stopped, with everyone cheering and saluting me. It was absolutely incredible."

At the race, Hyland was invited into the drivers' meeting. He thought he'd be a happy spectator and had no idea what was to occur. When the VIPs and dignitaries were announced, his was the last name called. His story was told, and the entire room broke into a rousing standing ovation.

"Every single NASCAR driver and crew chief got on their feet and was applauding me. I was so humbled and grateful. It's sometimes hard to accept the attention and favors we get; I was just doing my duty over in Iraq. But what Mr. Hendrick did for us was truly an unforgettable experience," Hyland said. To try to repay the gesture, Hyland gave Hendrick his Silver Spurs, one of the most coveted military awards received for heroic actions.

"I didn't want to take them, but John insisted," Hendrick said. "He continues to amaze me. You look at the pain he's been through, what he's lost and sacrificed, but he's not one time had a negative or bitter word. Getting to know John has been a humbling experience for me."

Hyland's physical therapy will continue for a long time. When he stands for extended periods of time, he feels the sensation of daggers thrust into his heels. Walking is a challenge. He's haunted by chronic pain. There will be more surgeries ahead. He refuses to feel sorry for himself.

"I believe there's a silver lining to everything," he said. "Events in our lives happen for a reason. After getting hurt, I got a do-over. Not many people get the chance to press the reset button and do what you really want to do."

By the time you read this, if I've done my job and presented my case to the right executives in a convincing way, the would-be opera singer from North Carolina who sacrificed so much in the Middle East will be scheduled to sing our national anthem at a NASCAR race, this proud and honorable man's rich tenor adding poignancy to each word while he balances a brave body held together by sutures and screws on one amazing titanium leg.

America's Anchor
Finds His Slice of Heaven

WHEN AMERICAN PRESIDENTS visit war zones, NBC anchor Brian Williams often tags along. It's a humbling responsibility to beam to televisions the first draft of history from hot spots around the globe. The downside of these hastily scheduled trips, aside from stinging windstorms, lousy hotel room pillows, and time away from the family, is missing NASCAR races.

Williams keeps Earnhardt paraphernalia in his office and No. 3 stickers in his briefcase. He stuck one on Saddam Hussein's former palace while covering President Barack Obama in Iraq. *Author photo*

But Williams always brings a piece of his beloved sport with him. For instance, when President Obama first toured Baghdad, he spoke to military personnel at the Al Faw Palace, built by Saddam Hussein and now occupied by the U.S. military. Williams decided to mark the territory in a fashion any fellow fan would understand. He plastered a Dale Earnhardt "3" sticker onto one of the palace's outside walls.

"As far as I know, it's still there, on the wall of a guest house on the bank of a skanky man-made lake," Williams said. "I figured it's time the Iraqis knew about the real 'Intimidator.'"

This was not an isolated incident. Williams goes nowhere without a supply of black No. 3 stickers in his bag. He has to replenish the stock frequently, especially since he slaps a number three decal on every car he rents.

"My goal is to eventually sticker the entire U.S. rental fleet," Williams explained. "Half the time I turn the car in, the rental guy thinks it's an official number, some code from corporate headquarters, and it stays on the car. I have to admit, when I'm driving, I keep an eye out for my Dale stickers. Haven't seen one yet, but it's only a matter of time."

Whether he is stickering the property of deposed dictators, rent-a-cars, and his own Mustang GT; injecting racing analogies into election-night coverage; or extending a business trip to attend a dirt-track race, Brian Williams could be the NASCAR fan wielding the largest and most persuasive megaphone. His appreciation of racing has percolated since his dad introduced the young boy to Joie Chitwood's thrill shows and local dirt races near their home in upstate New York where NASCAR's Bodine brothers ran. Listening to the throaty engines and crunching metal during beloved demolition derby nights ignited in Williams a lifelong passion for fast cars going in circles.

"It's plain and simple: I like speed," he said. "Just give me the first turn at Talladega, when they come around at speed on the second lap. I defy you to replicate that feeling anywhere else in life. You don't know if it's your heart thumping or the eruption of all that American horsepower coming around that turn. These are full-blooded, normally aspirated, American-built cars doing exactly what they are supposed to do, driven by men whose bravery is never fully discussed or recognized. And I love every second of it."

The greatest blessing in anchoring *NBC Nightly News*, Williams declares, is the opportunity to meet people he truly admires. Among the world leaders, captains of industry, humanitarians, scientists, and rock stars he's broken bread with, none ranks higher than Dale Earnhardt. Williams was able to meet and grow close to Dale after taking a job with *NBC News* in 1993. "Call it one of the perks of knowing the president of NBC Sports," he explained.

At the 1998 Daytona 500, Williams took his 10-year-old son, Douglas, to meet Dale. "My son asked Dale if he could put his hand on the number three machine—which is what Douglas always called it, 'the number three machine.' Without hesitation, Dale said, 'Absolutely,' and led us through a scrum to the car. He told my son, 'If we win, you come back for the trophy presentation.'"

Dale wasn't asking, he was ordering Douglas to do this.

Of course, Earnhardt dramatically won the race. The fans went bananas. Earnhardt did a few celebratory doughnuts in the infield grass. The racing gods must have been making up for the two-decade curse because his spins in the grass took the uncanny shape of the number "3." Brian and Douglas Williams watched as a group of fans ran to the beaten-up turf. Some jammed chunks into their coolers. Others laid their bodies down in the deep tire tracks, communing with the celebratory ruts.

Victory Lane was rocking like a van on Lover's Lane. Earnhardt memorably shouted, "Daytona is ours! We won it, we won it, we won it!" Dale found time during the rollicking celebration to call over Brian and Doug to pose for pictures. Those photos, along with Dale's No. 3 die-cast car and hats he signed, are proudly displayed next to signed letters from past U.S. presidents in Williams' Rockefeller Center office.

"He was that kind of guy to remember us at such a big moment," Williams said. "The King, Mr. Richard Petty, opened the door to drivers carefully crafting a media image, and Dale took that to a new level. Dale realized 'the Intimidator' was a title that worked for him and the sport. He knew the value of that iron-headed reputation and how to market it. But he didn't always follow that image in his personal life. He made it very big but never got rid of that regular guy side, fixing ball joints and front ends. And he had a marvelous soft side few saw. I'll always remember his smile more than any glare. He had a warm, crinkly, wry smile and loved to tease people. Dale started racing when the family was down to its last can of beans, and he clearly relished becoming a successful, self-made businessman. By the end, he was very happy with where he was. He'd tell us, 'If I die racing, please understand that I died doing what made me happy.'"

Three years after standing in Victory Lane with his son and his racing idol, Williams was on vacation watching Earnhardt's final race on television. "Having seen him flip seven times and walk away, I didn't think anything of his last-lap crash at the Daytona 500," he said. Soon after, word came through that NASCAR had lost its greatest driver. Williams rushed back to his New York office. A host of messages was waiting for him. One was absolutely haunting. "There was a voicemail on my answering machine—it was Dale checking in to say hello, wanting to know if I was coming to Daytona. It stunned me. I put the message on an audio CD. To this day, it's hard to listen to."

Many in the media—clueless about NASCAR but hip to Williams' curious passion for racing—came to him for comment. "It was one of those Margaret Meade moments for mainstream media, as if they were discovering a new civilization: 'Brian, tell us about those NASCAR fans and NASCAR Nation.' I was a rare member of mainstream media asked to explain the meaning of it all. I wrote an essay about Dale for *Time* magazine. It was a horrible week."

It's been said NASCAR needed Dale Earnhardt's passing to reach its full potential for coast-to-coast popularity. Following the tragedy at Daytona, many new fans discovered big-time stock car racing. For Williams, some of the old magic disappeared. "It's not that the sport immediately changed. It's just that *my guy* was gone. I still look for his car when they come around on the first lap. I'm still subconsciously scanning for the black No. 3. I am hopelessly devoted to his memory."

Following Earnhardt's death, Williams ventured deeper into the roots of the sport, the racing that first sparked his love of automobiles, those small local tracks he loved as a kid and now could sample during his journalistic travels. The steel-skinned newsman becomes earnestly poetic when discussing small-town racing. "These tracks are glowing islands of light, smoke, and noise that dot the countryside and roar to life on Friday and Saturday nights where fans encounter the sport in its purest form," he said.

Growing up in Elmira, New York, Williams first attended races at the Chemung County Fair. His family moved to the Jersey shore, where the inquisitive and well-read teenager became a regular at Wall Township Speedway, Flemington Speedway, Stafford up in Connecticut, even head-

One of the best perks of his job comes when he gets to meet his real-life heroes. Brian Williams, seen with Dale Earnhardt and his son Douglas at the 1998 Winston 500, is happy his boy had a chance to meet the complex champion fans saw as John Wayne in a driver's suit. *Courtesy Brian Williams*

ing up to Portland, Maine, for short-track races. "Ours was a pure American home—the garage was for stuff, and the driveway was where you kept your car so everyone could see how you rolled. You kept meticulous care of that machine, and on Saturday, everyone could see you washing it."

As Williams rapidly ascended to the pinnacle of TV journalism, he bought a summer cabin in Montana and became part owner of a dirt modified team. He'd already driven Talladega, reaching a very impressive 181.5 miles per hour. He makes a point of emphasizing the additional half mile an hour in recounting the feat. "That's the definition of being alive," Williams proclaimed. With his place out West, the East Coast newsman could get seat time running dirt on Friday nights at a small dirt track outside Bozeman ambitiously called Gallatin International Speedway, feeling the heat coming up his legs and a special kind of claustrophobia sliding into the turns.

"A dirt modified car is a different animal, 800-horsepower monsters, really," Williams said. "Your whole life is one controlled skid. Asphalt is great—it's sticky and fast and hot and lot of fun. But dirt is a whole different experience. I have so much respect for dirt drivers. And, as a fan, you can measure your good time by the amount of track you wear home on your body."

Scruffy, dirt-kicking, splintered-grandstands, small-town NASCAR appeals deeply to Williams, who was once a volunteer firefighter and maintains his Irish-Catholic working-class roots. He is known mostly for work performed solo behind a desk while wearing an expensive suit, but he appreciates the camaraderie and profound bonds forged among sweat-stained men on a team getting dirty to pursue a common goal.

"The sport of NASCAR is a reflection of America, a place with a real romantic side, which I see in hard-working people asking to be entertained at a small race track on a Friday or Saturday night," Williams said. "NASCAR is a great slice of America. If I have a layover for a weekend, I will always find out where the small tracks are. There, I feel at home, watching working mechanics, contractors, firemen, builders, school teachers by day, and on the weekend driving a car put together with chewing gum and baling wire. All available money goes into the car, and if they're lucky, they can steal away Monday night in the garage to pound out Saturday night's dents.

"NASCAR fans don't ask for much. They save up all week for a few hours of entertainment. They find being at the track preferable to sitting in an air-conditioned movie theater. It's like being in on a wonderful secret—sitting in the infield, the smell of the track, the lights coming up. It's just a hugely patriotic crowd—a tough, largely working-class crowd, but don't get me wrong, decent people. During the national anthem before the engines fire, you can hear a pin drop. The fans come out to see family and neighbors running super stocks, modifieds, just basic entry-level stock car racing on a dirt track, on a Friday night, capping off a long work week. I tell my children not to root too loudly against any given driver, because that might be his wife, mother, or kids sitting directly in front. It's a true slice of heaven."

Harry How/Getty Images

PART III
FLIRTING WITH FAME

In the early days of NASCAR, the gates under the flag stand opened after the race and spectators streamed down to pit road to mingle with the drivers. Letting fans onto the field and into the "locker room" to get close to the sport's biggest stars was part of the charm and allure of NASCAR. And it still is.

Today, teams, tracks, and sponsors are doing creative things to make fans the stars as well. They've named race events after fans. Fans have shouted the most famous words in motorsports, "Gentlemen, start your engines," and waved the green flag to start races. Their names and faces have been emblazoned on the race cars' paint schemes for millions to see. One fan even had his marriage proposal on the car. (She said, "Yes.")

Some fans win contests to gain NASCAR immortality. Others find their own creative niche in NASCAR's weekend carnival to draw the limelight and flirt with fame. Whether fans have created a dynamic persona that gets noticed or simply got lucky in a random sweepstakes, all have had a grand time basking in their "15 minutes" and dutifully serving as the newest ambassadors for the sport. Here are a few of their stories.

There's Nothing Flat About Tire Man

THROUGHOUT HISTORY, a host of useful and important inventions have come from unplanned accidents.

In China 2,000 years ago, legend has it a cook mixed charcoal, sulfur, and saltpeter. The concoction exploded in vivid colors. Fireworks were invented, and life immediately got better for teenage boys.

In 1879, a researcher spilled a chemical on his hand. He went off to lunch, forgetting to wash his hands. The bread he munched on tasted unusually sweet. The world would get its first artificial sweetener, saccharin.

Penicillin was discovered by chance in 1928 when a British scientist was experimenting with bacteria in petri dishes.

Chris MacNicol (a.k.a., "Tire Man") sporting the most photographed tire on the circuit. During a race weekend, Tire Man will pose for photos with hundreds of fans. Many stay in touch. *Courtesy Chris MacNicol*

Twenty years later a Swiss engineer returning from a walk found some burrs stuck to his clothing. He looked at them under a microscope and came up with the idea for Velcro.

And so it was for Chris MacNicol, who for five dollars purchased Joe Nemechek's right front qualifying tire at the 2004 Daytona 500. The tire was heavy. MacNicol put it down. Looking at that tire, he had an epiphany. Wearing only shorts, he sat in it. When he got up, the tire stuck. Hilarity ensued. Fans gathered around. Photos were taken, autographs signed. Tire Man was born.

Most celebrities need a build-up to develop their base. It's usually gradual. The biggest stars of modern times, the Beatles, played for years in relative obscurity before the madness began. Tire Man, however, happened instantly. Fans saw the buff dude in the Goodyear and frayed straw hat and instinctively called out, "Tire Man!" He was an immediate pied piper for the enthusiastic NASCAR masses, who formed a bellowing impromptu circle in the infield.

A Florida state trooper was called in to investigate the ruckus. She approached the well-built young man mugging for the cameras in a role he'd been waiting his whole life to fill. Picture the scene: female state trooper in her snappy uniform addressing 30-year-old Chris MacNicol, ostensibly naked, save a race car tire.

"Please tell me you have something on under that tire," the officer said.

"Why don't you look?" Tire Man suggested.

The cop was flustered and embarrassed. Here was this good-looking, muscular guy, could have been a Chippendale's dancer, his formidable, well-rounded pecs dancing a happy jiggle when he laughed. They didn't cover this in the training academy.

Tire Man respects the law. His dad is a retired cop. He wasn't about to let the trooper lose face, particularly in front of dozens of preening fans awaiting the outcome of this peculiar showdown. He reached into the Goodyear. A hush settled over the crowd. He yanked up his shorts. Major cheers.

The state trooper tipped her cap and moved on, utterly relieved about the quick and suitable ending, escaping the awkwardness of hauling in a guy for what? Wearing nothing but a Goodyear? Was she supposed to impound the tire and take it back to the NASCAR research and development center for inspection?

On the day Tire Man was born, so many fans wanted their photos taken, it took Tire Man and his dad six hours to walk from Turn Four to their campsite in Turn One. Chris sensed what Superman felt wearing that cape. He innately knew he'd be inside this tire at other tracks . . . especially his beloved Talladega Superspeedway.

"He put on that tire, and the whole thing was absolutely immediately hilarious," said his dad, Bruce MacNicol. "It was the best scene at any sporting event I've ever seen. All the women wanted to know what he had on underneath. Chris said, 'an inner liner.' A few of the ladies got a little risqué, but it was all in good fun."

Tire Man's supportive wife wasn't there, and maybe that was a good thing. "As lucky as I may be to be married to the guy, I have not yet ventured to the track to see him wearing the tire 'live,' though he has put it on at home and modeled it for me," said Chris' wife, Tonya. "The funniest part is seeing pictures of Chris, and in the background there's a large crowd taking even more pictures . . . and then there's the line of people waiting to meet him. Just amazing!"

Tonya and Chris met in college, where he was pursuing his degree as an exercise physiologist. Chris had back problems and took to swimming. Tonya was a lifeguard, and they'd swim together when Chris wasn't doing cannonballs off the diving board. It took more than four years, but he made her laugh till her sides hurt and finally got his girl.

Even though Chris is hoofing around the track mostly *au natural*, posing for pictures with scores of strange women of unknown repute, Tonya completely supports her husband's alter ego. "Chris is not shy about anything. He loves the sport of NASCAR and anything that puts him in the center of it. I love the whole idea of Tire Man because I know Chris loves it. He is such a people person, and whatever he can do to make people smile makes him the happiest. I look at his website and Facebook page in awe of the friends he's made and the loyalty they show. The man they see is the same one I'm at home with every day, who makes me smile and makes me crazy all at the same time. I have nothing but pride when I hear someone say, '*That's* your husband? I just saw him at the track.'"

"I just love making people laugh," Tire Man said. "I was the class clown, the guy always doing the stupid stuff no one else does. I'm kinda like Mikey, the kid in the TV commercial, who will eat anything."

If you take an informal poll of NASCAR fans, many have seen Tire Man, in person or through Internet photos or in features in NASCAR-friendly outlets like *The Sporting News* or SPEED TV. When ABC's *Prime Time Live* ran an in-depth series on NASCAR, producers found Tire Man. Even Will Ferrell, appearing on talk shows to promote his film *Talladega Nights: The Ballad of Ricky Bobby,* remembered venturing out into the infield late at night and marveling at this gregarious guy in a straw hat with a tire around his waist.

During the week, when Tire Man goes back to his civilian "Clark Kent" persona, he is a sales rep for a medical supply company, specializing in breathing devices. At the company's annual sales meeting, a photo of Tire Man went up on the big screen to motivate hundreds of managers from all over the country.

"It's an amazing and diverse bunch that congregates around Tire Man," said MacNicol, who, like Bo Jackson and Charles Barkley, frequently slips into referring to himself in the third person. "Tire Man has met everyone from CEOs to the gainfully unemployed. But for five days twice a year, we hail from the same place and hoot and holler side by side. After doing this a few years, I've built a lot of friendships, and going to races is really like a reunion."

Tire Man is built like a bull that goes to the gym. Still, the first time wearing the tire, he was supporting its full 45 pounds against his skin. "I suffered a severe tire rub in my right quarter panel," he said. He still has a scar on his hip where the tire sat that day.

He went home, got out a sawhorse and circular saw, and went to town on the tire. There was all kinds of noise, and smoke and rubber all over the place, but also a method to the madness. Tire Man sliced away some rubber to insert pipe insulation. He drilled holes for U-bolts attaching to two-inch heavy-duty Dickies suspenders. The tire now hangs from the suspenders, steadied against his hips.

The trickiest part is going to the bathroom. Tire Man has to lean back and use a side wall for required stabilization and leverage. "At every race, someone will inevitably walk in the bathroom, and you'll hear, 'Holy S--t!'"

Even before the creation of Tire Man, Chris showed his devotion to NASCAR in curious ways. About a year after he married Tonya, Dale

Tire Man and Joe Nemechek in the campgrounds at Daytona. Known as "Front Row Joe,"
Nemechek has been one of the great qualifiers in NASCAR. His right front Goodyear from the
2004 Daytona 500 qualifying session was the inspiration and raw material used to create Chris
MacNicol's popular alter ego. *Courtesy Chris MacNicol*

Earnhardt Sr. won a race. Chris celebrated by diving into the biggest mud
hole he could find.

"You guessed it—off comes the wedding band," Tonya explained.
"Apparently Chris searched for nearly four hours for that ring before
having to come home and confess what had happened. Bystanders took
pictures, and he came home with a stack of photos showing him digging
through the mud pit looking for his wedding ring. I just had to laugh. I
guess everyone must have anticipated I was going to make his life miser-
able. They took pity on him and emailed me, vouching for how long he had
searched and how sad he was. Needless to say, the ring he wears today is
from WalMart."

Tire Man wasn't always so passionate about NASCAR racing. Although
his dad was a drag racer in Detroit and a friend of NASCAR driver
Benny Parsons (the two men belonged to the same Masonic lodge in the
Motor City), he grew up indifferent to racing. In fact, he'd never been to a

NASCAR race until college, making his first trip to the track under mild duress while at Jacksonville State University.

"My teammates on the baseball team wanted to hit the race at Talladega. To be honest, my first reaction was, 'I'm not watching that crap.' I just had no idea and, like a lot of people, resorted to the stereotype that it's not a sport and would be boring. I had no interest at all."

The fellas talked about how cool the race would be. Their resistant teammate was not swayed. Instead of Rusty and Dale at Talladega, it might was well have been Anthony and Cleopatra at the Metropolitan Opera. There was nothing intriguing about hanging around a race track. It sounded like a colossal waste of time. Then his buddies promised a big party. Bingo; that was the magic term the gregarious, outgoing class clown needed to hear. Now they were speaking his language. Six strapping ballplayers loaded into a pickup truck, heading for the Alabama border.

"From the moment we rolled into Talladega, I was hooked," he said. "I went just to hang with the guys. Seeing those cars going 'round and 'round, I started to ask questions, learning about the drivers and their history. It really grabbed hold of me. And to be 19 in the middle of that huge party. Oh, man, I was in heaven."

Since 1993, Tire Man hasn't missed a single Talladega race weekend. There have been big parties and sad, poignant times as well. "In the infield, if you go to the second to last light pole on Talladega Blvd. headed toward Turn One and Two, you will find a memorial plaque for Steve Citrano embedded in his camping site," Tire Man explained. "Stevie Wonder, we called him, because he was a mechanical genius. Stevie was always fixin' someone's motor home, and most of the fixin' was on his own, which kept breaking down on the way to the track. About five years ago, we lost Steve to a diabetic-induced coma. We found him on Sunday morning before the race. That race was rained out and finished on Monday. We stayed and watched the race in his honor, then somberly packed his things and left the track. At every race, we display checkered flags at his plaque because Stevie Wonder has finished his own race."

Tire Man started taking his dad, Bruce, to races in 1995. At first they rolled out sleeping bags and slept under the stars in the bed of Bruce's Ford Ranger pickup truck. He now travels in style to races at Daytona, Atlanta, Bristol, and Talladega in a 35-foot motor home with comfortable beds and satellite TV.

Tire Man and his dad have spent some of their closest times at the track. Chris is considering tires for his two boys, six and four. "Maybe a bicycle tire!" he said. Eternally level-headed Tonya is putting a kibosh on that for now.

"One day, I do want them to see the reaction their dad gets at the race track," she said. "I think Tire Man encompasses everything about Chris. It's really his character, his charisma, his charm that draws people in. Anyone can throw on a tire—but that doesn't mean everyone is going to like the man wearing it. When people meet Tire Man they are definitely meeting Chris—the guy that loves to smile, loves to laugh, loves NASCAR, and loves his family."

Toasting a Hero

ONLY IN NASCAR could a regular fan get selected like Willy Wonka's Charlie Bucket, led to the limelight, celebrated like he'd won the golden ticket, and permanently enter the sport's lore.

That happened to wounded U. S. Marine Sgt. Russ Friedman, who wrote an essay urging more support for the military and wound up as the namesake of a NASCAR race in Richmond attended by over 100,000 people.

Walking the track on race day with Russ, a regular guy from Long Island who went fluke fishing the previous night, was a surreal journey into the modern-day celebrity-making machine. The Russ Friedman name was everywhere. If one fan said to another, "Meet me by the Russ Friedman sign," it could have meant thousands of different places in these parts. The frequent repeated sighting of your name all over the place in giant letters must have been like strolling the streets of Manhattan when your driver's license says "Trump."

Outside of closing your eyes, there was no escaping the unmistakable "Crown Royal Presents the Russ Friedman 400" signs, backdrops, banners, and posters. The man's name was on the tickets, on the souvenir programs, on purple t-shirts fans were wearing, on TV ads hyping the

Sergeant Friedman was injured in two separate enemy attacks in Iraq. Back in the United States, he was banged up even worse in a car accident when he had a flashback on the highway. *Courtesy Russ Friedman*

Driver Jamie McMurray helped dedicate the race as the namesake of
Sgt. Russ Friedman. They visited wounded soldiers at McGuire VA Hospital
near the track in Richmond to thank them for their service. *Getty Images
for NASCAR*

race, on hats the winning driver and his team would don in Victory Lane,
and, of course, on the giant *Russ Friedman 400* logo painted in the grass
next to the front stretch.

Double-taking fans spotting newly famous Russ had a bemused expression on their faces that said, "Don't I know you from TV? Not *America's
Most Wanted* but maybe *American Idol?*" Fans did what comes natural for
fans. They offered Sharpies for an autograph. The 27-year-old Marine
obliged with smiles and laughs. After speaking from the gut in the VFW
hospitality tent about keeping alive the memory of our troops' sacrifices, he

received a standing ovation. Clapping men in wheelchairs, unable to rise, sat taller. A brother was getting his fair due.

Whirling to his next appearance on a golf cart, Russ admitted that these nods of assent—from muscular young bucks with razor-sharp crew cuts and weary, white-bearded men in stiff-crowned ball caps declaring their military affiliation, these knowing expressions of mutual understanding, signaling, "We get it, we hear what you're saying, we feel it, we too were there"—meant more than all the combined press interviews and autograph requests.

Fans knew that in a few hours, Jeff Gordon, now aging in front of fans' eyes with a daughter on pit road and gray-flecked sideburns sneaking down his face, might win the Russ Friedman 400. Or maybe it would be fan favorite Mark Martin, still full of smiles and aw-shucks gratitude at 50 years old following an emotional win two weeks before at Phoenix. Or maybe it would be young Brian Vickers who streaked fastest around the 3/4-mile track to capture the poll while the nodding vets applauded Russ. Whoever would take the checkered flag, Russ Friedman would be in Victory Lane to present the trophy. And rightly so. His name was etched on that hardware. It was his race.

But calling Russ a regular guy is not entirely accurate. He's a Marine from Huntington Station, New York; deployed to Iraq in 2001 weeks after the devastating surprise attacks on New York City, his city, 35 miles west; promoted to sergeant; injured on a mission; returned to service; blown up more severely; sent home; and awarded two Purple Hearts.

The first incident occurred in the town of Husayba outside of Baghdad while on a routine patrol. An improvised explosive device hidden in a pile of brush on the side of the road went off, shooting a load of hot shrapnel into Russ' arm. Fortunately, the shrapnel didn't hit any major vessels and Russ' injuries were relatively minor. With a bandaged limb, he rejoined his unit. Six days later, he wasn't so lucky. The U.S. base outside Husayba was taking mortar fire. Russ' quick reaction force was sent to locate the enemy. The Marines were ambushed. Russ ran to an abandoned building for a better angle to return fire. A rocket-propelled grenade blasted into the building and exploded, leaving shrapnel in his back, legs, and shoulders, while severing a nerve in his left arm.

Russ didn't know how badly he was hurt until he looked down and saw blood filling up his boot. He credits his vest and helmet for saving his life. This time, with shrapnel wounds in his leg, back, arm, and shoulder, he was going home. He was medevaced to a triage center, then airlifted to Germany, which, next to Iraq and Afghanistan, is the military's most-visited country among soldiers hooked to feeding tubes and beeping electronic devices monitoring their vitals.

"That kind of thing unfortunately comes with the territory," Friedman said, dismissing wounds that would earn him the military's highest honor. "You sign up knowing the risks and consequences. It's similar to a NASCAR driver hitting the wall at 200 miles per hour. It's part of what you do."

The Marine made it back to his boyhood home to recuperate. The adjustment from heart-thumping, adrenaline-fueled missions to resting at his family's home in Huntington Station wasn't easy. Yet his medical ordeal would truly begin when it was time to have the operation on his arm. On a Long Island highway, Russ was driving to the Northport VA Medical Center for surgery when an Iraqi insurgent jumped in front of his car. At least that's what he saw, clear as day.

Russ veered off the road flush into a telephone pole. I'd list all the bones he broke, but we'd run out of room. He woke up in a head-to-toe body cast like a character in the film *It's a Mad, Mad, Mad, Mad World*. Ironically, the injuries brought by visions in his head were significantly worse than those imparted by the insurgents' bombs.

Following the car accident, Russ was laid up in the hospital for 18 months. He recovered and met his fiancé April Willmott. They shared a passion for NASCAR, Russ rooting for Tony Stewart "who tells it like it is" and April pulling for Jimmie Johnson "only because Chad Knaus is his crew chief, this is a team sport, and Chad brought that team three championships."

As their relationship bloomed, Russ and April found a grounding common interest in NASCAR. They watched races on the big-screen TV at home, collected merchandise, and started taking weekend trips to attend NASCAR events. Each had a different "wish list" of races. Already displaying problem-solving relationship skills that will surely allow them to avoid counseling in years to come, the couple created a tidy method for choosing the races: drawing names from a hat. Once, Phoenix was picked. Another time it was Charlotte. And one track selected was Richmond for the Dan Lowry 400—named after a fan who won a contest for sharing the best Crown Royal celebratory toast.

When Russ found out "Dan Lowry" wasn't a company, he decided to compete for personal naming rights to the next "Your Name Here" race. But he added a twist. It wouldn't be about him. No, Russ was just doing his job overseas, and to be honest, so many had sacrificed so much more, not only in the Marines but every branch of the military. He worried that with all the crises happening in the world—brought to an edgy public via an endless CNN breaking news ticker—American troops, particularly the wounded warriors returning home, were being forgotten. No, this wasn't about Russ Friedman. Not at all. He wrote an essay calling for the race to be named the U.S. Armed Forces 400. That would help get his band of brothers the attention they deserved. But, in a series of conversations that could have been dialogue lifted from a Joseph Heller novel, government bureaucracy wouldn't permit the use of Friedman's proposed race name.

"Why that didn't happen is a decision way beyond my pay grade," Friedman said. "But the important thing was that Crown Royal let me make it completely about supporting our troops and showing them we're all behind them. They are protecting us and our freedom. There is no second-guessing. They are doing the right thing."

The blunt sincerity of Friedman's words, a direct and passionate plea for all Americans to acknowledge sacrifices being made on a grand scale, resonated with executives at Crown Royal. He was selected the contest winner. Friedman then wound up in another hospital. But this time it was with NASCAR Sprint Cup Series driver Jamie McMurray on a goodwill tour of McGuire VA Hospital near the track in Richmond to thank the troops.

On a misty May day, the NASCAR driver and Marine circulated among a group of injured soldiers on a patio outside the hospital. The men formed a large semicircle, a stunning wheelchair brigade. For the word *sacrifice* in the dictionary, this could be the photo. In the middle of all those wheelchairs were several men on flat gurneys. They were on their stomachs, elbows bent and forearms pressed into folded pillows to prop up their bodies, arching their backs into a position you'd see on the mats in a yoga class. Except the men's legs were gone.

As the wounded warriors waited patiently, Jamie McMurray signed 8x10 cards with his photo on one side and career driving stats on the other. In the world of sports, these are commonly called "hero cards," a description demonstrated this afternoon to be wildly inaccurate.

In no other major professional sport will you see a marquee event named after a fan. *Getty Images for NASCAR*

Inside the hospital, several veterans with fresher wounds confining them to their rooms waited for personal visits. One solider who couldn't use his arms sucked on a long, rubbery straw attached to the portable TV. I'd never seen an oxygen tank attached to a TV. Then I realized he was using the straw to change the channel. He'd been in the hospital six months and had watched all the NASCAR races on that small TV dangling less than two feet from his face.

Another soldier was propped in bed at an awkward angle, his frail, broken body sinking into a bank of pillows. There were more pillows than what remained of the body. Long red belts streamed down his bare torso. Taped to the wall was a color snapshot before the injury: a smiling young recruit, arms proudly crossed, muscles rippling below a faded green t-shirt. Next to the photo, a hand-printed sign read, "Please do not wake patient to tell him you are turning him or performing wound therapy. Just perform action."

The young Marine from West Virginia, who now has to look at that photo if he ever wants to see his legs, wowed Jamie and Russ with a remarkable sense of humor that must have been piped in from heaven. In a deliberate Southern drawl, slow from growing up in the South, or perhaps from having to catch your breath after a portion of your side has been blown away by a bomb, he deadpanned to McMurray, "I don't watch your Crown Royal car. But I do drink Crown Royal."

McMurray was wearing a short-sleeved knit shirt smartly emblazoned with his sponsor's fancy logo. The Marine commented he'd love to have a fine garment like that. The NASCAR driver took off the fresh garment, signed it, and handed it over. Without a second thought, McMurray gave him the shirt off his back.

McMurray, Russ, April, and I visited the spinal cord injury ward and the polytrauma unit, which we learned comprises soldiers with more than one serious injury. Russ had spent serious time in VA hospitals. But it was still like a bucket of cold water poured on his head to witness in room after room after room the multitude of ravaged soldiers slowly healing. So many young bodies, broken, battered, scarred, twisted, and utterly destroyed by war.

The government built this hospital—the second largest building in Virginia—next to a railroad line to unload injured World War II troops efficiently from rail cars. I wanted to proclaim with heartfelt outrage the senselessness of war and all the destruction it brings. But that would unjustly besmirch the honor, bravery, and sacrifice of Russ and his brothers. It would only show how much I need to learn about unconditional service to your country.

There was no bitterness in the air. The extraordinary veterans in this sprawling hospital are too broken to sit for a day at a desk job. Yet, none expressed any regrets about the outcome of his or her service. In fact, if they had their former bodies back, to a man they'd hightail it back to the front lines in Iraq. It would take a long time to process the concepts of duty and honor on display.

"The first thing the soldiers talk about is they want to get better to get back overseas to join their brothers and sisters and fight," Jamie McMurray said as we walked to another unit. "There's an incredible selflessness. Russ is just like that—a very giving person. His first response to the contest was to give back to the military. It says a lot about the guy."

Russ Friedman, 3rd Battalion, 7th Marines, fits the central casting mold of a truly selfless American hero. At the track, he was a good sport in putting on a purple crown for promotional photos, playing the role of Race King in Victory Lane as Kyle Busch rolled in his battered car and dove into the arms of his crew. He graciously played the part to get out his message, sitting for countless interviews, tirelessly deflecting attention to the men and women in the U.S. Armed Forces.

"I don't deserve special praise," Russ said. "We're all together as a band of brothers. This is about them. My name was on the tickets and the programs, but behind me is every single man and woman representing the armed forces, along with all of their families."

As his race weekend wound down and Saturday night turned into Sunday in a champagne-drenched Victory Lane, April looked at Russ and asked, "Are we really here?"

Following his tour overseas, making the toughest adjustment, the one inside your head, Russ may sometimes see things that don't exist. But this, of course, was real, and April's husband-to-be was at the center of it all. For a reserved, regular guy from Long Island who'd rather be casting a fishing line than talking into microphones, Sgt. Russ Friedman was an ambassador for the ages, beautifully serving the military, his sponsor, NASCAR, and every fan who has pressed a hand to his heart during the singing of the national anthem.

One weekend in May, NASCAR's traveling road show stopped in Richmond, Virginia, and Russ Friedman owned the joint. Wonka had turned over the keys, and it was Russ Friedman's chocolate factory. The M&Ms driver, Kyle Busch, even won the race.

As Russ and April strolled from Victory Lane hand in hand toward the garage where tools were being slammed into boxes, cars loaded, and race haulers rolling toward the infield tunnel and the next stop on the circuit, I heard Russ say this: "Sweet!"

NASCAR's Candy Man

Y NO MEANS AM I THE MOST QUALIFIED person to write this book. Others in the sport are stationed at Ground Zero for meeting fans who truly "bring it." Their jobs place them in the eye of the NASCAR hurricane blowing through a new market each week. They are the experts on the true NASCAR aficionados.

One of these people is Ryan Eichler, a.k.a. "Right Turn Ryan," who patrols the infield and the campgrounds of NASCAR Sprint Cup Series races, handing out M&Ms and imploring fans to enter a photo contest to be anointed the sport's most colorful fan. Wearing a snazzy M&Ms fire suit with hot flames shooting down the arm, Ryan is instantly associated with his sponsor's driver, Kyle Busch. But he's really an ambassador for the entire sport, disbursing copious amounts of candy like the Willy Wonka of Watkins Glen. Wonka declared, "Candy is dandy but liquor is quicker," and the combination of the two—yes, a fan or two has been observed enjoying a constitutionally granted right to adult beverages away from the grind in

Ryan Eichler, known as "Right Turn Ryan," patrols the infield handing out M&Ms in his search for the "Most Colorful Fan of NASCAR." *Getty Images for NASCAR*

the safe confines of the campgrounds—makes this outgoing 31-year-old bounding around with a large sack of M&Ms a veritable chocolate magnet for drawing fans into conversations about the sport.

Not everyone chatting with Ryan is fueled by Dutch courage. He usually makes the first move. Ryan only has to catch the glint of a stranger's smile or a hint of approachable body language, and he careens ahead to ask, "Where are you from? Who's your favorite driver?" If that fails, there's the failsafe conversation starter: "How about some M&Ms?"

Of course, fans don't root for every driver; Right Turn Ryan of M&Ms, so closely associated with Kyle Busch, the sport's newest villain, is not always greeted like a long-lost friend. He's fine with that. Not every driver can be universally beloved like Mark Martin, winning races at 50 years old and affectionately called "old man" by drivers young enough to be his son. The acronym *NASCAR* does not stand for "Neutral Athletes Stridently Courting Absolute Respect." Some drivers carry the outlaw streak of the rebels who formed the sport. Others could be choir boys. Razzing a driver you don't like (because he's the rebel or the choir boy, depending on preference for bad boys and good boys) and teasing that driver's loyal constituency can be more enjoyable than pulling for the guy you want to win.

In recent years, Kyle Busch has been the driver stirring the proverbial pot to elicit one of the most unique sounds in nature—the dissonant harmony of human voices simultaneously cheering and booing. Make no mistake, his antics are brilliantly entertaining and helpful to a sport seeking attention in a land of short attention spans and 500 cable TV channels. Busch is a supremely talented athlete who knows how to win and does it brazenly and often, savoring every second of his triumphs by metaphorically dancing on the graves of all he has defeated. He's the latest descendant of a long line of drivers who win in spectacular fashion while irking part of the fan base.

Young Darrell Waltrip ran his mouth to taunt King Richard Petty. Squeaky-clean, California-bred Jeff Gordon challenged Dale Earnhardt Sr.'s dominance while sporting a GQ look that shocked a sport full of cowboy boots and mullets. Similarly, the politically incorrect, guitar-smashing, Junior Nation–baiting, often-dominating Kyle Busch has shocked and awed and enraged and bedazzled every precinct of NASCAR Nation. Each fan has an opinion of Kyle, and some of them are unprintable.

"He's like the Yankees or the Red Sox," driver Jeff Burton said. "Millions love him and millions hate him; there's no middle ground or sitting on the fence." Many fans cheer like mad, and an equal number will voice displeasure with Kyle's exuberant bows after a win and hasty exits after a loss. Junior Nation collectively went ballistic when Kyle called them "crazy." Making the comment, Kyle was wearing a baiting smile, playing the media like an old fiddle the way Waltrip did two decades earlier, but that got lost in the game of telephone that passes this kind of news. And the cacophony of warring opinions about Kyle Busch and whether he's public enemy number one or perhaps tracking to be the greatest driver this sport has ever seen means Right Turn Ryan, guilty by association, isn't always greeted in the infield like the Pope walking into St. Patrick's Cathedral. Yet Right Turn has a knack for calming and neutralizing even an agitated Kyle basher. He's so earnest, a person would have to have a dark, corrupt soul—or no soul at all—to turn down his sweet peace offerings. Members of the anti-Kyle brigade walk away with a pack of the world's best-selling chocolate, and while these fans aren't known to make a beeline for the M&Ms merchandise hauler for Kyle's latest t-shirt, they also have a newfound (if begrudging) respect for an athlete they may not want to go hunting with but one who nonetheless has claimed the most wins before 25 years of age of any driver in NASCAR history. Amazing what a pack of M&Ms served with a honey-dipped delivery from a wholesome boy from Wisconsin can do. Maybe during the off-season, he should go to the palace in North Korea with his bags of candy. Print up the t-shirts: Chocolates for Nukes.

Right Turn Ryan had spent the morning in Pocono combing the infield for the best fan to feature on his popular "Most Colorful Fan of NASCAR" segment airing on SPEED TV's *Race Day* program. Visiting more than a dozen campsites, he was offered water, beer, scotch, tequila, a cigar, a turkey sandwich, a sausage hoagie, a cheeseburger, chicken wings, a hot dog, and shrimp and pepper kebobs. Over and over, he heard that universal greeting among fans: "You hungry?" "The generosity of these fans never ceases to amaze me," Ryan said.

A bald fan from Fayetteville, North Carolina, was on the side of the fence with those who believe Kyle Busch is exactly what NASCAR needs—a headline-generating personality who has outrageous fun when he wins and snarls like a hungry cat when he loses. He offered to paint

Wearing a snazzy M&Ms fire suit, Ryan is an ambassador for the entire sport, disbursing candy to hungry fans like the Willy Wonka of Watkins Glen. *Author photo*

his shiny pate bright yellow to resemble an M&M, with the same stylized number 18 that appears on Kyle's door. "Call me then, I'm definitely interested," Ryan said, taking his card.

A man from down the hill in Wackesville, Pennsylvania, was wearing a "Hat of Tomorrow." He mounted a black plastic wing on the back of the NASCAR cap, just like the wing on NASCAR's new car. "When you get drunk, it helps you hit the ground slower," he joked. His German girlfriend (this we know because he kept offering to introduce us to "my German girlfriend") emerged from their tent and asked for candy in German. Ryan, ever the international diplomat, gave her plain *and* peanut.

A striking young lady with dual silver studs protruding from her tan belly, appearing to be the eyes of a dragon tattoo disappearing into her terry cloth shorts, also could have been an intriguing interview. "I don't accept candy from strangers," she told Ryan, who smiled without breaking stride for the next campsite. M&Ms doesn't explicitly market to kids, and who knows how old this girl was.

A couple who drove to the Poconos from California was highly promising. "That's a pretty long haul; we can make that interesting," Ryan said. They were slated as his final choice until a band of merry firefighters from Patterson, New Jersey, came on the scene seeking candy like a pack of hungry trick-or-treaters.

"Who doesn't like M&Ms?" said Marty Krupinski, battalion chief for the Patterson Fire Department. Krupinski had spotted the fire suit, loved the flames, and began chatting with Ryan. "What I like about this scene is everyone has a common interest: NASCAR and having a good time," Krupinski explained to Right Turn, then invited him to a seafood dinner at his camper with his firehouse buddies in Bass Pro Shop hats representing New Jersey's own Martin Truex. "You get into your own world here—everybody's happy and everybody's your friend. They come here and leave all their problems at home. Look around. Everyone's smiling. Show me one unhappy person."

Listening to the firefighter who rushed across the Hudson into Manhattan on September 11 and plugged his pumper into a fire boat on the river to get water to the burning towers when none other was available, Ryan knew he had his segment. "I don't want the guys with their faces painted," he said. "Those fans are great, but they're all over the place, and we've seen them before. I'm really looking for the good stories, the Charles Kuralt human interest pieces you'd get from a world-class TV journalist."

It's an interesting gig, part journalist, part carnival barker; good work if you can get it and alternate between high- and low-brow in the same conversation. Ryan will talk track dynamics with fans and in the next moment is not above dancing around as if he's had a few and posing for fan photos at a makeshift beach party on top of a motor home. "NASCAR is an entertainment product, and I feed into that," he said. In Charlotte, one lady followed him around for 10 minutes, getting multiple "Right Turn Ryan" autographs. A fan in Darlington asked if Ryan wanted to marry his daughter. "He was looking for a good racer for her, liked the way I looked in the fire suit, and thought I fit the bill. I very respectfully declined." With his high-energy SPEED segments and Facebook videos attracting a strong following, a permanent TV gig may one day be in the cards.

Before his M&Ms role, Ryan was promoting GM and was chosen for on-camera work for the 12 Hours of Sebring American Le Mans race in central Florida. He was assigned to the Baja 500 in the Mexican desert for Team Hummer, where he became "Ryan the Race Master" in video segments for the endurance race. When his PR agency, Weber Shandwick, was brainstorming ideas to take the M&Ms Most Colorful Fan contest to a new level, and came up with the idea of "fanvocates," he became Right

Turn Ryan, joined at races by his female alter ego, Left Turn Lindsay. Together, the fanvocates have been a big success for M&Ms.

"I guess I never realized they'd pay me to do this," Ryan said. "I've always loved to have fun, and because I'm a big NASCAR fan, it's probably a lot easier for me to fit the role and help the program."

Whereas most kids go to baseball or football games with their dads, Ryan and his father attended local dirt-track races near their hometown of Racine, Wisconsin. The closest NASCAR Sprint Cup Series track, Michigan International Speedway, was seven hours away. Ryan's dad, who worked for 35 years at SC Johnson Wax making shaving cream and car wax, didn't want to make the drive. But hard-working Ryan was named "Carrier of the Month" for the Milwaukee *Journal Sentinel* in 1993, which brought free tickets to see the NASCAR Nationwide Series at the Milwaukee Mile.

He loved it and started attending races at Indianapolis and Chicago, often coming home with car parts. He's bought a front end of a car, a hood, four tires, and the wing of a midget car. Foreshadowing his track appearances as "Right Turn Ryan," he attended an Indianapolis 500 in a suit he made with checkered flag lapels and race patches.

Ryan became a Jeff Gordon fan, and when he scored a hot pass for an assignment with a Chicago PR agency and saw Jeff in the pits and on the track at Chicagoland Speedway, his NASCAR fandom took off to an interplanetary level. He was in the pits when the crews of Kasey Kahne and Tony Stewart brawled on pit road after Stewart rear-ended Kahne, spinning him head-on into the Turn One wall. "That's an odd moment to say, 'I really want to be involved in the business side of the sport,' but seeing that excitement and energy was when it happened," he said.

GM became a client, giving Ryan the opportunity to interview all the drivers from Chevy Racing. It wasn't an instantly smooth transition for a Gordon fan. "I once was asking Jeff Burton questions and calling him 'Jeff Gordon' on camera. Burton looked at me kind of strange, chuckled, and answered the question without a hitch."

Aside from the gaffes, there were poignant moments too, like interviewing Jimmie Johnson at the Woodward Dream Cruise of classic cars on the strip in downtown Detroit. Johnson was being presented a 1969 Camaro with a motor built by Randy Dorton of Hendrick Motor Sports. In fact, it was the last engine the team's chief engine builder ever designed. Dorton was on the Hendrick team plane that crashed into a mountain on the way to Martinsville, Virginia, on a foggy Sunday in October 2005, killing all 10 passengers on board. NASCAR learned of the crash during the race. When Jimmie Johnson took the checkered flag, he and his team were summoned to the NASCAR hauler and told the tragic news. The Victory Lane celebration was cancelled on one of the saddest days in NASCAR history. "When Jimmie got that car in Detroit, he was so happy to have this beautiful Camaro but sad about Randy. It was completely bittersweet because this was the last engine Randy Dorton had built. It made for quite an emotional interview. Jimmie was great about it. It was tough for him to talk about Randy, but he was going out of his way to make *me* feel comfortable. He was really professional and just a plain good guy in the way he conducted himself and helped us get through that."

Johnson, a three-time NASCAR champion, has been tagged by many as a milquetoast personality with a vanilla image. It's a curious opinion to voice considering that in winning three consecutive NASCAR Sprint Cup titles, Jimmie is one of the most dogged and accomplished champions in sports history, who during off hours, broke his wrist falling off a golf cart on boys' night out and once had his hair cut, badly, by kids at a birthday party. That's boring? If Johnson were a fan, he'd be a strong contender for Ryan's "Most Colorful" videos. Jimmie's biggest problems with media pining for "personality" are his grace and elegance. He makes winning look easy. He's calm in victory and the same in defeat. He doesn't start fights or drop bombshell quotes. Sounds a bit like Joe DiMaggio, who was fortunate to play in an era when a champion was given his due respect simply for his on-field heroics.

Now that Ryan is helping represent Kyle Busch, he faces a different PR challenge. No one in his right mind will ever write that Kyle is bland. But athletes who excel in a particular field are quite often complicated souls, and capturing the essence of recalcitrant Kyle has proven difficult. It's not necessarily that Kyle is inwardly complex. The media and many fans simply haven't decided what they want him to be. Perhaps Kyle needs a reality show. Absent that, Ryan wants to expose new facets of a driver who may turn out to be one of the greatest in NASCAR history yet remains underestimated and misunderstood, particularly in avoiding the hot media lights when he fails to win the race.

"Everybody thinks Kyle stomps away because he doesn't know how to articulate his feelings," Ryan said. "Hey, he's *frustrated.* He wants to win more than anything else. He runs every lap like it's his last. When he wins, he's highly entertaining. When he loses, he's furious. He's the epitome of a race car driver. He'd knock you aside on the exit ramp on the interstate if he thought you were trying to pass. Kyle would frankly rather drive the car than do press interviews. At the track, he is completely focused on that race car. He says what's on his mind. In today's sanitized age of speaking in pre-approved sound bites, that's a pretty cool throwback notion. As time goes on, I think fans will also start to see a side of Kyle they have no idea exists, which is his commitment to children's charities. He supports five children's orphanages, helping kids who are abandoned, abused, and disadvantaged. I've seen Kyle spend a whole afternoon with those kids asking questions and really getting engaged. It's a completely different guy than the one who can be demonized in the press and on the Internet fan boards."

Just as Ryan was explaining Kyle's unheralded affection for kids, two late-stage teenagers skidded up on mountain bikes. "Hey, you don't drive with Kyle Busch, do you?" one kid asked Ryan. "We like Junior, not Kyle."

"Yeah, Junior!" his sidekick said.

"Hey, I'm the most colorful fan, Right Turn Ryan! You guys want some M&Ms?"

They took a handful of packages and pedaled away on their fat-tire bikes, hooting and hollering like kids who should be riding tricycles. Amazing what a bag of candy can do. Maybe they'll be rooting for Kyle this afternoon.

The Fathead Guy

A HANDFUL OF LANDMARKS are very familiar to the fans populating the campgrounds of NASCAR. Everyone knows where the showers are located. If those facilities are too crowded, they can find hoses for a "pirate bath." They know the location of the tunnels to get outside for more steaks, ice, wood, and beer. And at NASCAR tracks in places like Pocono, Watkins Glen, Bristol, Darlington, Dover, Martinsville, Michigan, Richmond, and Talladega, everyone seems to know the campsite of "The Fathead Guy," Kenny Gregory, who has created an eye-popping homage to the often-controversial sport he's made part of his life for more than three decades.

Kenny Gregory brings his Fathead driver stand-ups to a dozen NASCAR races each year. He's interested in creating controversy, conversations, and new friends. *Courtesy Dave Nesi*

Kenny's innovation is to make Fatheads—the humongous player decals that kids and men in developmental limbo plaster on their bedroom walls—into a NASCAR prop. He brings the sport's biggest stars directly to the fans on their turf by mounting driver Fatheads onto plywood, cutting the figures into a precise silhouette, and attaching the drivers to a metal stake driven into the ground like a fiery tiki torch. The "starting grid"—Jeff Gordon, Dale Earnhardt Jr., Tony Stewart, Kyle Busch, Jimmie Johnson, and Kasey Kahne—stops fans in their tracks. Stumbling upon a group of proud NASCAR drivers standing tall in the middle of the smoky infield is a sight as remarkable as Stonehenge. Fans will rub their eyes and break into a trot for a better view. Closer, they see the drivers are just an illusion. Then it hits home: the cutouts must have been brought to the campground by *someone*—a mad genius, must be a rock-solid fan, who else could come up with an invention this perfect? They realize *he is one of us*, and that makes the discovery even better, maybe the greatest thing to happen in the grasses of NASCAR since Earnhardt ripped across the turf on the front stretch in Charlotte, kept control of the car, and seemingly picked up speed to win the NASCAR Sprint All-Star Race. Fans need to know more about this strange, wonderful sight and the person behind it, and dozens each race day will find out because the affable Gregory is inevitably lurking in the wings. He's 58 years old and has survived three heart attacks but still darts around his camper like a Red Bull–fueled bunny, wads of cash collected for race wagers bulging from his thin white socks, waiting to meet new friends and take more bets, if anyone's up for it.

"I've got these drivers out here because it brings people together," Gregory said. "Everybody has their favorites in NASCAR, and there are spirited arguments and a lot to disagree about, but it's all in the name of good fun."

On an early-summer Sunday morning at Pocono Raceway, Kyle Busch was planted in the turf head first. The previous night at Nashville Superspeedway, Busch won the NASCAR Nationwide Series race, and as is the custom in Music City, he was presented in Victory Lane a beautiful, custom-made, specially painted Gibson Les Paul guitar that serves as the revered trophy. True to his nickname, "Rowdy" proceeded to smash the expensive instrument like the Who's Pete Townsend during the final encore at the Isle of Wight.

"Now, a lot of people think that was not a good thing to do last night. So today, Kyle is upside down," Ken said, standing next to the overturned Busch, his elbow leaning on Jeff Gordon's shoulder as if the two were old army buddies. "I've never seen his kind of driving talent in a boy this age. He's got a gift from God, and even though Kyle's my driver, today he's in the doghouse. But you know what, when he smashes a trophy, or storms off after the race without doing his media interviews, or if Carl Edwards almost punches his teammate Matt Kenseth in the face, or if Tony's into it with Jeff Gordon, it's good for the sport. It's controversy, it's publicity, and it makes this sport bigger and more fun."

Relishing the side skirmishes produced by a sport featuring 3,400-pound cars bumping at fantastically high speeds, and courting a smidgen of controversy himself, Kenny chose for his starting grid drivers who set off the most sparks. In fact, simmering bad blood between Gordon and Stewart several years ago inspired Gregory to decorate his campsite with the driver Fatheads. "When they almost came to blows in Watkins Glen, I said, 'Let me get me a Stewart, put some boxing gloves on him, and bring him out to the camper,'" Ken remembered.

Today, Gordon is happily married and mellowed. Run-ins with his competitors are few and far between. He doesn't draw as many boos in pre-race ceremonies as Kyle Busch, but it's darn close. Fans harboring a grudge against Gordon make it personal. One woman regularly treks to Gregory's campsite to have it out with the four-time champ.

"Every night, she comes by to kick Jeff in the midsection. A few nights ago, she broke him in half, right below the belt, and I had to glue him up. I asked her, 'Now why would you do that? This driver is not bothering anyone.' She said, 'I hate Jeff Gordon, and I'm gonna come back and kick him tomorrow.' Now that's not a NASCAR fan. There are a lot of people here but very few disrespectful ones. Unfortunately, they surface now and then. If there's a bad apple here at the track, these stand-ups will draw them over, that's for sure."

Last season, Kenny woke up to find an obscenity scrawled on Gordon's face. "I look out from the camper and see two dozen women surrounding Jeff, fiddling with their makeup, choosing a shade to best cover up the ink on Jeff's forehead. They did a pretty good job. The next day, a little boy comes over and says to me, 'Mister, I wrote that, and I sure am sorry.' That's a good boy who learned his lesson."

Gregory is a kind, generous man who, during tough economic times, funds the race weekends of his guests. Here within the "starting grid," he poses with Julie Botts, a close friend he calls "my adopted daughter." *Courtesy Dave Nesi*

Gregory, a thin, animated man who has a face that seems incapable of harboring deceit or insincerity and likes to lower his chin to peer over his sunglasses when making a point, began following NASCAR decades before fans could get life-size facsimiles of their drivers. He started attending races 30 years ago at Watkins Glen and was at a Formula One event at the road course in western New York wine country for one of the most bizarre incidents in American auto racing history. A large group of people picked up Emerson Fittipaldi's bus, rolled it into the bog, and burned it. "The National Guard helicopters came in. It was the only time I got tear-gassed in my life."

When I first discovered Kenny with Right Turn Ryan, the M&Ms "fanvocate" gathering colorful fan leads for his SPEED TV *Race Day* piece, it wasn't easy to get these stories. Kenny didn't want the attention. Friends and family were materializing from everywhere, and he kept pulling them in, slinging his wiry arm around their necks, offering them to answer questions meant for him. Kenny wanted me to interview Julie Botts, a woman he's so fond of he actually calls her his "adopted daughter." Julie met Kenny through her husband, Rob, who worked with him at Joy Mining Machinery in Pennsylvania. The couple's 18-year-old son will come to the next Pocono race. "Ken is my sugar daddy without benefits," Julie joked. Kenny brought out his smiling sisters, Dee and Chris, who clearly adore their brother and nodded with great affection whenever I could get him to answer my questions.

Compared to the fans I'd interviewed at other campsites, Kenny's friends and family were bashful. It was as if a secret were being harbored, and for the first time in my research it felt like I was prying, a nosy NASCAR busybody with no business showing up unannounced to ask personal questions, only to go off once a few notes were taken in search of another life to invade. I later learned that Kenny, who was divorced in 2001 and had begun traveling to more than a dozen races a year, was treating the group to the race weekend—food and drink, track admission, everything. He did this at a dozen races throughout the season. Funding the entire trip was no big deal to the retired tool and die maker from Franklin, Pennsylvania.

"We all come from the same background. The economy has bad effects. So I pay their way," he said. "With the blessings God has provided me, I can share my good fortune with my circle of friends and meet a lot of new ones."

The Fathead stand-ups are this generous, open-hearted fan's calling card for other fans to congregate and connect. Ken stokes the party by handing out glow sticks to the kids and bestowing Hawaiian leis on the women. Sometimes he plants the stand-ups in the form of a mini-golf course, handing out balls and putters to whoever wants to play. But the extra props aren't really necessary. The sight of these drivers in the middle of the feast of exuberance that is the NASCAR infield is enough to get the fans' attention and allow them to meet a very special man.

"The best part of the driver cutouts is how they've allowed me to make so many friends," Ken said. "At the race track, I have good friends, and they treat me well. I love life and NASCAR and great people. I am blessed to get all that here."

Jeff Burton and the World's Fastest Grandmother

NASCAR DRIVER KEVIN HARVICK once sank into a hot tub—wearing his racing fire suit—with a group of NASCAR fans.

Jamie McMurray has shuttled many grateful (and tipsy) folks as designated driver for sponsor Crown Royal.

Michael Waltrip has been known to deliver a Domino's Pizza or two to hungry fans.

And during Speedweeks of 2008 Jeff Burton drove a purple Chevrolet Monte Carlo SS with the No. 31 Prilosec OTC paint scheme to the driveway of Kathryn Cooley of Barnesville, Maryland, adding his name to the roster of NASCAR drivers to surprise the heck out of a fan on behalf of his sponsor.

Cooley, 64 years old and utterly delighted to see the NASCAR driver, was washing laundry when Burton knocked on her front door with a

Kathryn Cooley won the Prilosec OTC "Victory of a Lifetime" sweepstakes, which included a new car, $20,000, and VIP treatment at 20 NASCAR Sprint Cup Series races.
Courtesy Jordan Futscher

camera crew in tow. You could say she entered the spin cycle of NASCAR in winning one of the most generous sweepstakes in sports, "The Prilosec OTC Victory of a Lifetime."

The spunky grandmother is still beholden to Richard Petty, though it's been years since the King ruled NASCAR by collecting seven titles. She most fondly remembers the King's theatrically timed win in 1984 at the Firecracker 400. President Ronald Reagan was aboard Air Force One when the race started but landed next to Daytona International Speedway. The presidential motorcade, an odd sight in Daytona Beach, raced over to make it to the track in time to see Petty win his 200th and final race.

Even though no driver has moved her like Petty did, Cooley continued following NASCAR when the King hung up his helmet. One driver she pulls for is Jeff Burton, a talented, clean competitor who she says is a good role model for the sport. Being an honest driver, treating each competitor as you'd like to be treated yourself, racing hard but fair, these traits that are spread unevenly throughout the field have always been very important to Cooley. When she spotted Burton in a Prilosec OTC newspaper ad featuring a coupon and the "Victory of a Lifetime" sweepstakes, she went looking for her scissors. It wasn't Burton's handsome, smiling, honest face she wanted to clip, or the offer of a new car and VIP trips to more than half the NASCAR Sprint Cup Series races next season. Kathryn suffers from acid reflux and wanted to save a few dollars on a box of Prilosec OTC. She nabbed the coupon and stuck the sweepstakes offer in her purse.

Kathryn thought about the sweepstakes and realized if most people suspected they'd lose and didn't enter, well, that raised her odds of winning. She filled out and mailed her entry, soon forgetting all about it.

Some months later, a notification letter arrived at her house. She'd won the Victory of a Lifetime sweepstakes. To claim the prize, Cooley had to have the letter notarized. Her bank was suspicious. They knew Kathryn as a loyal customer, a grandmother, a sweet lady, maybe a little naïve about financial matters. No one wanted an innocent, gullible woman to be swallowed up in what appeared to be an awfully creative scam. "They thought it was identity theft and didn't want to notarize the letter," Cooley recalls.

The bank helped investigate. Phone calls were made. This was no royal scam. Cooley was told Procter & Gamble, the maker of Prilosec OTC

Cooley's husband heard Kathryn "won a car" and waited to receive a die-cast in the mail. Instead, the Maryland grandmother got a house call from driver Jeff Burton, who delivered a hot new purple Chevy Monte Carlo SS. *Charles E. Shoemaker II/The Gazette*

and one of the world's most sophisticated marketers, was behind all this. Kathryn had won the contest and was ready to receive her new car. Who wouldn't want a new Chevy? But she was more excited about how she was getting it—through a personal visit from Jeff Burton.

"From watching races, I knew Jeff, who always races you fair and is considerate of his competitors, is a fine display of what NASCAR is and should be," she said. "It's important for my grandkids to look up to these drivers. Jeff, like so many others, is a quality family man who brings respect. I'm proud it was him who brought the car to me."

The conspicuous purple hot rod Burton drove to her house and the promise of an unforgettable 2008 season on the road with NASCAR made Cooley's experience all the sweeter.

"I never imagined I would be personally delivering a purple Chevy to a 64-year-old female race fan," Burton said. "It was pretty cool. The expression on Kathryn's face when she opened the door was priceless. She was overjoyed, which makes doing things like this worthwhile."

"When they first told us we won a car, my husband thought someone would mail us a little metal die-cast," Cooley said. "I don't know who was more excited, Jack or me."

After Burton dropped off the new ride, the Cooleys took a spin. The slick Chevy with lightning-bolt decals and 5.3-liter V-8 drew double takes on the streets of Barnesville, especially when Jack squealed the tires. Kathryn may now be the grandmother with the hottest car in all of Maryland.

Burton's visit bearing the new Monte Carlo SS was just the tip of the booty. Cooley attended 20 NASCAR Sprint Cup Series races in the 2008 season, a pretty serious swing through the circuit. She, Jack, and two guests flew first class and enjoyed VIP treatment at each track. She even met Richard Childress, team owner of the No. 31 car, toured the RCR race shop, and had lunch at Childress' vineyard. Oh, and there was $20,000 in spending money as well.

Prior to her 20-race adventure, Cooley, a lifelong resident of Barnesville, had attended races at her "local tracks"—Dover and Richmond International Raceway. She once took Jack to Daytona International Speedway as a gift. But with nagging health issues and the rising cost of travel, she hadn't had the chance to see other NASCAR venues or distant parts of the country. As she recovered from cancer, Cooley said Burton's surprise visit was "just what the doctor ordered." She particularly enjoyed races in places like Phoenix, Las Vegas, Los Angeles, and Loudon, New Hampshire.

"My whole life, I really wanted to see other parts of the U.S. I was unable to do so, and then I got sick. Now, with my health getting better and with NASCAR races thrown in, this experience has just been great," Cooley explained.

Her heartburn is gone too. The marketing department at Procter & Gamble named this one right. For Kathryn Cooley, the 2008 season was truly the "Victory of a Lifetime."

Friday Night Lights Lead into Saturday Night Racing

M URRAY ERICKSON, A FORMER hockey player from Calgary, Alberta, Canada, now transplanted to Odessa, Texas, home of "Friday Night Lights" and lucrative oil fields, admits he's an unlikely NASCAR fan.

"I'm the last person in the world you'd think would be into racing," Erickson said. "It's not in my family or a big part of where I grew up." But as I got to know Erickson, an attraction to racing and its close-knit community was by no means a giant leap of logic. He's an absolute adrenaline junkie who owns airplanes, sleek motorcycles, and fast automobiles and who, most of all, has the friendship of many "sincere and decent people" he's met in racing who share an interest in going faster than the other guy, or at least having a heck of a good time trying. Despite a background that's

Oilman, rare-car collector, track owner, and NASCAR fan Murray Erickson spent a few days with Michael Waltrip, getting a rare insider's view of the blizzard of commitment and distractions filling the life of a NASCAR driver/owner. *Courtesy Ferguson & Katzman*

different than the fans and drivers he knows, Erickson is now part of the racing community.

He was born in a frigid part of Canada where kids learn to skate before they walk. The speed of the game on ice foreshadowed the rush he'd seek on asphalt and dirt. Erickson's progression from hockey to racing was a steady gravitational pull. Those who wind up in the sport know the feeling: it feels like destiny, an inescapable path within the order of nature. Water seeks its level. Matter can neither be created nor destroyed. For every action, there is an equal and opposite reaction. And speed freaks will find other speed freaks.

A magnetic pull toward the top ranks of America's car culture may be one explanation for Murray Erickson's transformation from rough-and-tumble junior hockey goalie to wrench monkey, classic car collector, race car driver, and race track owner. Or, if you catch glimpse of his lower leg, maybe it's about the girls. Erickson's right calf boasts a tattoo of a curvy pinup girl pleasantly sitting in a cocktail glass. She's wearing a driver's helmet and come-hither look and has a steering wheel triumphantly thrust above her head. A pair of checkered flags crisscrosses the long-stem glass. Erickson's car number (8) rises through champagne bubbles toward his knee. It's a brilliant tattoo, the mark of a man with a healthy appreciation of racing and the benefits that may come with it.

Whatever the root causes of his sumptuous racing appetite, once Erikson developed a taste for the sport, and the like-minded people who inhale rubber-tinged air with the satisfied gusto of a nature lover sucking in the dewy goodness of a spring morning in the woods, there was no pulling away. He got in deeper and deeper. It was like being cocooned in a barrel careening over Niagara Falls. Once over the edge, there was no stopping.

As his passion for fast, beautiful, and increasingly expensive cars was growing, Erickson moved to Texas and launched a business to service oil companies tapping black gold in the barren fields of west Texas. The company thrived. He started collecting rare automobiles, including four vintage Corvettes, the most recent picked up at the Barrett-Jackson auction. His stable of cars runs heavy on Detroit muscle, including a 1969 Mustang, 1969 Firebird, and 1973 Trans Am. He also has a Ferrari, a vintage Mercedes, and a very rare Bengal Charger, which commemorated the football team's entry into the NFL. Only one other Bengal Charger exists today.

If the machine has wheels and goes fast, Erickson will likely be interested. He has several Harleys and a "crotch rocket," a New York City chopper. He was eying one particularly hot bike in an online auction, but NASCAR driver Tony Stewart outbid him. Then he caught wind of an auction for a "fan swap." Anyone willing to write a big enough check could switch jobs for a day with NASCAR Sprint Cup Series driver and team owner Michael Waltrip. Proceeds would go to the charities of Waltrip's sponsor, Best Western. Erickson could peek under the hood of Michael Waltrip Racing while doing some good. He sent in a winning $4,700 bid.

"I like to see how things work," the entrepreneur explained. "This was a chance to go behind the scenes and check out NASCAR as a competitive sport and big business. I'd get a real insider's perspective not available to anyone outside the sport."

Best Western sent Erickson to Waltrip's Charlotte headquarters, RaceWorld USA, where he tagged along for a day with the driver-owner and enjoyed a behind-the-velvet-rope experience that is probably unavailable in any other major sport. Over the course of two days, he sat on the set of NASCAR Media Group's Charlotte studio as Waltrip taped "The Week in NASCAR," a weekly retrospective show on SPEED, and participated in the taping of Waltrip's weekly SiriusXM satellite radio show. He accompanied the two-time Daytona 500 winner on a photo shoot for Coca-Cola's advertising and promotional materials. He feasted on an authentic North Carolina barbecue lunch with Waltrip, his sister Connie, and their charming mother, Margaret. And he shadowed the driver/team owner as he met with many of the 230 employees of Michael Waltrip Racing preparing for the coming weekend at Atlanta Motor Speedway. It would be Waltrip's 1,000th race in NASCAR. Only Richard Petty has made more starts at the sport's top levels.

"One thousand races," Waltrip told his new friend, accompanied by a low whistle. "You know what that means. Only one thing: I'm old!"

The Hallmark greeting card reads "Life begins at 40." That's about right for Erickson, who hit the big "four-oh" and began competitively racing sprint and midget cars—smaller vehicles with powerful engines that often run on dirt tracks, sliding through the turns and bouncing off one another. Racing against drivers half his age, Erickson hooked up with driving coach Jimmie Sills, a four-time USAC Silver Crown champ whose father was a driver in NASCAR's Grand National Division, which is today the top-level NASCAR Sprint Cup Series.

Erickson set up his own race shop and bought a run-down race track, which he called "a bunch of weeds." He completely refurbished the neglected 3/8-mile dirt course. He rebuilt the bathrooms, redid the concessions, and painted the grandstands, which quickly filled up with new race fans. Champion Motor Speedway puts on shows to packed houses every other Saturday, all summer long. "We are four hours from Dallas, and there's not a lot to do here," Erickson said. "This community needed a race track. I felt I was doing a public service."

Before becoming a track owner, Erickson had deeply enjoyed competing. He's had the opportunity to race in the Chili Bowl—the year's biggest dirt event each January that pits the top stars of all forms of racing against each other in a festive indoor race in Tulsa. When competing at demanding dirt tracks like Belleville High Banks in Kansas, he could feel the intensity of the revved-up, gung-ho crowd even while inside a loud, eardrum-busting car. "Belleville is a place where the entire crowd boos any driver who gets off the gas. I took my two qualifying laps on the gas the whole time, holding on for dear life. I'm pretty sure they were cheering when I got out of the car, but all I really could hear was my heart pounding inside my helmet."

The journeyman race car driver never got to spray adult beverages in Victory Lane. He simply didn't have that rare combination of an all-your-waking-hours commitment in the shop during the week with blind win-at-all-costs courage behind the wheel on Saturday night. He realized a driver's ability to block out any fear with each approaching turn is as crucial for winning races as raw driving talent.

"I did love the times when I was side by side with kids who have absolutely no fear in the world. Maybe I was too old when I got started. I wasn't prepared to go that distance. I didn't want to get in the way of the faster drivers. I didn't have an attitude and driving style completely devoid of fear. I didn't have that win-at-all-costs mentality."

Sinking into chairs scattered about the cozy SiriusXM radio studio located above Michael Waltrip's airy race shop, the former goalie accustomed to taking pucks in the face said he wasn't prepared to pay the price in racing. Waltrip, a jolly jokester from Kentucky who turns stone serious in the race car and has been in his share of stomach-turning wrecks,

shrugged off the consequences of pushing a car to the precipice of catas-
trophe. "When you hit something out there, you might get hurt. That's
why they put you in a fire suit and put a helmet on your head," he said.

Through the job swap, Erickson saw a different side of Waltrip. Exposed
to his incessant media appearances, some fans view the driver as a goofy,
sponsor-plugging PR machine whose better days are behind him. Yet the
45-year-old NASCAR veteran possesses marketing and entrepreneurial
talents that belie the cut-up caricature he creates as NASCAR's clown
prince rarely passing up a chance to ham it up on TV. Waltrip is more
dimensional and complicated than the flip court-jester image he enjoys
projecting. "Some people might say I'm two different people, but I think
it's more like seven or eight," he said.

On the track, he's achieved far less success than his older brother
Darrell. Then again, few drivers match the retired legend's 84 wins, which
ranks third of all time in NASCAR's top series. But rather than disappear
in the formidable shadow of the man known as "DW," Michael managed
to forge a long and profitable career that includes two Daytona 500 victo-
ries and the more recent formation of a three-car NASCAR Sprint Cup
race team he oversaw while driving the No. 55 NAPA Toyota. He started
Michael Waltrip Racing in his backyard a few years ago; today, there's visible pride in his step as he walks the shimmering floors of 142,000-square-
foot RaceWorld USA.

"What Michael has done is a significant feat," said Erickson, who has two
full-time employees in his race shop building three cars for the next Chili
Bowl. "Successfully breaking into team ownership at this level of expectations and performance is nearly impossible to do from a standing start. But
he did it. I'm really impressed with what a bright and focused man he is."

That ability to concentrate on constantly rotating tasks amid a blizzard of commitments and distractions is perhaps as difficult a feat as
maneuvering a 3,400-pound race car through heavy traffic. The life of
a NASCAR driver is a hodgepodge of endless appointments and obligations . . . with heated racing thrown in the mix. Erickson watched
Waltrip hopscotch a dizzying set of transitions from the ridiculous (in
the sponsor photo shoot, vamping on his back like a calendar girl while
sprawled across a set of Goodyear race tires) to the sublime (working on
his car's setup for NASCAR's fastest track where speeds will touch 200
miles per hour).

The ad shoot included other drivers in the Coca-Cola racing family: Waltrip's fellow competitors Tony Stewart, Kevin Harvick, Jamie McMurray, Elliot Sadler, and the highly touted rookie Joey Logano. Fans regularly see these Coke-sponsored drivers during post-race TV interviews on pit road and in Victory Lane, pulling sips from their Coke bottles, the labels expertly tilted toward the camera. (Each time a driver takes an on-camera slug, NASCAR's official soft drink donates money to charity.) To accommodate the various photographic backdrops—including one tongue-in-cheek setup requiring the drivers to lean against a ladder in kitschy poses for a 1970s-era Sears portrait studio look—the shoot was spread among three spacious houses on Lake Norman north of Charlotte. These were big homes, though not as large as some of the houses Erickson is accustomed to in Texas. They were not quite McMansions. More like McMansions on the Dollar Menu.

He may have the proverbial racing tattoo, but Erickson is not your typical hardcore NASCAR fan lathered in driver merchandise from head to toe. He owns none of the usual apparel and accessories wallpapering the typical fan. Inside RaceWorld USA, he snapped more pictures of engine parts and fabricating equipment than of the driver. While he did bid generously for the job swap and enjoyed his time with Waltrip immensely, the trip to Charlotte wasn't to fawn over a driver who's the object of an intense cheering experience. As an entrepreneur and former race car driver, Erickson wanted to view the whole enterprise, to observe how a driver-owner balances running a state-of-the-art race shop building more than three dozen race cars while fitting in media appearances, ad shoots, and impromptu autograph sessions with fans paying 15 bucks for the run of one of the most accessible garages in the sport.

Erickson's fascination with NASCAR is not with the individual drivers, though he respects each of them. He marvels at the entire enterprise. He has a keen appreciation for the collection of guts, courage, and extraordinary technical prowess on display in the Big Show every Sunday.

As he nears his 50th birthday, he has mothballed his fire suit but is closer to the sport than ever. The car counts at Champion Motor Speedway are strong. The sounds of wrenches banging metal can be heard in many local garages. Odessa, Texas, may be best known for "Friday Night Lights," but it's the Saturday night dirt track racing more and more people are looking forward to as the work week draws to a close.

Sam Greenwood/Getty Images

PART IV
ALIGNED WITH THE STARS

One of the first questions I'll ask a NASCAR fan is, "How did you start following the sport and become a fan?"

Family or friends usually turn them on to the sport. Once watching, the race cars might be the draw—the numbers, the colors, the way a car looks on the track. Sometimes a sponsor helps create fans. (When Kyle Busch is old, retired, and cutting people off in his wheelchair, on Halloween he should give the kids nothing but M&Ms as a token of thanks for the millions of happy introductions his sponsor has made.)

Whatever the path, fans are eventually drawn to a particular driver. Something about him—and now, increasingly, *her*—is intriguing. Maybe he was down to earth and funny at an autograph signing. During the race, he may have blown through holes in traffic that didn't seem to exist, and no one else mattered. Maybe they saw him on a TV talk show, liked his attitude or the way he talked or the things he said, and wanted to find out more. That's how fans are born.

The most intense fans learn a lot about their drivers and come to loathe his rivals. They voraciously consume trivial tidbits about his performance on the track and his life away from it. Even from afar, and through the lens of the media, they feel an intimacy, as if they know and truly comprehend the person behind the glossy image created in sponsor commercials and pre-race features. This understanding, along with the hours upon hours spent watching races and reading the blogs, builds powerful emotional connections. The driver becomes, to a fan, more than someone turning fast laps on a Sunday. He can inspire, even heal. And sometimes the fan tries to heal the driver. After you meet our next group of remarkable fans, you'll see what I mean.

Spencer Roy Sees
the Other Side of Smoke

WHEN LITTLE SPENCER ROY was six, he wanted a tattoo. Not one of those temporary Cracker Jack ones. No, he asked for a real tattoo—needles in flesh. A Tony Stewart tattoo.

That was, of course, out of the question. There are laws. But the boy's mom, Stephanie, had an idea. She watched every NASCAR race at home with Spencer, and Tony was her driver too. Mother and son named their cat "Tony Stewart." The family's pet fish is "Tony Stewart." Step out of their shower, and your wet feet meet a Tony Stewart bath mat. You don't have to be a mentalist to guess Stephanie's computer password. Then there are the Tony Stewart cars and cups and flags and stickers throughout the house.

Spencer and Stephanie Roy met their hero, Tony Stewart, prior to the spring 2008 race at Richmond International Raceway. Stewart treated the boy like a long-lost friend, spending extra time and nearly missing his next meeting. *Courtesy Stephanie Roy*

Considering the various and sundry ways the Tony Stewart name infests the Roys' home, the idea of branding a family member's skin with "Tony Stewart" wasn't so outlandish. Maybe Stephanie, as an agent representing the Roy clan, would get the tattoo.

A race was coming up at Martinsville, Virginia, Stephanie's home track. The Roanoke mom knew Tony would be doing an autograph session in the Salem Civic Center. She showed up, inched to the front of the line, and offered her bicep. This wasn't the first time Stewart had been asked to sign a body part. He laid pen to flesh with big, confident strokes—a John Hancock with verve and flourish, the kind of assuredly bold signature you'd expect from a driver Stephanie and Spencer love because "he will move your butt out of the way or put you into the wall if he has to."

Stephanie found a phone book and a tattoo parlor. For 40 bucks and a little bit of sting, she could again show how far she'd go for the boy she loves so much who is suffering from a serious heart condition. It took about 20 minutes to make Tony's signature permanent. Stephanie had to keep hitting the brakes, she was driving so fast to get home. Little Spencer was just tickled pink. To this day, he'll gleefully lift his mom's shirt sleeve to show total strangers the tattoo of the only driver in NASCAR who matters.

Six years later at Richmond International Raceway, courtesy of the Make-A-Wish Foundation, a wonderful organization helping children with life-threatening medical conditions, Spencer got his chance to meet the driver on his mother's arm.

Tony Stewart met Spencer and Stephanie Roy at his motor home in the drivers and owners lot before September's Chevy Rock and Roll 400 race. Stephanie came prepared with orange fingernails with jet-black tips and the No. "20" etched on. Stewart showed up wearing his orange fire suit and a big smile. He greeted Spencer with a fist bump and began to treat the boy like a long-lost friend.

Spencer flipped his program open to Tony's page, pointing to his man.

"Who's that goofy guy?" Tony asked. "You picked the ugliest guy in the whole book!"

Spencer laughed and turned to another photo of Tony.

"You're laughing, but I don't get better looking in any of these photos, do I?" he asked. "No wonder I don't have a girlfriend."

Stewart spent 15 minutes making Spencer crack up while signing a heap of paraphernalia handed over with assembly line precision by his PR man Mike Arning.

Bad weather was headed for Virginia as tropical storm Hannah moved in. The 37-year-old two-time NASCAR Sprint Cup Series champion did a rain dance jig, attempting to ward off the precipitation so Spencer Roy would be able to see his first NASCAR race. Stewart promised the boy if he won the race, and he had every intention of doing so, he'd climb the fence at Richmond just for him. Together, they'd celebrate in Victory Lane.

A hospitality tour was waiting. Stewart's PR man motioned to the group, reminding the driver of obligations backing up. Stewart said goodbye to Spencer, then found a way to kick-start a conversation he didn't want to end. The cycle of attempted goodbyes followed by more joking repeated itself a few times. Finally, after a series of high-fives, it was time to go.

"Remember: after the race, Victory Lane," Stewart said as he walked back to the garage.

Spencer and Stephanie had seats directly in front of the No. 20 pit stall. Spencer was physically in Virginia but more accurately in heaven, throwing up his hand every time Tony's race car flew by.

The boy had been a NASCAR fan almost his entire life and only had two favorite drivers. First was Ernie Irvan, known to some as "Swervin' Irvan." He was the favorite driver of Philip and Georgia Gregware, who lived above the Roys and took care of Spencer for several years when Stephanie worked weekends. Phil's nickname was "Curly," but before Spencer could talk, he couldn't say that. He just called Phil "Ernie."

When the real Ernie retired from NASCAR in 1999, Spencer immediately switched allegiances to Tony Stewart. The boy's medical condition, prolonged QT and myocardial disease of the muscles, makes comprehending complex things difficult. While traditional learning—the Pythagorean theorum and the Magna Carta, and the arcane a + b = c equations and historical events each of us suffered through and mostly forgot—is difficult, Spencer has strong intuition and is sharp as a tack. Watching the races on TV with the Gregwares (every Sunday the families would share a home-cooked meal and the race), Spencer would pick his own driver.

Spencer didn't get his Tony Stewart tattoo, but he did sit in a prime spot to see his driver and Jimmie Johnson battle to a fantastic finish at Richmond. The race was so exciting Spencer's goose bumps got goose bumps. *Courtesy Stephanie Roy*

Spencer liked Tony Stewart's personality, his driving style, everything about the guy.

After adopting Tony as his driver, he'd followed him on TV for years. Now he was at the track in Richmond, watching this momentous freight train of race cars zooming by, close enough to make his wheelchair shake. It felt to Spencer like the whole earth could be thrown off its axis. Spencer wanted Tony to lead the pack. He was rooting hard, encouraging Tony to go faster and faster as the laps ticked off. Stewart had a solid car and was running up front. He was in contention. Would he take the checkers, climb the fence, and meet Spencer in Victory Lane? As the laps wound down, it was turning into a battle between Tony and reigning NASCAR champion Jimmie Johnson. The Home Depot and Lowe's cars battled on the final laps in a thrilling bumper-to-bumper duel. They tore around the 3/4-mile track, Stewart on Johnson's bumper, fast into the turns, moving alongside Johnson on the gentle banks but unable to fully carry the momentum he'd built through the sweeping curves and fading as his rival burst ahead on each straightaway. The cat-and-mouse game continued, lap after lap, Tony inching up, drawing even, falling back. The crowd of more than 90,000 was on its feet. Spencer was shaking with excitement. Could goose bumps get goose bumps? Spencer's arm shot up each time Tony rocketed past, right on the No. 48's tail. But this day, this race, was not to be for Spencer or Stewart. They couldn't catch Jimmie Johnson, and Tony finished second.

Spencer was crushed. He didn't make it to Victory Lane. He was quiet and withdrawn, not himself for an entire week. But as the days passed, who won at Richmond didn't seem to matter as much. The end of the race faded in his mind. Spencer Roy's weekend in Richmond holds a sharper, more intense memory that grows in prominence as other recollections fade. Spencer had met his hero, and he was larger in life than even in the boy's grandest dreams.

Ryan's Hope

CHRISTINE DEUKER WAS DEVASTATED when her son Joseph died after a sudden, undiagnosed illness struck him in July 2001. Joe was a smart, curious young man who loved to read. He played the trombone in the school marching band. He wanted to be an orthopedic surgeon. Joe was 18 years old when the pain became too much, and he took his life.

There were terrible, dark days ahead for Christine. At times, she wondered, why go on? She had two other wonderful children she loved very much. After being divorced, she even found her soul mate in her kind and gentle husband, Steve. But losing Joe was like falling through a cold black hole with no bottom. "The loss of Joe left us in devastating shock," said Steve Deuker. "Life went on day after day, much of it unmemorable today."

Ryan Newman holds the NASCAR Hall of Fame brick etched with the memory of the son of Christine and Steve Deuker. Newman's uncanny resemblance to their departed son helped the Deukers through a period of enormous grief. *Getty Images for NASCAR*

Steve was a lifelong racing fan who had saved money from every two-bit job he could find to race open-wheel cars at dirt tracks in Arizona. He introduced Christine to NASCAR. Witnessing her fiancé's passion for NASCAR, watching his face brighten when recounting racing memories, she was completely open to the sport. She wanted to investigate and experience what made Steve so happy. She quickly became a fan. Then she lost Joe.

The following NASCAR season, Ryan Newman appeared as a rookie on the NASCAR scene. Christine immediately noticed him. She's a well-educated high school social studies teacher who observes people to understand them and to try to make sense of the world. Watching Ryan Newman in interviews, she noticed stunning similarities between the then 21-year-old driver and her departed son.

There were obvious shared physical characteristics: eyes, eyebrows, hair, and the hunched-up shoulders. Somber faces that would break into an impish smile. Two shy, patient, and introspective young men who would surprise you with their dry senses of humor. But it was recognizing eerily similar mannerisms connecting Joe and Ryan that drove Christine to think about the new NASCAR driver more and more. When listening to a difficult question he didn't want to hear, Ryan was a spitting image of Joe. Both men would cast their eyes down, lost in thought. They'd stammer when searching for a specific word. That's the sign of a person with much more going on inside than shows outside, Christine realized. Just like Joe. She constantly thought about Ryan Newman and was riveted to NASCAR on TV for a chance to see him.

Through preordained fate or dumb luck or random events or however you make sense of the world, Christine would soon meet Ryan. A NASCAR fan had extra Bristol tickets he couldn't use, and he wanted his coveted passes to go to someone who would genuinely appreciate them. He found out Steve was a big fan and offered him the tickets. When the Deukers got to Bristol Motor Speedway, they heard Ryan would be signing autographs, and to Christine, this was more than simple luck. She believed destiny was bringing her to Ryan. When have you ever heard of an impossible-to-score Bristol ticket offered by a total stranger to someone who hadn't even asked?

In meeting Ryan, Christine's welled-up feelings were confirmed. "His eyes, his smile, his halting speech, how he used his hands when talking, it

Watching Ryan Newman's interviews and remembering her departed son Joseph, Christine saw the same introspection, dry sense of humor, and mannerisms. Meeting Ryan was a deeply emotional experience aiding her healing process. *Courtesy the Deuker family*

was like watching my son," Christine said. Afterward, she broke down for half an hour.

Christine was relieved to share common interests and values with the Newmans. Ryan and his wife, Krissie, rescue dogs. Christine volunteers for the humane society in Minneapolis. Ryan, a graduate of Purdue University, established a scholarship for students and talks about the value of education. She is a teacher.

Dealing with their grief, the Deukers began to lose themselves in Ryan Newman and NASCAR. "Ryan, in just being himself, offered us a glimpse of the face of the son we had lost," Steve said. "If you've ever had a dream where you 'saw' someone you missed badly, when you wake up and reality hits, you're saddened the person is not there. But you still feel good that you got to see him in your mind. That's what it is like. To us, Ryan just being himself was helping us to heal and continue to claw forward."

In grief counseling, Christine was advised to keep her mind occupied. When she wasn't preparing school lessons or in front of her classes, the growing preoccupation with Ryan Newman helped her generate positive thoughts. During the week, school kept Christine busy; on weekends, watching Ryan compete in NASCAR and journaling about it eased her grief.

"The whole race weekend helped carry me though," she said. "It would start with qualifying, right through to Victory Lane on Sunday. NASCAR was like a train that pulled me through the year. I got on the Ryan Newman Express. I learned how to start having fun again."

As Steve explained it, "There will always be a hole in our lives. We're just learning to not step in it as much."

Steve heard the NASCAR Hall of Fame was offering bricks for sale and allowing fans to inscribe a personal message. He bought one and had it etched with a tribute to Ryan, reading:

TO RYAN NEWMAN:
YOUR DEMEANOR
REFLECTS A SOUL
U NEVER MET. IN
YOU WE SEE OUR
SON, JOSEPH HELD

One day, when listening to an interview on Sirius Radio about the progress of the coming NASCAR Hall of Fame, Steve nearly crashed his car. The Hall's director, Winston Kelley, mentioned a poignant brick memorializing a boy with a connection to Ryan Newman.

"I was shocked Winston had [even] seen what we had written, much less remembered it to share in an interview," Steve said. "I was very touched and thankful."

He wrote to Kelley with the full story behind the brick. He wanted people to understand how Ryan had helped make a difference. He also wanted to assist the Hall of Fame. "I thought our story might be used to raise more funds than we could send ourselves. Years from now, no matter how many races Ryan wins, he will always be our driver, based on the ladder he unknowingly offered so we could climb back to the life we're now living. Although Joe will *never* be forgotten, we're able to smile again."

The note to the Hall of Fame was forwarded to Newman. The story of Joseph Held moved him deeply. He printed the email and placed it on his desk at his home in Indiana.

"I was completely touched and knew I'd want to write back to Steve and Christine," Newman said. "Adversity is a part of everyday life. The difference is how you deal with it. This was obviously a very tough situation of unfathomable grief. It was gratifying to be able to help, even without knowing it. In my mind, it's the ultimate fan tribute. I'm just myself, and they applauded me for that. This is way more than just a brick to me. It's how two people overcame a great challenge, and I'm honored to be even a small part of that."

After Newman responded, the NASCAR Hall of Fame arranged for the Deukers to meet him prior to the 2009 Daytona 500, a race he had won the previous season.

It would be a chance for Christine to thank Ryan for his part in her recovery, diverting her mind from the destructive thoughts preventing a person from healing. Yet Christine also realized some people hearing her story might consider her unbalanced. She was concerned about meeting with Ryan. What if he thought she was a stalker?

"We were worried Ryan might feel this was a bit creepy. You lose someone you love and start creating that person in someone else. I could see how anyone might think, 'This woman is out of her mind with grief.' But I know Ryan is different than my son. Joe was not a racer or mechanical. He loved music. He grew up under different circumstances. Even with their stark similarities, I focused on their differences so I wouldn't make Ryan out to be Joe. He's not Joe. But Joe's spirit is recognizable in Ryan."

The Deukers were to meet Ryan on February 14. As part of a "thank you," they made a Valentine's Day box for Ryan and Krissie. Christine knew which cars Ryan and Krissie drove and scoured the Internet to find "his and hers" die-cast cars: a red 1957 Thunderbird and 1949 Jaguar XK120. The cars went in a glass case Steve and his daughter built. Steve drove around Minneapolis to locate a pet store that had heart-shaped Valentine treats for each of the Newmans' dogs: Digger, Socks, Harley, and Mopar.

The morning of the face-to-face with Newman at Daytona, Christine again grew worried she might fall apart. "But then this opportunity to say thanks would pass me by," she said. Christine remembered pulling herself together in front of her students when the Space Shuttle *Challenger* exploded on live TV and again on September 11, 2001.

With gifts in hand, she was ready to talk about Joe in an informal and positive context. "This will not be a tragedy that happened and the rest of your life is hopeless," she said.

An hour before the scheduled meeting, Newman and his new teammate (and team owner) Tony Stewart were running practice laps on the track's high banks. Stewart was drafting behind Newman when his teammate's Chevy veered right into a skid. He'd blown a tire. Stewart mashed the brakes, but he was doomed. His car plowed into Newman's. Both were totaled. The drivers would have to go to backup cars in the Daytona 500.

Christine saw the wreck unfold on a TV hanging from the ceiling in the media center. All she could say was, "Oh my God, oh my God, oh my God." She and Steve wondered if Ryan would have to skip their meeting. It would be completely understandable. Teammates had just wrecked before the biggest race of the year. They needed to huddle with their crews and devise a strategy for furiously preparing back-up cars. But Newman, looking as relaxed as if he'd stepped off a cruise ship, showed up at the U.S. Army hauler not a minute late, eager to meet the Deukers. He put what happened on the track completely aside. He was easygoing and affable. His regular-guy manner and casual sincerity reinforced everything Christine had been feeling about the kindred spirits who had never met—her dearly departed son and this special NASCAR driver.

Ryan got a kick out of the dog treats and vintage cars. News photographers snapped photos. Sirius Radio was on air asking about the brick. Local newspaper scribes were thrusting tape recorders under her chin. So many things were happening. Ryan stood with her and Steve for all of it. They embraced and said goodbye. The meeting had passed in a blur. Christine felt relief, joy, sadness, and the lightness of a burden removed. She sat on a tire next to the army hauler and had a good cry.

Before we parted ways after an extraordinary day at the race track, Christine said, "Ryan was totally gracious; an everyday guy. Just 'Newman being Newman,' as they say. He was what I expected—low-key but forthright, plain spoken in a simple, Midwestern way. A lot like Joe was. It's a massively comforting thing to see my son's qualities out there. They haven't disappeared from the face of the earth. I won't look at pictures of Joe much anymore. I don't have to. I see him alive in Ryan."

A Bad Case of NASCAR Disease

S HE HOPED THIS WOULD BE the final leg of a 16-year pursuit to meet Jeff Gordon, and Carolyn Hastings showed up in Miami in grand style. For the cross-country flight from Northern California to southern Florida for NASCAR's season-ending race and a planned rendezvous with Gordon, she had packed a special bag to decorate her hotel room with No. 24 posters, flags, and die-cast cars. She slept with a Jeff Gordon blanket. In the morning, she walked across a Jeff Gordon rug, put on a silver No. 24 necklace, and painted orange flames on her fingernails.

The carefully constructed portable shrine would make for a good photo in Hastings' newsletter, *Jeff Gordon No. 24 News*, which she distributes free of charge to hundreds of Gordon devotees. The impish grandmother from Redding, California, spends 40 hours a week on this "labor of love," often cranking out three issues between races, many with barbs aimed at Jeff's unlikely new teammate, Dale Earnhardt Jr., particularly when he "needs

---

Carolyn Hastings and her daughter Tracy met Elliott Sadler on pit road before the season-ending Ford 400 race in 2008. *Courtesy Rob Kinker/Carolyn Hastings*

a shave." Her devoted readers from all over the country will send gifts—Gordon coffee mugs, event pins, life-size cardboard cutouts, displays pilfered from supermarket aisles, and those DuPont-blue Gordon blankets that seem to bring peaceful sleep better than any pill from a bottle. Several subscribers are elderly, and she checks on them every day.

Carolyn's affection for NASCAR and the editorial service she provides to fans has brought intimacy with a widening circle of like-minded Gordon boosters, which now includes Jeff's mother. They met at Infineon Raceway in California's wine country. Carolyn was there for the race when her sixth sense kicked in. Someone important was nearby. She could feel it, similar to the way you can sense when someone's staring at you. She turned around and spotted that important person—Carol Bickford, the woman who brought Jeff into the world in August 1971. Carolyn had been keeping track of Bickford for years. The two ladies hit it off immediately, and Carol shared a very big scoop: Jeff had gotten engaged to Ingrid Vandebosch the previous evening at a polo match. Carolyn Hastings got the news before anyone else in NASCAR.

Arvil, Carolyn's husband of 45 years, doesn't go to the races with his wife. NASCAR is Carolyn's "off time" from him, strictly an "all girl thing." (Listen from afar to the couple discussing trips to watch deafening race cars traveling at perilous speeds, and you can be lulled into believing Carolyn is headed to a Tupperware party.) Arvil accepts but doesn't completely understand this all-out obsession with stock car racing, and neither, for that matter does the local pastor, Al Rountree. Reverend Rountree was visiting the Hastings' home in Northern California and came across the permanent Gordon shrine on her second floor, complete with every newspaper clipping and magazine article she's gotten her hands on since the immensely talented young driver broke into NASCAR in 1992. The pastor was taken aback at the wall-to-wall magnitude of photos and posters and racing magazines. The tribute crept clear across the ceiling. Didn't the good Lord in Exodus proclaim, "Thou shalt have no gods before me"? Was this mania not unlike a golden idol of Egypt? In church the next week, Reverend Rountree asked members of the congregation to lay hands on Carolyn Hastings, for she had a strange "NASCAR disease" that needed to be healed.

It may seem odd to a clergy member and his flock to witness a 67-year-old woman displaying devotion of biblical proportions to a young man wearing a shiny racing suit, a fervent tribute consuming every inch of a room in her home where she toils for hours at a stretch, writing, laying out, and distributing her devotional newsletter. A pastor may view such fanatical heights of obsessive loyalty as the dead-end province of teenage girls consumed with hopeless crushes on the latest pop star, a state of celebrity worship no proper older woman should emulate. But Carolyn's too busy finding new Gordon photos and merchandise to worry about that. She's more concerned the room doesn't merely become evidence of former glory. If Jeff and his crew chief, Steve LeTarte, could only take more chances and venture into the grey area of the rules like his teammate Jimmie Johnson and crew chief Chad Knaus, she's sure more championship headlines will come. For now she'll keep collecting Gordon's photo layouts and cars with the latest paint schemes. She's added two more No. 24 die-casts from the souvenir bins at Homestead-Miami Speedway and is mighty proud of her latest purchase. In all, she's catalogued 2,500 Gordon items and plans to continue the collection until her house busts a beam or they stop making new stuff and writing new things about Jeff.

"I don't care about the economy," she said. "I make wedding cakes and use that money to attend races and pick up my NASCAR merchandise."

Hastings is a season-ticket holder at Infineon Raceway, a road course in Northern California about 200 miles south of her house. She likes to get close to the blustering stock cars without any protection for her ears. "Ear plugs take away from the race," she said. After nearly half a century as an avid race fan, she still has most of her hearing but not much of her voice, at least this weekend in Miami, after screaming for Todd Bodine and Johnny Benson in the NASCAR Camping World Truck Series season finale. The truck race was her first NASCAR event at an oval, and she couldn't contain herself. But she's an energetic cheerleader back in California too. At the twisting Infineon road course, her seat is a concrete slab off of Turn Nine. "It would be a pretty uncomfortable seat, except I'm on my feet screaming the whole time," she said.

Carolyn stays at the Redwood Valley Inn when attending the NASCAR Sprint Cup races near home and has grown accustomed to a particular parking spot. One trip, hotel construction was underway, and she asked a worker why he had taken her space. When she left the track and returned to the hotel, the spot was cordoned off with a large checkered flag and sign announcing, "Reserved for Carolyn Hastings and Jeff Gordon." All

Clowning around with Hellmann's driver Elliott Sadler in his hauler.
Carolyn did her homework and rattled off the sandwiches on which
Sadler uses his sponsor's mayo. *Courtesy Rob Kinker/Carolyn Hastings*

weekend, fans were running from their rooms to see if Jeff was in Carolyn's special spot.

Ever since, in early June each year, when NASCAR comes to Northern California, Carolyn and Jeff Gordon have a permanent, roped-off parking spot at the Redwood Valley Inn. "Wouldn't it be a kick if one day Jeff decided to park there?" she asked.

Carolyn recently missed that June race for the first time in years. Arvil had fallen ill, and she needed to stay with him. "It was very depressing to watch on TV," she said. As sublime as a high-definition, surround-sound TV broadcast has become, sitting at home can't compare to the track. With her husband sick and the season coming to a close, 2008 would be the first time in many years Carolyn would not be attending the Northern California race. Then a newsletter reader started emailing her about a Hellmann's contest to find the "NASCAR Real Fan of the Year." The grand prize would be a trip to Miami and VIP treatment during

Ford Championship Weekend. Carolyn was naturally skeptical about her chances of winning any contest. She paid no attention to the messages. "This reader was bugging me two, three times a week, telling me to take a shot because there's no bigger fan than me," Carolyn explained. "Finally, I entered the contest to get her off my back."

Carolyn had never won anything in her life. When a woman she'd never met left a congratulatory message on her answering machine about some sort of NASCAR contest, she ignored it. Then an email from Hellmann's announced her grand prize as fan of the year. With the phone message, it all added up. "Knowing I won, I was awake all night long," Carolyn said. "I literally did not sleep a wink. I never shut my eyes once!"

The news, of course, was a lead story in *Jeff Gordon No. 24 News.* More than 100 congratulatory e-mails flew in. If anyone deserved to be Hellmann's Real Fan of the Year, it was Carolyn. Her eldest daughter made the trip down from Portland to take care of Arvil, and Carolyn was off to the races, as they say.

But would she finally meet Jeff?

I'D HEARD A LOT ABOUT CAROLYN, and she was all I'd hoped for in the legion of remarkable fans. We met at a NASCAR breakfast to thank sponsors for their support during difficult economic times. The spunky grandmother immediately began recounting how she became the fan of the year, punctuated with asides on her 45-year marriage to Arvil. (When they wed, she was 23 and he was 48, four months older than Carolyn's mother, but "we've had a great marriage and proved everyone wrong that it wouldn't last.") The breakfast event is held in the garage, and while NASCAR's sponsorship group had set up tables with white linen and real silverware, it still was a race track, and the aroma of stock cars can overpower even simmering eggs and bacon. Carolyn took a deep breath and said, like Robert Duvall in *Apocalypse Now,* "Ah, there's the smell I like in the morning. Burning rubber! If they bottled that, I'd wear it every day."

This V.I.P. experience in Miami was one of the best times her of life, she said. In addition to watching all three of NASCAR's top series close out their seasons, Carolyn got to wave the green flag for Elliott Sadler's qualifying run and then hang out with the tall, affable driver in his trailer.

They'd barely exchanged hellos when Carolyn reached up and touched Sadler's wooly black beard.

"Why do you have this?" she asked.

Sadler replied in his Virginian drawl, "'Cause deer hunting season starts in the morning."

Carolyn is an encyclopedia of NASCAR knowledge; she even won a fan trivia contest at the track once. She explained to Sadler what a great time the Hellmann's people were giving her and noted Elliot should, of course, expect to hear about that kind of first-class treatment, since he always puts Hellmann's mayonnaise on his bologna sandwiches.

"How'd you know that? You're a sponsor's dream!" Sadler exclaimed.

Carolyn giddily shared mayonnaise suggestions with the Hellmann's driver, but her Fan of the Year experience wouldn't be complete without one additional attempt to finally meet Jeff Gordon, whose tastes in egg-based condiments remained a mystery even to a lady who had read virtually every book, article, and blog post chronicling the life and times of the four-time NASCAR champion. She'd been seeking out Gordon since 1992. Perhaps in Homestead, her luck would change. Carolyn knew Gordon would be coming to his hauler after final practice. She camped out there with her daughter Tracy. Suddenly, Jeff appeared, walking directly toward her. "As much as I wanted to meet him, he was at work. I wanted to be respectful," she said.

She'd spent 16 years trying to meet Jeff and was willing to wait another 16 rather than rudely interrupt the driver only steps away. Two burly fans shoved in front of Carolyn's five-foot-two frame. The men stuck cards in front of Jeff to sign. Amateurs, Carolyn thought. They have nothing to write with. Carolyn Hastings goes nowhere without a Sharpie.

Jeff Gordon looked at Carolyn and smiled.

"May I use your pen?"

"Sure," Carolyn responded, schoolgirlish.

Gordon signed the pictures and looked sternly at the men who had just cut off Carolyn. "Hey guys. Next time try to be more careful. You almost knocked this nice lady down."

Gordon spotted the die-cast cars Carolyn was holding—one for his sponsor, Nicorette, and a snazzy black car for the Jeff Gordon Foundation.

"Do you want one of these signed?" he asked.

Jaimie Fish, senior brand manager for Hellmann's, declared Carolyn the "NASCAR Real Fan of the Year" on stage at Homestead-Miami Speedway before the race. *Rob Kinker*

Carolyn offered up the black car.

"Great choice," Gordon said. "Not too many of these have been made. This one might actually be worth something someday!"

Jeff Gordon turned to leave but in the next pace spun around.

"Thanks for letting me use your pen, ma'am," he said.

Carolyn's eyes crinkled up in a delighted smile. Everything with Jeff happened so fast. She felt warm and glowing. She drifted backward, trancelike, into the road of the garage area. She didn't hear the No. 48 car rumbling into the garage. A NASCAR official ran over and whisked her off the ground to save her from being run over by Jimmie Johnson tearing toward his stall.

"I would have been crushed, but what a way to go, getting Jeff's autograph and then run over by the guy who's about to become a three-time champ!" she shouted.

The Sharpie Jeff used has been retired. Carolyn framed the marker along with the two die-cast cars from Miami. The custom case was mounted on the wall of her racing workroom, right over the computer monitor where she diligently creates *Jeff Gordon No. 24 News*. Carolyn Hastings, NASCAR Real Fan of the Year, wants to be able to look up from the screen and see the pen used by her NASCAR idol. She's got an affliction for NASCAR and seeks no cure. Just don't tell anyone at the Valley Christian Center.

Nursing Junior to a Championship

S OME PEOPLE LIVE to save the world.

Barbie Robbins lives for Dale Earnhardt Jr.

One time, Junior wrecked and was shaken up. Barbie, who was at home, thousands of miles from the race, put on a nurse's outfit. She was channeling healing vibes to her number-one driver.

Every morning, the 49-year-old Californian wakes up underneath a collage of Dale Jr. photographs pasted above her bed. Before shedding her No. 88 pajamas, she makes a beeline for the computer to vote for her man in the NASCAR Most Popular Driver contest. She then punches up her MySpace page, checks the guest book for new NASCAR friends, and gazes at the latest Dale Jr. photos posted. In one shot, the driver is sleeping peacefully in his race car. Thought bubbles, like those in cartoons, rise from his head to a superimposed cloud framing Barbie's smiling face. A photo of Dale's car speeding past the start/finish line has the caption, "Junior looks at Barbie." A shot showing Junior with chin on clenched fist, deep in

Known as "Junior's Baby 88 Girl," Barbie Robbins of San Diego has a legitimate claim to being called Dale Earnhardt Jr.'s biggest fan. *Courtesy Barbie Robbins*

thought, is captioned, "Hmmm…should I call Barbie?" A photo of Junior appearing surprised is tagged, "Is that Barbie?" In another one, NASCAR's biggest star is with fellow driver Tony Stewart who exclaims, "Look Dale, there she is again. I think Barbie is stalking you!"

Barbie sends daily notes on the life and times of Dale Jr. to dozens of friends met on the web. On race day, members of the virtual club sit with their laptops in front of the TV telecast, typing bulletins to one another. If Junior is rammed by another driver, Barbie will fire off sailor-worthy cusses. She's known online, and among many in the physical world, as "Junior's Baby 88 Girl." Some in her San Diego neighborhood call her "NASCAR Chick."

Most days, she puts on a Dale Jr. t-shirt, which was ironed and carefully set out the night before. She selects a Dale Jr. hat. There's a set rotation: on Sunday night, shirts and hats are matched to days of the week. She has been unable to find Junior underwear and will take any leads offered. At the corner store in her San Diego neighborhood, the counterman catches a glance of her NASCAR garb and long Stevie Wonder–style braids and invariably shouts, "Hey, NASCAR Chick!"

Barbie Robbins, formerly of Chicago, Illinois, and a nondescript civilian life, now of San Diego, California, and a minor celebrity in her neighborhood and at Auto Club Speedway 104 miles due north, became Junior's Baby 88 Girl after seeing the driver in a TV interview. The attraction was mystical and instantaneous. The Sicilians, as any fan of *The Godfather* knows, have a term for such otherworldly instant connections: "The Thunderbolt." The thunderbolt is deeper and more complex than what Americans might call "love at first sight." This is not puppy dogs and floating hearts. The thunderbolt is serious, life-altering destiny not to be messed with.

In Sicily, the thunderbolt is called *lu lampu.*

In San Diego, Barbie Robbins said to the TV screen, "Damn, he fine!"

The hour she first believed, she watched Dale Jr. answer the reporter's questions, slightly impatient, index finger prone to reach up and clean his ear, a plain-spoken North Carolina boy saying "y'all" and "ain't" whenever he darn well pleased, a man of unkempt, rugged good looks who'd rather be hunting or fishing than facing questions about the so-called Earnhardt family legacy. Barbie saw beautiful unvarnished authenticity in a glossed-up world populated with too many pretty boys, and she was zapped by the thunderbolt. She started tuning in to NASCAR races to see the free-

Robbins has made new friends at every race she attends at Auto Club Speedway in Fontana, California. She says the only color that matters to her friends at the track is "Dale Jr. green."
Courtesy Barbie Robbins

spirited cowboy ride. He was courageous and could drive that car. He had his own chocolate bar. She hates chocolate, but it was the sweetest candy she'd ever tasted.

Junior's Baby 88 Girl is never to be bothered on Sunday even during family emergencies. She is always eager to display the Dale Jr. tattoo covering one shoulder blade and to speak forcefully about "Junior Nation," one topic leading to the other. She never shies from a chance to promote the individual who is the object of many of her waking thoughts and desires. And some thoughts and desires while she's asleep. Ask Barbie about her life, and she'll flatly tell you, "It's all about Junior!" There's a twinkle in her lagoon-green eyes, and she's not joking.

Junior's Baby 88 Girl wasn't the kind of woman to go trawling for celebrities to occupy a central position in her life. It was out of character for her to feel an intimate connection with any pop-culture icon—those distant figures of tabloid renown captured by the media to satisfy the public's insatiable appetite for unconsummated fantasy, tart gossip, and computer wallpaper. The possibility of Barbie connecting with a NASCAR

The apple doesn't fall far from the tree; Barbie's son Jordan won't miss a race at Auto Club Speedway either. *Courtesy Barbie Robbins*

driver was more remote. It wasn't because most African-American women in Southern California have little in common with the front men of a sport rooted in Carolina moonshine. Barbie had watched the IndyCar Series races with her cousins, and she wasn't much of a race fan. She wasn't opposed to it. Racing was cool, but there were so many other things to do on a Sunday afternoon. She actually prefers connecting with people personally in the flesh, over a Bud Light and a Benson & Hedges menthol, rather than plumbing the lives of public figures through supermarket checkout magazines. Then came the *lu lampu*. She didn't plan it. No one asks for the thunderbolt. Now there's an unmistakable connection, a spooky empathy at play.

"When Dale Jr. does an interview and I see he's sad, it makes me sad," Barbie said. "I will pick up on his moods and will really feel the same way."

After Dale Jr. left the team formed by his father—which after Senior's passing was run by his stepmother, Teresa—to join the NASCAR powerhouse Hendrick Motorsports, Barbie noticed the driver was relaxed, freed from the politics and pressure of the family business. The days following his shocking move from Dale Earnhardt Inc. to join Jeff Gordon and Jimmie Johnson as a new team brought relief to the driver and his biggest fan.

"Watching Junior talking about his new team in the press conference, you could just see how happy and excited he was. And so was I." As she likes to say in her emails, "Life is Gr88t!!!!"

Even cocooned in her car on the freeways of California, Junior's Baby 88 Girl is identified by a batch of Dale Jr. bumper stickers drawing odd looks. "Sometimes on the highway, a driver will pull alongside. He's seen my Dale Jr. stickers. The look on his face, says, 'That is *not* her car.' Yes, it's my car, and I'm a NASCAR fan! I'm a redneck with a permanent tan! But when I get to the track, I'm just another race fan, fitting right in. I'm probably the most crazy fan, like an Energizer bunny but doing all I can to not jump over that fence and grab onto Dale Jr.'s car. But I'm still just a fan. Every other NASCAR fan I've met has been awesome. They don't care if I'm black, pink, or orange. I'm not into black or white. I'm into green. No. 88 green! That's all that matters"

Getting close to the driver of the No. 88 green car is this and every racing weekend's main goal. "I have my Junior Station setup where I lay out my hoochie outfits . . . oops, I mean respectful, family-friendly, NASCAR-themed clothing," she said. To look her best, Junior's Baby 88 Girl sits for eight hours to get her hair specially braided. Getting ready for the drive north, she cranks up Jackie Wilson's *Baby Workout*. Grilled foods are wrapped in foil. The ice chest is filled with Bud Light. Most of the beer will come back, since NASCAR fans offer theirs to her all week-end. "NASCAR tailgating rocks," she said. "Oh my God, two times a year, drinking beer at 8 a.m., it's the only way to party. Those other so-called big sports events have nada on NASCAR."

She loves seeing the new crop of Dale Junior t-shirts and having her picture taken in his colors. She once bought a bunch of new tees in the parking lot and began dancing for fans snapping her picture. She didn't know it, but the goods were illegal knock-offs. The police snuck up and busted the counterfeiter. Nearby at her SUV, Junior's Baby 88 Girl was posing in her new wares. She explained to the police that it was her car, and she bought the shirts not to sell but to use for herself, since she is *the biggest* Junior fan. She said the photos were not to encourage the sale of illegal merchandise but to promote her favorite driver. No, she was not being compensated. Yes, she does this at all the races. Yes, OK, it's a little over the top. No, she's not kidding about all this.

The cops shook their heads and pulled away.

She's found a niche, has made dozens of friends at the track, and is on a first-name basis with Auto Club Speedway president Gillian Zucker. Yet she still feels on the outside, nose pressed against the glass. Myriad websites, fan magazines, TV, and satellite radio coverage bring Barbie and other fans their NASCAR fix whenever they want. But not all the time, anytime. Life beckons. There's a job to go to, assignments looming, appointments to make, groceries to buy, a boy to raise. Thankfully, her son drinks the NASCAR Kool-Aid too, and they've not missed a single race at Auto Club Speedway since 1998. Pit passes bring them close to the drivers. At one race, Junior nearly bumped into them before the drivers' introductions.

"I reached out and touched Junior for a hot second, rubbed his arm, spoke to him," she said. "I said, 'I want a hug,' just to let him know, 'Dude, I love ya, I'm always loyal, dedicated, and right there with ya.' His smile was priceless." Telling this story, her eyes filled with tears.

Try to squeeze Peyton Manning's shoulder before a game. You'll be handcuffed and thrown in jail. The chance to get up close is what Junior's Baby 88 Girl likes most about the sport. But as near as she can get to the drivers, it's only twice a year. When race weekends start, and she's at work punching information into the computer, there's no way to know what's going on in the race shop and at the track. The data-entry position is a job, not a career. Her dream is to be employed at NASCAR, on the inside, living a life with no barriers to the information about what's happening with Dale Jr. exactly when it's happening. She brings her resume to each race she attends. You never know.

At work on a Friday afternoon, cut off from NASCAR, a fan like Barbie can get very frustrated. She sometimes has a premonition, as she did before the race at Talladega. She felt something was wrong and snuck a peek at the Internet. Dale had blown a tire during a practice run and crashed. A feeling of dread washed over her.

The online NASCAR network kicked into gear. Friends with jobs allowing them to follow NASCAR on SPEED or Sirius sent news. Junior was fine—checked out in the infield care center and released, walking to the garage to set up the backup car.

This time, Barbie could leave the nurse's outfit in the closet.

Paying It Forward

M ATT KENSETH AND TONY STEWART occasionally run in the NASCAR
Nationwide Series to get extra seat time, fulfill sponsor obligations,
and do what they love most—race cars. When the drivers competed
in the 2009 season-opening race for NASCAR's number-two series at
Daytona International Speedway, little did they know they'd also be helping to save a fan's home.

It all started on Valentine's Day when Connie Bradley, her husband,
Ron, and their nine-year-old daughter Jordyn drove to lunch at a steak-
house in Mount Pleasant, Michigan. Connie is a protective Stewart fan
who fires off letters to the NASCAR trades if anyone even remotely dis-
respects her driver. Jordyn is an enthusiastic member of Matt Kenseth's
fan club who mails homemade congratulatory cards to Kenseth following

After the home of Ron, Jordyn, and Connie Bradley was destroyed in a fire, Office
Depot joined with Michigan International Speedway and NASCAR to give the family a
very special day at the track. *Getty Images for NASCAR*

race wins. Ron has been going to races since he was 11 years old and has followed Jeff Gordon since Ward Burton retired. But it's the mother and daughter who are the real NASCAR fanatics in the Bradley household. So on this busy Saturday, the family ate a fast meal so mother and daughter could get back home to watch the race, while Ron went off to attend a niece's basketball game.

Connie and Jordyn pulled their Pontiac with the "14 Tony" license plate into the driveway of their ranch house in Claire, Michigan, and were running to claim their spots in front of the TV. What they really ran into was the surprise of their lives.

"I opened the front door, and smoke came pouring out, so thick and big I thought a person was coming out of the house," Connie said. She slammed the door and called the fire department. Local firemen arrived on the scene in minutes and were able to save the house. However, the master bedroom, where an electrical problem under the flooring caused the blaze, and Jordyn's bedroom were torched.

"If Matt and Tony hadn't been entered in the [NASCAR] Nationwide race, we would have stayed in Mount Pleasant instead of rushing home to watch the race. The whole house would have been destroyed," Connie said.

The Bradley girls missed the race, of course, but later received a glimmer of good news on a grim day. "That night I went online at my parents' house to check the [NASCAR] Nationwide race and saw Tony won. It was the only time I smiled that day since opening my front door. I was glad to hear that outcome but definitely would have been happier seeing Tony win it on TV."

Though she was happy for her mom, Jordyn's spirits were low. Her treasured Matt Kenseth memorabilia had gone up in smoke, including autographs she gets each year at a special all-star race Kenseth's dad arranges in Madison, Wisconsin. Yet, the day after the fire would produce another silver lining to the dark cloud hovering over the family. From her new hotel room that would be home the next few months, Jordyn watched Matt Kenseth win the Daytona 500.

Connie was luckier with her Stewart swag than her daughter or husband, whose prized Ward Burton–autographed hats were destroyed. Before the 2009 season, Connie had dedicated a room to Stewart and had painted it in Home Depot orange. But when the longtime Home Depot–sponsored No. 20 driver moved to Office Depot and Old Spice for the 2009 season, Connie packed up the memorabilia collected over the years and stashed it in the garage. She planned to paint the room a shade of red matching his new sponsors and put in new team merchandise. It turned out to be another fortunate turn of events; the empty racing room was heavily damaged by smoke, while the garage holding the Stewart items was mostly unaffected by the fire.

The Bradleys' story came to light through a twist of fate. Connie had entered a racing pool through the local newspaper and came in second place. Several days after the fire, a reporter called with congratulations.

"What a great way to start the week," he said.

Connie responded, "Not really," and shared the story of the house fire.

"That's a good story," the reporter offered.

"Good story for you, not so good for us," Connie said.

It actually turned out to be not such a bad story. While the family lived in a hotel as their home was rebuilt, the ensuing publicity about Connie and Jordyn rushing home for a NASCAR race to find their home in flames would make things a little bit better. Michigan International Speedway president Roger Curtis heard about the Bradleys and offered to host them at his next race. The family could attend the closed-off drivers meeting and watch the race from the track's luxury skybox. He'd even set up a quick meeting between Jordyn and Matt Kenseth.

"When we called Connie, she started to cry," Curtis recalled. "She couldn't believe that the president of MIS was on the phone. That's the kind of call I really like to make—when you can do special things for people. Certainly, we don't like to reach out because someone lost their home in a fire, but it is very important for MIS to use these opportunities to recognize the real VIPs in NASCAR—the fans."

Meanwhile, Mindy Kramer, head of public relations for Office Depot, heard Connie was a big Stewart fan and jumped into action. She sent a box of Tony's new merchandise—t-shirts, the No. 14 car, a flag, a clock, a mug, even a life-size cutout of the driver. For the race, Kramer arranged for a track tour with an up-close look inside the Office Depot team hauler capped by a personal meet-and-greet with Tony. To top it off, she sent a $1,400 gift card—Stewart's car number times 100. "These gestures were unbelievable. I immediately picked out a new camera to take to the race to replace the one lost in the fire. Mindy is now my hero," Connie said.

Connie Bradley was moved with how folks in NASCAR helped her family after their house fire. She "paid it forward" by donating her Bristol race tickets to charity so someone else in need could have an unforgettable experience too. *Getty Images for NASCAR*

The 44-year-old card dealer at the Soaring Eagle Casino & Resort in Michigan didn't start out a NASCAR fan. Living in Indiana she was drawn to open-wheel cars and the Indianapolis 500. "Everyone there was an Indy car freak," she said. "To see what it was all about, I went to the Indy 500 when Tony was racing open-wheel cars. I began following him. He was the Indiana boy, and I love his personality. What you see is what you get. He doesn't sugarcoat anything. If you don't want to hear the truth, don't ask him. I like people who are real, and he's a real person."

When Stewart moved from open-wheel cars to stock cars in 1999, Connie's allegiance jumped to NASCAR. "People say I'm a freak about it. My entire life is basically scheduled around the races. If you know me, you know not to ask me to do *anything* if a race is on."

Connie tried to groom her daughter to follow Stewart, but the independent-minded lass gravitated to Kenseth. "Matt flies under the radar, so I have no idea how she picked him, but I'm glad. She saw Matt's just a plain good person."

The family travels each year from central Michigan to Madison, Wisconsin, to watch Kenseth's all-star race and chat with Kenseth, who is from Cambridge, Wisconsin, during his generous meet-and-greet sessions. Kenseth's sister Kelley is always on hand, eager to spend time with Jordyn. Following Matt's Daytona 500 win, Jordyn made him a congratulatory card. She mailed it off to Kelley, who sent back a load of Kenseth goods. "Kelley and Matt knew Jordyn had lost a lot of things in the fire and sent her a new zip-up hoodie, t-shirts, hats, a beanie bear, tote bags, a parking sign, just a whole box of stuff with his name and number on it."

After the traumatic fire, the unexpected response from so many quarters of NASCAR deeply touched all of the Bradleys. "As a fan, you always read articles on how the racing community comes together in circumstances like this. When it happens to you, it's really unbelievable. There's no way we could experience this without the help of Michigan International Speedway and Office Depot and NASCAR. I'd heard about 'paying it forward,' and Roger and Mindy did that by giving us an experience we'd never otherwise have."

The ordeal of the fire, and the response of people she'd never met, gave Connie a chance to learn about paying it forward too. "We have season tickets at Bristol and drive 23 hours to get there. For the 2009 spring race, we were still out of our house living in the hotel with too many things going on in rebuilding the house to go to the race. I was thinking about putting the Bristol tickets up for sale on the website. When I saw what a nice thing was being done for my family, I thought I could give back as well and donated the tickets to Speedway Children's Charities. Now somebody else will experience something great. I think we all learned a lot of life lessons from the fire that we will never forget. It seems a lot more important to do things you should always do—simple things—and not take anything for granted."

Indeed, there are many lessons to be taken from Connie, Jordyn, and Ron's story. One of them may be this: Tony Stewart and Matt Kenseth need to run in more NASCAR Nationwide Series races.

Getty Images for NASCAR

PART V
STUPENDOUS FEATS OF OVER-THE-TOP FANDOM

Ever notice a song you really like sounds so much better on the radio? You have the exact piece of music on your iPod or in your record collection, but when you hear it on the car radio while pulling up to work, it doesn't matter if you're already late, you will sit in the parking lot until that song is over.

Songs on the radio are better because they're a larger, shared experience. The DJ chose the tune for you . . . and thousands of others are simultaneously enjoying something special.

It's the same with NASCAR.

The sport is a sacred part of fans' lives, but no one wants to keep it a secret. We walk around smiling and ready to tell all like teenagers in love for the first time. NASCAR fans want you to celebrate their passion. They feel a magnetic sense of belonging to something much bigger than themselves. Wearing their driver's colors, flying their flags, and even boasting a tattoo signals membership in a community driven by a common purpose. They are part of a club, are proud to be fans, and want you on board.

As "NASCAR Fan of the Year" Julie Geary said, "Where else but a race can you be at a sporting event with 160,000 of your best friends? You're part of a bigger family, the NASCAR family, where everyone has a place at the table!"

Whether it's the spectacular NASCAR museum Julie and her husband built in their basement for others to enjoy, the heartbroken fiancé getting unexpected help from fans of a rival driver, or the mountain climber embraced by NASCAR's faithful, the over-the-top acts of fandom among our next group make them part of a national fraternity you're welcome to join.

The Summit of Fandom

THE LOYALTY OF NASCAR FANS to their favorite drivers and sport, and the measures they'll take to prove it, is legendary.

There's the iconic gentleman whose photo of the number *3* shaved into his prodigious hairy back lives in Internet infamy. There's the ambitious farmer in Ohio who, like Michelangelo on a Yardman tractor, marvelously groomed green acres into an expansive tribute to Michael Waltrip and the No. 55 car (www.jayski.com/schemes/misc/NAPA-Nascar-Corn-Maze.jpg)

Not to be outdone, a fan near Dover took a chainsaw to a tree in his front yard, carving the stump into a huge *8*. You'll even see examples of chainsaw art at the track. Another fan of the Earnhardts, Craig Reda of Frankenmuth, Michigan, cut a large cottonwood stump into the shape of the number *3*. "It stunk to high hell and took two years to dry out," he said. When the stench subsided, Reda permanently bolted his Dale Sr. tribute onto the roof of his converted 1972 Ford school bus.

Dr. Pat Hickey, who has a debilitating fear of heights, took the NASCAR flag to the top of Mt. Everest. The Jeff Gordon fan had less than a minute to take this picture, before his hands would develop frostbite. *Courtesy Pat Hickey*

These are obviously noteworthy examples of fan devotion. But extreme NASCAR devotees boldly venturing where no others have gone before have a new mountain to scale. A mild-mannered gent by the name of Patrick Hickey upped the ante to a much higher level. His was a feat of extreme danger and borderline lunacy. Hickey, who has a deathly, debilitating fear of heights, took a NASCAR flag to the top of the world: the summit of Mt. Everest.

Adding to this incredible accomplishment, the mountain climber, registered nurse, and nursing professor at University of South Carolina, managed to time it for May 24, matching the number of his favorite driver, Jeff Gordon. When Hickey stood on the roof of the planet, he had completed a dangerous eight-year quest to scale the "Seven Summits of the World"—the highest mountain on each of the seven continents. He joined an elite group of fewer than 150 people in history who have attained this "Holy Grail" in mountaineering. "The Seven Summits was the fulfillment of a quest so wild and fanciful, few have ever dreamed it, and fewer have experienced it," Hickey said.

As he charted the course for conquering the final—and most dangerous—summit, Hickey wasn't planning on taking a piece of NASCAR with him. As with so many things that go down in this sport, the fans had a say. In a blog tapped out during 64 days on Everest, Hickey wrote that he could deal with the cold, isolation, and constant danger. But there was one very distressing, depressing thing about the trip. He was cut off from NASCAR. What was happening with Jeff Gordon, Hickey wondered? Soon, online updates from strangers in 20 different countries began pouring in.

"All kinds of hits came in from so many NASCAR fans. They were giving race results, points updates, and news like Dale Jr. leaving DEI," Hickey said. "Co-workers were amazed to learn I was a NASCAR fan, when I had no idea they were fans too. Of course, the best part was being up on the mountain and hearing Jeff was doing so well on the track."

Hickey noticed something else: NASCAR fans were giving generously to the Summit Scholarship he had created to promote nursing amid the growing shortage and to support the education of nursing students at USC. The goal was to raise $29,035—or a buck for every foot of altitude of Mt. Everest. (Donations can still be made at www.sc.edu/everest/scholarship.html.)

One blog reader, Elizabeth Henry, was also tight with Kristin Nave of NASCAR Corporate Events. Henry was following Hickey's fascination with Jeff Gordon, and she contacted Nave to see if NASCAR could send something to him. Presto, a NASCAR Nextel Cup Series flag was heading from Daytona Beach to base camp at Mt. Everest. Eight days later—and two before his climb—the flag arrived on a U.S. medevac helicopter, which swooped in to take away two sick climbers.

Up on the summit, completing the most challenging physical task on the planet, Hickey quickly removed his insulated mittens, grabbed the NASCAR flag, and posed for a photo. He had to be fast—after 30 seconds, frostbite will set in at temperatures reaching 40 degrees below zero and winds gusting to 125 miles per hour. Hickey had serious business to attend to as well. Stowed in his backpack were the ashes of his dear friend, Sean Egan, who had perished on Everest in 2005. Since 1921, the mountain has been climbed by more than 2,200 people. More than 190 have lost their lives—frightening odds for not making it down. Hickey would worry about that soon. For now, he opened the urn and released Egan's ashes high into the raging winds and across the wide expanse of mountains.

While Hickey downplays the danger associated with the climb, it is wickedly perilous. The mountain's top 3,000 feet are considered the "Death Zone." The digestive systems of the climbers start to shut down just when their bodies need nourishment the most. There is increased risk of high-altitude cerebral edema, an often fatal swelling of the brain, as well as pulmonary edema, where fluids gathering in the lungs can drown a person. Basically, the human body is not built to survive such heights and will rapidly deteriorate.

Moving upward in the Death Zone, on his way to the summit, Hickey had been caught in a violent windstorm. His legs went numb, and he couldn't move them. He luckily spotted his climbing team's tent and used his arms to pull through the ice to safety. He could only speak in unintelligible grunts and was unable to offer his comrades any clue about his condition. Fellow climbers diagnosed advanced hypothermia, and Hickey was revived in a tent only three hours before the final climb to the summit. Once there, he lost sight in one eye and had extremely limited vision in the other.

If you meet Hickey at a race, he looks like any other fan. But don't let his slight frame and easy smile fool you. He's a tough, stubborn, experienced

Dr. Hickey at base camp on the way to becoming one of fewer than 150 people in history to scale the Seven Summits of the World—the highest mountain on each continent. *Courtesy Pat Hickey*

mountain climber. Even so, the elements on Everest are brutal, and at the top of the mountain, Hickey was completely beaten up. He knew making it to the top didn't mean a thing if you didn't make it down. He'd heard about the difficulties of the three-day descent—where 80 percent of climbers lose their lives—but would now personally experience the hazards when it was his own depleted body wanting to shut down. More than once he sincerely believed he'd be another well-dressed carcass eternally frozen on the face of Everest. "Your emotions are riding on the exhilaration of summiting Mt. Everest, which turns to sheer terror when you remember you have to get down," Hickey recalled.

Unable to see much, he was confronted with a series of frightening moments that stretched to agonizing days. Deprived of oxygen and woozy—and battling his paralyzing, stomach-turning fear of heights—he had to cross deep crevasses by crawling over aluminum ladders in strong winds. On the verge of complete exhaustion, he fell down. Instead of tumbling toward Tibet (10,000 feet below) or taking a steeper drop into Nepal (12,000 feet downward), he crashed to a stop on a very forgiving part of the trail and was snagged by safety lines preventing him from taking a sure death plunge.

"Everest is the ultimate high and the ultimate risk," Hickey said. "You're not eating or sleeping, you're not hydrating, your legs are going rubber. My needle was past the E, and I still had to make it down a vertical ice wall. The steepness of the canyon walls and the radiation of the intense sun reflected off the snow and underlying glacier combine to sap your fluids until your tongue seems glued to the roof of your mouth. I knew I needed lots of water, but every time I swallowed it felt like sharp pieces of glass were tumbling down my throat, so raw from the wind."

For Pat, worse than his severe dehydration was not being able to see. So he visualized his wife, Carol, holding in his head her image and the thought of seeing her again. Virtually blind, freezing to death, and malnourished, Pat managed to dig deep and find reserves of courage and determination he didn't know existed. He kept moving forward, taking one small step, crawling, getting up, then taking another step, then another. "With each step, I kept repeating: I'm coming home, I'm coming home," he said.

Home is where Hickey became a NASCAR fan, but not until he was in his 20s. He grew up the eldest of nine on a 100-acre farm in rural Canada. As a boy, he was plagued by his bad asthma and that fear of heights. Once he missed dinner because he was stranded in the barn, holding onto a plank in the rafters for dear life. He felt awkward in school, wearing secondhand clothes and mismatched gloves from a bus depot's lost-and-found due to the family's meager finances. He did poorly in class, his mind wandering to dreams of exotic places far away. A guidance counselor directed him to study nursing. He was initially confused and put off; wasn't that a women's profession? But he was a tender, caring soul and realized the possibility of traveling the world, saving lives. A lifelong passion for helping others and visiting strange lands began. While studying for his advanced nursing degree at the University of South Carolina, Pat kept the TV on "for background noise." One Sunday the race was on, and he grew interested.

"I got caught up in the soap opera of the sport," he explained. He was entertained by the changing alliances on the track and the simmering grudges in the garage. He was immediately drawn to Jeff Gordon. In Jeff, he saw an admirable leader who remained positive no matter the present circumstances, qualities that would preserve his own life climbing on several continents. He liked that Jeff was a staunch competitor, always quick to praise unsung team members, which would be his philosophy on hospital trauma teams and in developing new nurses. He was impressed that

Gordon was an ambassador for goodwill in channeling millions of dollars for the needy through the Jeff Gordon Foundation. After all, Hickey's own desire to help others inspired him to become a nurse and then to train and mentor future nurses as a university professor, nursing advocate, spokesperson, and creator of the Summit Scholarship.

Hickey's first NASCAR Sprint Cup Series race was at Darlington Raceway in 2006. He sat three rows from the track, riveted by the thundering procession, aiming his mobile phone at the passing rush of cars. A year later, as he was climbing to the "roof of the world" and tackling the seventh and final summit, Jeff Gordon was racing at that same Darlington track. Before heading to Nepal, Hickey had told his good friend Judy Barr, a Tony Stewart fanatic working at the University of South Carolina, "If Jeff Gordon wins at Darlington, I want Jeff to know somebody will be smiling on top of the world."

"The whole time I was at Darlington, I kept thinking about Pat's words," Barr said. "When I climbed to the very last row in the stands for the race, I thought of Pat climbing. I was right in front of Jeff's pit box. Throughout the race, Jeff had water issues. There was just no way he was going to win the race, let alone finish. Steam was pouring from the engine. When Jeff ended up winning, even he said he had no idea how the engine held up. Drivers talk all the time about the 'racing gods.' The way Pat's climb and Jeff's win worked out, I like to think the racing gods were looking down on both of them that weekend."

Word about Gordon's win got to Hickey on the mountain, and he was naturally elated.

After hearing Hickey's Everest tale and Seven Summits accomplishment, NASCAR helped arrange for him to attend the NASCAR Sprint Cup Series race in Charlotte in October 2007. At the pre-race ceremony on pit road, he presented the NASCAR flag he took to the top of the mountain to NASCAR president Mike Helton. It will reside in NASCAR's Hall of Fame in Charlotte when the facility opens in 2010.

Pat finally got to meet Gordon prior to the race. The two world-class athletes who tempt fate in an often hostile and unpredictable environment stood in the narrow hallway of the No. 24 DuPont Chevrolet hauler. Hickey peppered Gordon with questions about maneuvering a stock car around at track at 180 miles per hour inches from good friends and respected rivals. Gordon wanted none of that. He was hitting Hickey with questions on making it up—and then down—the treacherous ice amid howling winds on a mountain so breathtakingly majestic and satanically cruel at the same time. Hickey pulled from his backpack a rock retrieved from the top of the world and handed the unique keepsake to his NASCAR hero. The race car driver said to the mountain climber, "Some people question what I do. But I think you're the crazy one here."

Hickey keeps another rock from the top of Mt. Everest in his office desk at the university. "I want to remind myself of the great potential we have within us to do anything we put our minds to, and also the great responsibility I have to find that potential in my students," he said. "Each of us has a sense of adventure within us. [My adventures] are just more noticeable because they're more extreme. For some, the adventure can be to climb a mountain, run a marathon, learn a new language, travel to a foreign country, or seek a more challenging job or position within an organization. We all have the potential to do better in our lives. I hope my Seven Summits helps show that."

The next time you're confronted with a daunting, seemingly impossible task, maybe you'll remember fellow NASCAR fan Patrick Hickey. Asthmatic and afraid of heights, Pat went to the highest, thinnest air on earth. He ventured far outside of his comfort zone, testing his limits way beyond reason and discovering what he's truly capable of: anything.

It was Pat's idea to bring the banner of his favorite sport to the top of Mt. Everest, but if NASCAR had its choice for a flag bearer, there would be no better selection than Dr. Patrick Hickey, a giving man who could have been robbed of his full potential by deep, dark fears. Pat decided to do what few attempt. He got down on his hands and knees, and he crawled right over those limitations.

Houston, We Have a Fan

I T'S NOT UNUSUAL FOR NASCAR FANS unable to tune to a race—maybe they're on the job or waiting to get a root canal—to sneak a quick online update. One fan, Doug Hurley, got his NASCAR fix at work on a laptop computer in a unique place: 250 miles above the earth moving at 17,500 miles per hour in zero gravity. "Now that's the definition of a hot lap," Col. Hurley wrote to me in an e-mail from the International Space Station.

Hurley, the pilot of Space Shuttle *Endeavour*, which completed its 16-day mission on July 31, 2009, hadn't missed a race in eight years since being introduced to NASCAR at Watkins Glen and feeling a rush of excitement he could only call "indescribable." He wasn't going to let a small thing like manning the controls of the most complex machine ever built get in the way of finding out how Joey Logano did at Chicagoland Speedway.

Space Shuttle *Endeavour* pilot Col. Doug Hurley watched his first race from crew chief Greg Zipadelli's pit stall and was "unequivocally, unbelievably, completely, and totally hooked on NASCAR." *Courtesy Col. Doug Hurley*

"It's not a very well-kept secret at NASA that I'm a pretty big NASCAR fan," Hurley said. The second line of his official NASA biography states, "Recreational interests include hunting, cycling, and attending as many NASCAR races as possible." While training in Star City, Russia, with cosmonauts preparing to work on the International Space Station, the Marine Corps colonel watched NASCAR Sprint Cup Series races on the armed forces television network deep into the night. On board the *Endeavour*, he took DVD copies to two of the most notable races in the history of stock car racing: the 1979 and 1998 Daytona 500s. He's lobbying to have these classic races included in the permanent library on board the International Space Station.

Hurley grew up in Apalachin, New York, a town so small it had no stoplight. On cloudless nights, he'd gaze at the wide sky, densely speckled with the twinkling lights of stars from galaxies billions of miles away. Doug was only two years old when Neil Armstrong set foot on the moon but remembers news clips of Sky Lab missions sandwiched between the Saturday morning cartoons. "As a young boy, you think, 'Wow, that would be pretty neat to go there and do that,'" he said. He liked what the military stood for and to help pay for college enrolled in the Navy ROTC program at Tulane University. During college, he spent a week at a navy jet base in Jacksonville and got to ride in a fighter plane. "That was the defining moment. I knew what I wanted to do." Hurley excelled as a naval aviator and a test pilot. He was the first Marine pilot to fly the F/A-18 E/F Super Hornet.

Despite his fondness for speed, Hurley never paid much attention to NASCAR, even though he'd lived 45 minutes south of the road course at Watkins Glen. That changed when his cousin Nanette began dating Greg Zipadelli, then Tony Stewart's crew chief for Joe Gibbs Racing. Nan and Doug had spent many holidays and summers together as kids and remained close as adults. He jumped at her invitation to watch the race from Zippy's pit stall at the Glen. "From the moment I heard the first engine roar to life, I was unequivocally, unbelievably, completely, and totally hooked on NASCAR," Hurley said. Since then, he's attended more than 20 races, holds season tickets at Texas Motor Speedway, and has become close friends with Zippy, going on hunting trips during the off-season and cooking up big steaks at Zipadelli's motor home on Saturday night whenever NASCAR visits Texas Motor Speedway. "I like being around Doug because he's simply a great guy, fun to be with, and just incredibly passionate and intense about what he's doing with the space program," Zipadelli said. "He is incredibly smart and could have done anything he set his heart to in life. I have to say, going into outer space is probably the coolest thing he could have picked."

Nanette and Zipadelli are now married with three kids, while Tony and the crew chief he called "the big brother I never had" have parted ways. After a stellar decade with the No. 20 Home Depot car, including two NASCAR Sprint Cup Series championships, Stewart left Joe Gibbs Racing following the 2008 season to form his own team, becoming the most successful driver-owner in NASCAR since Alan Kulwicki won the title in 1992. The separation was a tough, emotional time for Zippy. "Loyalty is a big thing with Zippy, and he decided to stay with Joe Gibbs, who gave him a huge opportunity. That's where his heart was."

Most No. 20 fans also guided by their loyalty simply followed Stewart to his new No. 14 ride. Hurley stuck with Zippy and his new driver, teenage phenom Joey Logano, nicknamed "Sliced Bread," as in "the greatest thing since." "Joey is amazingly grounded for a person his age facing tremendous challenges and responsibility," Hurley said. "If you compare him to Zippy or me, we were selected for our jobs—Greg as crew chief and me into the astronaut program—in our early 30s. Joey is 19 and handling the pressure of big-time auto racing very well. At the outset, there was skepticism about his abilities in a [NASCAR Sprint] Cup ride, but his true talent quickly became apparent. NASCAR banned testing for 2009, which was the right move to save costs, but it hurt newer guys like Joey. And then you have him going into a new car much different than the NASCAR Nationwide Series cars he was driving. Considering all that, he's figuring out a lot of things pretty quickly. Joey's been blessed with tremendous talent and the help of a core group of guys who have been with Zippy from the beginning. He and Zippy have been a great team, which they proved when Joey became the youngest driver ever to win a [NASCAR] Sprint Cup Series race at New Hampshire in 2009. Joey battled hard all day, and Zippy made a great call to win the race. I'm predicting Joey is going to do very well in the years to come. Plus, he is just a super nice guy. He's got solid support from his parents, and it shows."

Hurley, who is 42 and favors the flattop hairstyle reminiscent of the flight directors and flyboys chronicled in Tom Wolfe's book *The Right Stuff*, sees many parallels between the sport he loves to watch from the pit stall

Hurley and Zipadelli celebrate in Victory Lane at Texas Motor Speedway following a dominating Tony Stewart win in 2006. When Stewart left Joe Gibbs Racing to form his own team, Hurley started rooting for Zippy's new driver, teenage phenom Joey Logano. *Getty Images for NASCAR*

and his own job strapped into a rocket soaring toward the wild blue yonder. "My background is as a fighter pilot, so the speed, the adrenaline rush, the eye-hand coordination is somewhat similar. A big part of the excitement for me is getting so close to the action. Fans can feel a bit of that, sitting off the turn with the cars coming right at you. They can get some of that speed adrenaline rush a fighter pilot feels."

In some ways, NASCAR drivers face tougher challenges than astronauts, Hurley said. It's a surprising perspective from a decorated navy test pilot who was snapped up by the astronaut development program as soon as he was eligible, a four-time recipient of the NASA Superior Accomplishment Award who helped orchestrate the mind-boggling tasks of an upside-down rendezvous with the International Space Station, five space walks, the replacement of half a dozen 250-pound batteries in the unforgiving blackness of space, and the transfer home of a Japanese astronaut.

"The biggest difference is NASCAR is much more in the public eye than what we do as astronauts and what I did as a fighter pilot," he said. "When we launch shuttles into space, of course that's highly publicized, but months of training are largely done without constant scrutiny. NASCAR drivers live in the limelight virtually year-round. Being in a dangerous, high-pressure environment, it's not easy to manage outside eyes prying in."

There are obviously many differences between astronauts and race car drivers. Flirting with danger—the lurking, unpredictable set of unseen circumstances that can snuff a life out in a blink—is something they have in common. Hurley was avidly following the sport when Adam Petty, Kenny Irwin, and Dale Earnhardt Sr. passed away. A few years later, he personally strapped the STS 107 crew into the Space Shuttle *Columbia*, which disintegrated upon re-entry over the southwestern United States in 2003.

"Nothing prepares you for losing seven friends in an instant on a national scale," he said. "NASA had a tough decision after the loss of the *Columbia* just as NASCAR had a tough decision after losing its most famous and maybe greatest driver. Where do you go? What do you do? The right answer is you fly again, and you race next week. You just make sure you've learned from the previous events so it won't happen again.

"The danger of what we do is always in the back of my mind. But I think human space flight is better from the *Columbia* accident, despite losing seven people who can never be replaced. It's the same with NASCAR. We lost Dale Earnhardt Sr. and will never get him back. But some very positive things came from that tragedy. The sport made significant improvements to the cars and tracks and has never been safer.

"What happened with Dale and the *Columbia* are eerily similar. We'd seen foam fall off the Shuttle for years. We tolerated it. NASCAR had some bad accidents that seemed like freak occurrences. It took a huge event in both cases to bring about productive change—losing the most famous driver in what looked like an innocuous crash and the shuttle burning up over Texas after a piece of foam dislodged. But some pretty smart people worked hard to fix the problems. And we're much safer as a result."

Just as NASCAR is seeking expansion opportunities, so is NASA. Missions are being planned for the U.S. to return to the moon and possibly beyond to Mars. Perhaps one of our own remarkable fans will be at the controls. Whatever is next for Doug Hurley, all of NASCAR Nation wishes him "Godspeed."

Bob's Party Bus

ᴛALLADEGA SUPERSPEEDWAY has a notorious reputation as the loudest, most raucous party stop on the NASCAR circuit. It's also the place where Kevin Kent was sent to surrender to Christ.

And if that's not enough of a man-bites-dog story, before Kevin Kent went stone cold sober on October 6, 2007, dedicating himself to Jesus in the middle of the throbbing infield after 31 years of drinking and drugging, he was the good-time ringleader and captain of an amazing psychedelic bus that had probably served up more suds than Busch Stadium in St. Louis.

After his spiritual awakening at Talladega, Kevin became a brand-new man. His one-of-a-kind party bus still draws crowds at the races. It's just taken on a different role, now helping to tell a remarkable story of grace accepted and redemption pursued. The bus remains an amusement-park-

---

After his friend Bob passed away, Kevin Kent became caretaker of "Bob's Party Bus." Once a legendary partier, Kevin now hands out Bibles instead of pasties at the bus. *Author photo*

worthy attraction thousands of fans experience—covered inside and out in drips and streaks and splatters of florescent paint, colorful gobs slung on the walls and seats and floors, as if Jackson Pollock worked at Earl Scheib Paint & Body. When darkness falls over the race track, fans still wait their turn to climb aboard, putting on 3-D glasses to view a twisting, oozing menagerie of electric blues, hot pinks, ruby reds, canary yellows, and lime greens, a demented mix of color in a shifting landscape that throws anyone walking through the bus into a trippy, 1960s frame of mind. Kevin continues to be a fixture by the back emergency exit at the end of the tour, wearing a coat and hat speckled in neon paint. But instead of handing out beads and booze, he offers Bibles and church service DVDs.

"Before I was saved, this bus was the scene for one non-stop, hardcore party," he said. "I used to put pasties on girls coming through. Now I give them my testimony. You could say we went from the Pasty Bus to God's Bus."

The 1960 Chevrolet had been shuttling Indiana school kids before it was purchased by Kevin's friend, Bob. "About six of us got an assortment of paint and just let it rip," Kevin said. They feverishly coated the bus top to bottom in a freaky freehand style of which acidhead Ken Kesey's Merry Pranksters would have approved. When the black lights were installed and 3-D glasses brought in, the old Chevy became a favored party destination, particularly at Michigan International Speedway in the late 1990s. Word spread, and Bob's psychedelic bus became *the* place to visit in the infield.

In 2002, an aggressive cancer snuck up and took Bob's life. Kevin purchased the bus from his friend's estate. "I wanted to keep Bob and his dream alive, so I bought it and simply named it, 'Bob's Party Bus.'" Kevin and the bus would make regular pilgrimages to NASCAR's two summer races in Michigan.

The legend of the psychedelic bus grew, as did Kevin's appetite for beer. He could drink four or five cases a weekend. He had started drinking when he was 14 and never let up, even after getting kicked out of school for good at 16 and being convicted of DWI several times. Drinking led to drugging, and over the years, getting blotto as often as possible cost Kevin his driver's license, two marriages, and a few jobs. But he had no intention of stopping.

Being at a race was a good excuse to get knee-crawling drunk. In the infield of Michigan, Kevin roamed freely with a drink in his hand, except for one spot. He'd always come across a hot band playing catchy music and having a good time. He stayed away. "They were a Christian rock band, and I just knew Christians never had any fun. I didn't need to know about God, and I kept my distance," he said.

At the 2007 August race in Michigan, he noticed a guy named Mike unloading a trailer for the band. He offered to help. Mike was fine on his own; he only had one box. "What? I'm not good enough to carry your box?" Kevin joked.

The men hit it off, and Kevin invited Mike and a bandmate to visit the magic bus. Naturally, they were impressed and returned with the rest of the band that evening. Each band member autographed the inside of the bus.

On Saturday night, a fellow in the band who went by the name of Preacher Man Berry told Kevin that a big-time executive would be at the concert to hand out shirts, sign autographs, and thank the fans. Kevin spotted the exec at the show and invited him to see the bus. The buzz had spread further than anyone imagined, and the exec was eager to check it out.

Kevin and his friends cleared everyone out to give the executive a special tour. They chatted and snapped a few pictures. On the way back to see the band, the executive told Kevin he needed to take his amazing party bus to Talladega.

"I've always wanted to go, and I have a friend down there, but I can't do it," Kevin said.

"You didn't hear me. You really need to get this bus to 'Dega," the executive repeated.

Kevin gave the same answer. The executive asked why.

"This bus doesn't do too well on gas. And we need to eat. It costs a lot to get down there and back, and I just don't have the money," Kevin said.

"What about if I split it with you?"

An offer like that was the last thing in the world Kevin expected to hear. Too shocked to even speak, he nodded eagerly. The executive took out his wallet and handed Kevin $500.

Kevin was in awe of the gesture. He had found a steady job as an iron worker in Ohio, but he feared how much the trip would cost. And the bus needed immediate repairs. He sputtered, "I'm really not sure, my wife is gonna kill me...."

Before he could finish, he was handed another $200.

"I really want you to come to Talladega, and [I] hope this will make her happy," the executive said.

Kevin couldn't thank him enough. But what the executive said next surprised him even more.

"Thank you for being such a good fan," he said, extending his hand.

Kevin looked him in the eye as they shook.

"I'll be there," he said.

"I know you will."

The motorsports executive didn't know it at the time, but his extraordinary impromptu gesture likely saved Kevin Kent's life.

Even as his drinking escalated, Kevin worked nonstop over the next month to prepare the bus for the long haul to the Deep South. He got new tires and added a generator and air conditioner. He'd heard about the awesome bunched-up restrictor-plate racing at NASCAR's longest track, but he was more hopped up planning how he'd cut loose in the party capital of NASCAR. "I was so excited knowing that I'd be able to go crazy. And once we got there, party I did: Thursday, Thursday night, Friday, and Friday night," he said.

Everyone in 'Dega who saw Bob's Party Bus loved it. The story of the bus spread to the other camps. Big crowds were flocking at the entrance, with fans calmly lining up for the incredible tour. One of the fans who'd mounted the bus, Mark, was a member of the Christian band, the River. Saturday morning, within earshot of Kevin, Mark told Kevin's wife, Debbie, he wished Kevin would stay sober. "He'd be so much more fun, don't you think?" Mark said.

It wasn't an angry challenge or an aggressive intervention, more in the tone of a caring person disappointed with the way someone's life has turned out. Now, Saturday night in Talladega is like Fat Tuesday in New Orleans. That didn't seem to bother Kevin. For the first time since he was 14 years old, he decided not to drink. "I really didn't spend too much time thinking about it. I just decided not to have that first drink, and the night unfolded. Amazingly, it was the most fun in my life I had ever had. Without a single drink, I had a blast."

As day turned into night, Kevin was chatting with Wes, another member of the band. Kevin casually mentioned he was thinking about getting a Bible.

"I'll see what I can do," Wes said, before the men went to sleep.

On Sunday morning, Kevin woke up with a headache. "I'd been drinking so much my body just assumed it had to feel horrible in the morning,"

Kent brings the psychedelic bus to half a dozen NASCAR races each year. On a weekend night, fans will wait in line for a chance to put on 3-D glasses for a tour of Bob's Party Bus. It's easy to find: the lighted cross atop the bus can be seen from all corners of the infield. *Author photo*

he said. He and Debbie had such a good time with Mark and Wes of the River, they decided to head over to the church service the band organized between the track's first and second turns. Wes spotted them and announced he had a Bible for Kevin.

This wasn't a spare Bible gathering dust on a shelf. It was the Bible Wes' kids had used through five states, the Bible he had taken around the world twice on his mission trips, the one Wes had received after he accepted Christ into his life.

Kevin couldn't accept Wes' personal Bible, but Wes insisted.

"God has answered my prayers. He's led me to give this to you. Take it," he told Kevin.

With tears of happiness in his eyes, Kevin accepted the Bible. At the church service, he raised his hands and told God he was sorry for all he had done in his life. He prayed, "Jesus, please forgive me, I'm giving my life to you." He saw a bright flash, more intense than lightning or a welder's flash, brighter than anything he'd ever seen. When the light was gone, he could see more clearly, as if God had removed the plastic from his eyes. The air even tasted better.

"At that moment, God removed my desire for alcohol and drugs. He took away the anger from my body, and I began to love my family even more, with all of my heart. He helped me love from the inside out and not the outside in. The song 'Amazing Grace' is the story of my life—I once was lost, but now I see,"

Kent, who is now 47, has been clean and sober since that weekend in Talladega. He's still not sure why one of the top officials in motorsports was so insistent about him taking Bob's Party Bus to Talladega, putting his life on a new path, other than that it was God's will. "Can you think of any other reason?" he asked. Bob's Party Bus is still mobbed at a half-dozen NASCAR Sprint Cup Series races each year. It's easier to find than ever, now bearing a 30-foot cross illuminated with colored Christmas lights visible clear across the track. The bottom is rusting badly, and Kevin is praying for additional divine intervention.

"You could say we did a conversion on the bus, from R-rated to G-rated," Kevin noted. "It's still Bob's Party Bus but with a different purpose—to share the love of God with other people. When people come to visit the bus, I have their attention and can witness that there's much more to life than alcohol and drugs. I share my testimony with them so they know what God can do in their lives. I've replaced booze on the bus with Bibles. Anyone who needs one is welcome."

Hearts Big and Brave

H IS NAME IS CRAIG, and he "lives" just down the road from Bob's
Party Bus. His neighbors at the track, who visit bearing strong,
peach-flavored drinks in mason jars, call him "Braveheart." It's the
beard and charged-up Zeus hair. His wife, Jackie, will sometimes call
him "babe." She is a beautician who wears long, flowing, flower-child
dresses, serves food and drink like a one-woman 24-hour diner, and
correctly refers to herself as "the hostess with the mostest." I'm happy to
call Craig and Jackie my friends.

The couple from Frankenmuth, Michigan (a place not to be forgotten since Jackie presented and forced me to break in a Frankenmuth
Brewery shot glass) collects NASCAR signatures on the inside of a

---

Craig Reda, with his wife, Jackie, display the cottonwood carving honoring Dale
Earnhardt Sr. on top of their 1972 Ford school bus. Reda cried harder when
Earnhardt died than when his own father passed away. *Author photo*

converted yellow school bus. More than a hundred cover the cream-colored, domed ceiling. There are shiny black names of Goodyear tire changers. Driver David Starr is there, as well as crew chiefs Harold Holley, Brad Parrott, and Todd Parrott. There are track workers and guys who used to sling gas cans for Jimmy Spencer. It is a roster of marvelous signatures forming a tapestry of lives intersecting at the race track, some scribbled with the fine-art intricacy of Arabic, some in chunky bold caps—could be a back-of-the-pack, over-the-wall jack man not getting much attention but now the recipient of a special moment immortalized on the sloped roof of the 1972 Ford bus, courtesy of two down-home NASCAR fans.

I had been taking pictures of buses in the infield at Michigan International Speedway, and between Turn Two and Turn Three I spotted a large *3* carved in wood and mounted on a picnic table attached to the top of a school bus. Most fans who buy an old bus for the races repaint the hull, usually the color of a favorite driver. This one proudly held its original yellow. I headed over, and through the open rear emergency exit I could see a gent sporting a bushy ponytail. He was kneeling on the shag to put on a new record—yes, a grooved, black, vinyl platter on a real turntable next to a long row of albums housed in flaking covers with photos of the Allman Brothers, Creedence Clearwater Revival, Mott the Hoople, Led Zeppelin, Foghat, Neil Young, the Beatles, the Rolling Stones, the Who, and so on.

"Hey man, I'm taking pictures of buses. I dig them; can I take a shot of yours?" I asked.

With an easy smile, Craig Reda waved me in. He's a carpenter who has built a few churches. I had already detected a mellow, charitable, judicial, Jesus-like presence, and that, along with Craig's barely tamed Woodstock-era hairdo, may explain why I was slipping into hippie speak, leaking out "Hey man, can you dig it?" intonations and tie-dyed inflections you'd imagine from Sadie Atkins and Squeaky Fromme on Charlie's Ranch.

Far out.

Craig saw the bus abandoned in the woods in 1995, found its owner, and bought it for a few hundred bucks. It was to be used to transport tools and materials for his construction business. A race at Michigan was coming up, and the Redas brought the bus into the infield. "Three laps in, Jackie announced, 'This is our race bus.'" Craig put in a queen-sized bed, a sofa, a deck on the roof, and the stereo below. The idea of the signatures took on a life of its own once a few guys from Roush Racing signed. Craig pulled out a marker and asked for my signature too. I protested. Well, it was a half protest. OK, it was an extremely life-less rebuff. I said, "no, no I can't, no thank you" in a lame, uncommitted way to ensure I'd get to sign. Never turn down a chance to be on TV or to give an autograph.

Craig didn't have to work hard to lead me to an open spot, and Jackie easily talked me into signing a die-cast car especially for an eight-year-old in the camper across the way. I proudly squeaked out my name with a moist Sharpie, thereby devaluing the NASCAR-licensed merchandise. It was invigorating to be seen as "someone," and at the same time I wanted to take a shower to wash these sins of vanity from my body.

It was oddly discomforting to be considered a minor celebrity among the population of several camping slots on the big backstretch at Michigan. To all their friends, Craig and Jackie introduced me as a NASCAR PR director, as if I were a dignitary from an impor-tant, faraway government. Jen Irelan is a Dale Jr. fan from Traverse City who's been a regular at the track since she was two years old. Pete Monahan lives on a 1961 Chris Craft boat, only touching dry land during the summer for the races at Michigan. His girlfriend, Erin Glauch, was sitting on the horse saddle mounted next to the Reda's wooden bar alongside the bus, grabbing the horn when she laughed to keep from falling off. A parade of friends would drop in throughout the weekend, take a seat at the bar to catch up on all the news since the last race, ask how good it is to be back, and say, "Isn't your worst day at the track a thousand times better than your best day at work?"

With the fans out in these parts, when you're introduced as a NASCAR executive, it's as if Oprah has instantly become your aunt. There is a prevailing faith you can grant special wishes and impart general wisdom. Folks hang on your every word. To work for NASCAR is to pull levers behind the curtain at Oz. For a fringe player like me to be paid somber respect like this is a tribute to the honor and appreciation NASCAR fans have for the sanctioning body, even while all of the thanks should go to the fans. That's the twisted part of being a NASCAR PR guy hit up for an autograph: the fan is the star here.

You bet, these folks were highly impressed with NASCAR. They were here to see a race and were grateful for the presence of an employee with NASCAR credentials in a NASCAR shirt. But then I became friends with these fans and began to do the ordinary things friends do and joke around about the stuff friends kid about. I began to love them for the normal reasons any friends converge; the Redas are fun people with big, generous hearts and a knack for making me laugh. And I also started to get mildly annoyed at the routine minor transgressions among friends. Like snoring.

Jackie had generously invited me to crash on her couch, a world-class idea following spirited revelry for Craig's 50th birthday. As the clock flirted with 4 a.m., I sank into a surprisingly comfortable sofa next to the stereo in the rear, ready to chainsaw a stack of logs. We were on our backs cracking each other up like 12-year-old kids up way too late at sleep-away camp when Jackie, whose voice was now crushed auto glass soaked in whiskey, issued a warning: "Andrew, it is deathly hot in here. I'm taking off my clothes."

Cool and quiet, the Redas plunged into deep sleep. Within minutes, a foghorn sounded. Then another. Inside the bus, it was like angry dueling foghorns, one trying to outperform the other in a longstanding global grudge match. Craig let out a prodigious, full-air, gurgling blast that could have burst his uvula. This nice fellow may swallow his tongue, I was thinking. Craig's whopping wail was like a taunt, prodding and coaxing Jackie to return volley. And his beloved wife of 18 years didn't disappoint, coming with aircraft carrier guns ablaze, unleashing a fearsome cruise ship–worthy blast that would have blown the Gorton's fisherman from his boat.

I don't recall sleeping much, and at the first glint of light peeking through the bus curtains made of aprons rescued from a Frankenmuth German restaurant, I nearly tumbled out the back exit in order to freshen up and meet a CNBC crew for interviews with Tony Stewart, Carl Edwards, and our vehicle partners, since media here in Michigan were doing the "fate-of-Detroit-in-NASCAR" story. (Our drivers correctly pointed out Chevy, Ford, Dodge, and Toyota sell a heckuva lot of cars to NASCAR fans and are getting a significant return in the sport.)

That evening I returned to see the Redas, and our deep sleepers just ate up the eyewitness account of the grudge match and how the Gorton's dude was now hard of hearing and soaking wet after their blasts knocked him off the fish-stick boat and me from the bus at the crack of dawn.

"Yeah, if Jackie wakes me up, I'll just turn her over, and she does the same for me," Craig said, sipping homemade wine he received from an old man he does work for. He met Jackie on ladies' night at a local German beerhouse nearly two decades ago. "She was the funniest, prettiest, loudest girl in the bar. I could hear her over the band. I was single with a boy, and she fell in love with my kid . . . and me too, I guess." They're now inseparable. During a race weekend about the only time you won't see them nearly attached at the hip is when one trudges toward Turn Three for the bathrooms and showers. In fact, Craig was offered a garage pass on a Saturday but declined because he didn't want to spend a few hours away from Jackie.

I'm not the only NASCAR person who has observed this true love story while welcomed with open arms into the wide and expanding circle of Craig and Jackie Reda. They're good friends with Michigan International Speedway president Roger Curtis, first meeting in 2006 when security stopped their bus entering the track gates. Craig wondered which rule he'd broken. He pushed open the tall double door like a driver picking up a kid on the way to school, and the new track president bounded up the stairs, introduced himself, and thanked them for coming to the race. "Right there, we knew Roger was a different breed," Jackie said.

At this June 2009 NASCAR Sprint Cup Series race, as Curtis worked the infield, catching up with friends and thanking new fans for their patronage, he rolled up to the Redas' campsite in his Chevy Tahoe. He motioned for the Redas to jump in. They got a big surprise when Curtis pointed the vehicle onto the track and floored it. "Roger was laughing the whole time, saying, 'Oh boy, we're gonna get in trouble for this!'" Jackie said. Track security came blasting onto the scene as the president and his fan friends barreled around the two-mile oval. The men in badges started to reprimand Curtis, then realized it was the boss man wheeling this late-night hot lap.

Curtis once came by the campsite for one of Jackie's steaks. He asked Craig to name the one thing that would markedly improve his fan experience. It was an intriguing offer. Craig had been at these races since getting the bus in 1995. And he could draw on the collective memory of friends at the track. One of them, Jen Irelan, a fixture in the infield since she was in diapers, recalls in the dead of night, fans cranking their music as loud as they wished, and during the days their lady friends engaging in "European sun bathing." With all that fan history at the Redas' bus, and Craig's own experiences, he could have griped about tougher noise restrictions or other minor rules created as more families populated the track's campgrounds. But hearing Roger's "your wish is my command" tone, Craig knew what he wanted. "A big-screen TV right over there," he said, pointing to the outside wall in the middle of the 2,200-foot backstretch.

At the next race, when Reda was pulling the bus into his spot, he looked up and there it was: a giant screen right where he wanted it. It was, of course, for every fan's viewing pleasure, but damned if Craig didn't accept it as a personal gift from Roger Curtis, the coolest racing executive around. Roger even stopped by, elbowed him in the ribs, and said, "Hey, what do you think of that!"

Of course, it was a typical "customer is king" Curtis upgrade for the entire back half of the infield. For his pal Craig Reda, Curtis had something more personal in mind, showing up on the night of the carpenter's 50th birthday celebration at his campsite with a sheet cake made to look like a race track. Roger and Craig locked elbows and fed each other the way newlyweds will do before smashing it into one another's faces, which they did as well.

"Roger sees his job as 'How do I make you happy? What can I do for you today?'" Craig said. For his part, the track president said he's simply a fan at heart who has never let a pursuit of "market share" cloud a much more important goal: making every single ticket holder's experience memorable. From his office in the administrative building, Curtis can see the seats he had as a fan for so many years near the start-finish line. He remembers what it's like to buy a ticket simply to have a blast at the track . . . and what it's like to be caught in traffic afterward. His first time at Michigan, it took seven hours to make it to the highway, an untenable situation he's helped fix.

Also in Craig and Jackie's NASCAR circle are International Speedway Corporation PR man Lenny Santiago and Michael Printup, president of Watkins Glen International. After Printup spent time with fans at Craig's birthday bash, a handful of them are expecting to drop the green flag, drive the pace car, and sing the national anthem. Printup, who was asked to run Watkins Glen in summer 2009, is learning how to delight and amaze fans at the knee of Roger Curtis, so fans should expect the unexpected. At the next road-course race in western New York, if you see a long-haired guy resembling Sir William Wallace shouting, "Gentlemen, start your engines," with a smiling woman in a flowery sundress by his side, that may be Craig Reda. The honor will be well deserved.

Always in Victory Lane

SIX MONTHS AFTER HER DEAR BOYFRIEND, John Bookie, had passed away, Christine Kavka was devising a plan for spreading his ashes at the race track.

This is what John wanted. He'd said it.

John was healthy as an ox, as they say. No one had any inkling he'd suddenly be gone. But there was that eerie conversation at a Michigan versus Michigan State football game. From out of the blue, John declared a final wish: to be cremated when his time was up. This would be no squat jar of ashes gathering dust on the mantelpiece, however. John wanted his remains spread at a NASCAR track where Jeff Gordon raced.

Two weeks later, John Bookie died from accidental carbon monoxide poisoning. His body was cremated.

Now, carrying John's ashes, Christine was getting ready for the NASCAR Sprint Cup Series race. Sports had brought her and John together—first Michigan State football, then NASCAR. It figures that she met John at a game. He was in the team colors, this big gregarious

---

Christine Kavka's fiancé, John Bookie, was a boisterous Jeff Gordon fan, who made new friends wherever he went. *Courtesy Christine Kavka*

man in green pants. He was crazy and fun. Soon she was head over heels for this larger-than-life guy completely nuts about college football and Jeff Gordon.

Christine tucked John's ashes into her jacket. Eight years earlier, he'd introduced her to NASCAR. There were lots of good times built around watching the races, such as the time they visited friends in Florida. Everyone was in the Jacuzzi relaxing with drinks, the TV pointed at the hot tub and showing the race. John couldn't get in the water. The No. 24 Chevy was leading. John was a ball of energy, a big man pacing back and forth like a little kid, as if the harder he concentrated, the faster the car would go. Gordon held off the pack and took the checkers, and John just exploded in fist-pumping celebration. Christine smiled as she remembered, touching the container with John's ashes in the pocket of her DuPont jacket.

Head-to-toe in Jeff Gordon garb, she would grant his wish. Just as Christine had steadfastly maintained the shrine to Jeff Gordon that her boyfriend had built in her house, she'd find a way to spread his ashes at the race track. Doing these things kept him around.

On the tram from the parking lot, some members of Junior Nation began ribbing her. The colorful Gordon gear can rankle an Earnhardt fan.

Christine is no shrinking violet, but before she could speak up, one of John's loyal friends took over.

"Don't mess with her," the friend warned. "Her dead boyfriend is in her pocket."

The fans were confused, speechless.

"Yep, my boyfriend passed away," Christine volunteered, matter of fact, like chatting about NASCAR Sprint Cup weekend weather. "He loved NASCAR, and of course Jeff was his driver. His ashes are in my pocket. I'm looking for a spot inside the track to spread them."

John used to have an uncanny knack for making instant friends. He'd walk into a room of strangers and within minutes everyone knew who he was. At parties, he was the new guy to have a drink with. On vacation in Orlando, John befriended a bartender at the NASCAR Grille. The race was on, as it always was if there was a Sunday between February and November and a TV signal. John convinced the bartender to let him use his employee discount so he could buy an armful of Jeff Gordon shirts, and John's big arms equaled a lot of shirts. He just had a way for making friends in any situation. No stopping that, even now, on the tram again with Christine.

John told Christine that if he died, he wanted his ashes scattered in Victory Lane. Ironically, Bookie was killed two weeks later in a tragic accident at work. Christine carried out his wishes and captured the moment. *Courtesy Christine Kavka*

The former anti-Gordon brigade shook off the effects of the beverages they'd been enjoying. If their beers had "drinkability," Bookie had "likeability," even from inside Christine's jacket. He'd reached them too, and now they had a purpose on a Sunday morning.

One fan said, "We'll never say anything bad about Jeff again. We will help you!'"

The rest of the tram ride, John Bookie's newest batch of friends in Dale Jr. gear brainstormed with the redhead in the Jeff Gordon jacket, an unlikely new association concocting hare-brained schemes for properly disbursing human ashes on a race track.

Christine eventually found a place, with the help of a track employee who went above and beyond duty's call. She bent down and spread John's ashes in the shrubs next to Victory Lane. "Best seat in the house," Christine whispered. John used to show her the goose bumps on his arms when the grand marshal bellowed, "Gentlemen, start your engines." Now she had goose bumps too.

I'd like to tell you where John's ashes rest. But due to confusing and conflicting state laws, varying religious beliefs, and impossible-to-monitor sensitivities surrounding the presence of human remains in public spaces, the track wishes to remain anonymous.

As we honor that request and keep the attorneys at bay, think of it this way. The next time you see Jeff Gordon in Victory Lane, one of his biggest fans just might be there, unseen by you or me but undoubtedly sporting the biggest grin in the whole unfolding celebration.

Moments Missed,
Encased as Indelible Memories

Indomitable Spirit,
Like the Force of the Wind
Shall Drive on....

DALE
EARNHARDT
1951-2001

Some of the most avid NASCAR fans make a habit of missing the sport's best moments. But they preserve them in special ways.

When the checkered flag drops, these "super fans" are pumped about their favorite drivers. They're wearing that driver's number and colors, strutting around like a peacock in the paint section, talking track smack, and willing the car to the front of the pack. But the bluster doesn't last, and if the driver is on the verge of a big victory, the race can become

Julie painted a mural to greet those entering their marvelous basement containing thousands of driver items and a separate room dedicated to Dale Earnhardt Sr.
Author photo

unwatchable. You'll find these fans clipping nails, washing dishes, cutting grass, cooking dinner—basically finding anything to distract them from watching those crucial last few miles.

If this were a crime, they'd call it "fleeing the scene of a NASCAR race."

Some fans simply can't bear the pressure of a close race. The superstitious fans fear they'll jinx their driver. Others simply can't enjoy what they deserve.

Russ Geary is similarly challenged when his driver appears headed to victory. As the sun disappears behind the grandstands and the laps tick down, this big man with the wooly rust-colored beard of a lumberjack will dash from the TV room.

"I don't want to make him mess up," Russ said. "If I keep watching, I'm afraid that will happen. If you're not there to see it, it's not your fault if they slip up."

The most memorable instance of "fleeing the scene of the race" was the 1998 Daytona 500. Russ was glued to a 13-inch color TV in the kitchen of his girlfriend Julie's apartment. His man Dale Earnhardt had battled years of futility at Daytona's season opener. Now Dale was out front. Would the monkey finally be knocked off his back?

With five laps to go, Russ was feeling the pressure. The burly mechanic who fixes Caterpillar construction machines for a living couldn't take it. He bolted. Earnhardt led the field to the checkered flag, and Julie screamed, "He did it, he did it!" Russ flew into the kitchen, jumping up and down like a nine-year-old on a pogo stick. The racket was so great, a concerned tenant from downstairs banged on Julie's door. "We are large people. She thought we'd come crashing through the ceiling," Julie explained.

Russ and Julie were married and moved to Lindenwold, New Jersey, not far from Philadelphia. After Earnhardt's death, Russ poured his support into Dale Jr. Less than five months after the tragedy that shook the sport, Junior was leading the Pepsi 400. The son kept flying through that same turn at Daytona where his father was killed, pacing the field across the start/finish line. Would he hold on? Russ couldn't take it. He ran for cover in the laundry room. Dale won, Julie shouted the good news, and another celebration began.

Russ was missing big moments as they happened, but he and Julie were preserving them in a fantastic way through an extraordinary collection of NASCAR merchandise. Russ was focused on amassing unique items from the Earnhardts. Meanwhile, Julie, a self-professed "gear head" who has built cars from the ground up and is as intense in her NASCAR loyalties as her husband, was nabbing anything interesting bearing the name of her driver, Tony Stewart. By the time Dale Sr. passed away, the couple's burgeoning collection had taken over their basement. They decided to build a special extension solely for Earnhardt's gear.

"We wanted a reverent place," Julie said. "We didn't want Dale Sr.'s items mixed in willy-nilly with the other drivers."

Today the room dedicated to Dale Sr. is a mind-boggling collection of time-capsule-worthy memorabilia, encompassing lifelike figurines, painted plates, die-cast cars and haulers, train sets, lottery tickets, Pez dispensers, bobblehead dolls, bears, lighters, flags, posters, lamps, commemorative car hoods, playing cards, darts, postage stamps, ash trays, candy dishes, knives, coins and dollar bills, paperweights, tote bags, piggy banks, Coke bottles, snow globes, golf balls, sunglasses, shot glasses and old-style steins, a fighter plane, a skateboard, a working thermometer, a Snap On air ratchet and die grinder set, and even a No. 3 helmet that plays the Intimidator's actual in-car radio transmissions.

That's only part of the eye-popping collection—thousands of rare and sundry items representing more than 100 drivers are painstakingly placed in lighted glass cases and custom-made wall displays. A Christmas tree adorned with driver ornaments stands in a corner year-round. The swath of merchandise in "Russ and Julie's Race Place" fills every available inch of the Gearys' basement.

Asked about the wall-to-wall, ceiling-to-floor, museum-quality collection, Russ said, "Yeah we have a few things."

Each item has its own story. A neighbor visiting Reno found a bowling pin carved with Earnhardt's face. Julie met Tony Stewart at a dirt track in New Jersey where he signed one of his die-cast cars. She nabbed another Stewart autograph at a Home Depot in Jersey. "I told my boss, 'Gotta run! Gotta get Tony's autograph again!'" Perhaps the most difficult item to secure was Dale Earnhardt Jr.'s Coca-Cola car from NASCAR's 1998 exhibition race in Japan, ordered as a gift for Russ. Two years later, the car finally arrived. "You could call it the *piece de resistance*. We're rednecks, so we call it the 'Pasty Resistance,'" Julie said. "It was the pulling-teeth of collectibles but worth the wait in the end."

Many of the best "gets" were unplanned purchases, such as a "Last Lap" photo in the Earnhardt room and the Earnhardt versus Earnhardt poster from that tragic Daytona 500. Julie had taken the train to Atlantic City with her girlfriend Mel and her two daughters because the kids wanted to take a train ride. She spotted the framed Earnhardt items in a store while strolling the boardwalk.

"We weighed the possibility of getting them home in one piece on the train, stuffed in like sardines. Above all, we are NASCAR fans, so we decided to chance it. We bought these two monstrosities packed in cardboard. On the way back to the station, we passed a Wilson's Leather and saw in the window a beautiful Earnhardt Legacy leather jacket. We found one in Russ' size and bought that too. So here we have these two 40-inch pictures, a large jacket, and two kids on the train back to Lindenwold for 45 minutes. It was a fun and expensive day to take the kids for a ride on the train."

Everyone in the Geary's circle knows about Russ and Julie's Race Place, making birthdays and Christmas a breeze. Julie received a Mark Martin ceiling fan at her bridal shower. Russ got five different racing haulers for a birthday. As a Christmas present, Julie's brother commissioned a Pennsylvania art school student to paint an Earnhardt tribute. The one-of-a-kind oil painting—with the number 3 in a sunburst and heavenly rays illuminating the driver whose sunglasses reflect the rest of the race track—is one of the couple's prized possessions.

Some items become near and dear to the couple even when they don't particularly care for the driver. For example, Julie's aunt picked up a rare Jeff Gordon blow-up car, about three feet long, with the old No. 24 "rainbow" paint scheme. "She figured, 'Hey, it's NASCAR, they'll love it.' She didn't know Gordon is not a fan favorite around here. It was great to see Russ' face when he opened the gift and was like "uh, wow. . . .""

Russ didn't want to hurt any feelings, and he blows up the Gordon car at the Gearys' annual Daytona 500 party. "It's become a tradition, and everyone we know gets a kick out of that," Julie said.

There's so much stuff to take in, friends attending the couple's weekly race parties like to spend time in one section. They'll see more at the next race. A racing collectibles dealer noted there's more NASCAR merchandise packed into the Gearys' basement than in his entire store.

"You don't plan it this way," Julie said. "It didn't start out as us wanting notoriety. We were just excited about Earnhardt going for his eighth championship. Along the way, the collection took on a life of its own. It grows larger, becomes a beast, and you have the Loch Ness monster in your basement!"

She may call the room a monster, but she treats it with reverence. Children are banned from venturing down the stairs, past the hand-painted murals paying tribute to Dale Sr. "Little people like to touch things. Our basement is the world's biggest toy store, and every toy is worth a million dollars to me."

While the lion's share of the swag is displayed underground, the Gearys' over-the-top passion is telegraphed to the locals in Lindenwold through a most unusual calling card: a colorful above-ground swimming pool Julie painted to look like a combination of NASCAR paint schemes. When out and about, she uses an ancient Tony Stewart Nextel phone. Now that Stewart drives the Office Depot Chevy, she won't be caught dead in a Staples store. She and Russ only drink Coca-Cola, the official soft drink of NASCAR.

She's still loyal to Tony's previous sponsor, Home Depot. "I walked into the store with my orange Home Depot racing jacket, and a man asked me to get on the lift to pull some merchandise for him. Every time I go there, someone thinks I'm an employee. Then they offered Aflac at work, and I signed up without a blink. We will do whatever we can to support the sponsors of NASCAR."

Ironically, supplemental insurance would come into play when Julie was diagnosed with kidney cancer. To make matters worse, the family-owned printing business she worked for shut down. Being sick and jobless was the lowest point of her life.

"I was really trying to hold it together, and then [I] heard about the Official NASCAR Members Club's Biggest Fan contest," she said. "I'm a bit of a computer geek, and this became my project. Russ didn't want me to get my hopes too high. He said, 'Normal people don't win this.' But I reminded him we are not normal people."

For days on end, Julie retreated to the basement to take photos, tweaking the light at different angles and writing a script to narrate a video that would once and for all prove she and Russ were the sport's biggest, most passionate fans. The video of the Gearys' NASCAR collection can be seen at www.nascarbiggestfan.com/video.php?id=d8db27b5490f.

"With kidney cancer, by the time you find out, it's usually too late. I had a bunch of tests performed to find out what could be done. The contest kept my mind and hands occupied as I waited for the final prognosis. Doing that video saved my sanity."

After a frustrating delay, doctors determined they could operate to remove Julie's tumor. "It was the lowest time, but then the Members Club told us we were finalists in the contest and invited us to Daytona. That took us on a real high, which got even better when we were named NASCAR's biggest fans and given the $25,000 grand prize."

Julie is now in remission and can barely feel the effects of her illness. She's back in perpetual motion, working for a local printing company, hosting weekly race parties, cooking up a storm for family and friends as they root on their favorite drivers in the underground museum.

Russ is still pulling for the No. 88 car and slowly getting used to Dale Jr. being a teammate of his dad's former archrival, Jeff Gordon. When a Gordon fan arrived at one of the Sunday parties, Russ spotted the telltale stickers on his car and made him park in the street. But once the group retreats down below into the NASCAR museum, rivalries turn friendly. It's hard to hold grudges in a wondrous room full of racing history.

Russ and Julie have a running joke about their amazing collection, a light conversation that married couples who are comfortable in a daily rhythm will volley back and forth as banter to pass time.

"We fantasize one day Lloyd's of London will auction it off. We'll retire, buy a Winnebago and chase races all year long," Julie said. "In reality, the whole is definitely the sum of the parts. Every piece is important. We couldn't even sell just a few. It would be like, 'This car is my favorite, no, that plate is my favorite, no, it's that lunch box.' You couldn't begin to choose what to part with. Once you get this far, there's no turning back. It all becomes very near and dear to your heart."

Next time the race winds down and Dale Jr. is in the lead, think about Russ and Julie, NASCAR's biggest fans. In the waning miles, as fans in the grandstands rise to their feet, you can bet Russ will bound up the stairs into the backyard, unable to bear the pressure of contributing to a possible screwup. Julie will announce the results, and he'll scramble back for the happy replay. In the coming days, to commemorate the win, Russ will search for the special car or hat, or maybe it will be a lunch box or model train, that will be a perfect addition to the sparkling case dedicated to the son of the driver he loved so much.

The Big Apple's Biggest Fan

THEY SAY THERE ARE 8 million stories in the naked city.

This is one of them, about a NASCAR fan named Jody Dupuis.

Smart alecks may be thinking, "A NASCAR fan in New York? Let me touch the ground to see if hell has frozen over."

Not so fast.

It's common knowledge NASCAR has some of the most rabid fans in all of sports. (That's rabid as in "crazy about NASCAR," not "infected by bat bite.") However, people often overlook how many of those fans reside in New York City. On any given weekend, New York is one of the top five markets in the country for total NASCAR viewership. Makes sense, when you think about it. Anyone who's been in a New York City taxi cab can appreciate the white-knuckle thrills of trading paint during dangerous turns at breakneck speeds.

(Once, when taking a cab uptown, my driver chose an out-of-the-way route. "Why are we going up Eighth Avenue?" I inquired with hot indignation as the meter clicked away. "Because the cops are looking for me on Sixth," the cabbie replied while jerking the wheel to dodge a pothole as big as a piano case. Now he may not have been outgunnin' the law while haulin' questionable goods down a moonlit country road, but that wasn't bad for

---

Following a bad motorcycle wreck, Jody Dupuis talked his way out of the hospital to watch NASCAR at a Manhattan sports bar. After the race, he went back to his hospital room. He hadn't even been home yet.

genuine *Dukes of Hazzard*–worthy highway excitement on Manhattan's Mean Streets.)

When NASCAR got its big network TV contract in 2001, the sport had arrived. The New York audience grew. And, for a time, a group of the NASCAR faithful enjoyed the races at Buster's Garage, a downtown sports bar hosting "EA Sports NASCAR Race Days" each Sunday.

Buster's was a terrific place to watch the races. It once was an exotic car dealership selling Ferraris and Lamborghinis. The space was turned into a sports bar, and management kept the car motif with its huge, clanging garage doors that during the summer opened up to the warm city air. The space took on a down-home feel, which stood out in the TriBeCa neighborhood, where the famous Japanese sushi chef Nobu had opened a high-price eatery nearby. Also in the neighborhood, Robert DeNiro had established an acclaimed film festival, and John F. Kennedy Jr. had purchased a spacious loft to settle down with new bride, Caroline. However, anyone walking into Buster's felt as if they'd entered one of the NASCAR-friendly joints that dot winding two-lane highways all over the country. Places like Buster's weren't typically found in Manhattan, but here nevertheless was this wonderful NASCAR-friendly scene playing the races— with the sound on! It was as if Dorothy's twister picked up a bar from South Carolina and lovingly deposited it near Nobu.

NASCAR fans started to notice. They came from all over the tri-state area to watch races at Buster's. Alec Fleming and Sherri Davis drove in from Long Island for the big screens. Quinton Loder, a native Midwesterner living on the Upper East Side, was a fixture on the right side of the bar in his red Budweiser jacket, a jack-hammering fist in the air, screaming for Junior. Danny Conway of New York took the No. 1 subway line to Franklin Street, a stone's throw from Buster's, to root for Kasey Kahne. Native New Yorker Lily Knighton rounded up friends to make a usual Sunday stop. Staten Island's Jon Grogan, a NASCAR fan for 20 years, vowed to watch NASCAR at Buster's until a track comes to New York. Unfortunately, before this could happen, two-story Buster's, which sat on valuable land and wasn't cashing in its valuable "air rights," would be razed to make room for yet another condominium in the trendy neighborhood.

But for a time, rebel yells for the boys of NASCAR were heard in a neighborhood where apartments sell for $1,500 per square foot. EA Sports NASCAR Race Days reached a pinnacle in late July 2004, when Jody

Dupuis decided to watch the NASCAR Sprint Cup Series race at New Hampshire Motor Speedway at the sports bar. Unlike other fans walking into Buster's, Jody arrived in a wheelchair. He was accompanied by chaperones from the Dewitt Rehabilitation Medical Center, where he'd been on the mend since a nearly fatal motorcycle accident a month earlier.

Jody had been airing it out on the FDR drive, a highway that runs up the east side of Manhattan island from the Battery to the Bronx. It was early morning, and he was late and speeding. He cut into a lane too fast, lost control, and flew hundreds of feet, bouncing over cars and off the pavement like a rubbery Evel Knievel. The paramedics who carefully removed Dupuis from the wrong side of the highway and rushed him to the hospital couldn't believe the young man was alive. Dupuis was about as banged up as someone can get while living to tell the tale.

He was confined to hospital rooms at Cornell University (New York Presbyterian), where he was held in intensive care for nearly four weeks, and then taken to Dewitt Rehabilitation Center in Manhattan. As his body grew a little stronger day by day, Dupuis's one respite had been to watch NASCAR races on TV. However, as summer's races on cable TV approached, there was a problem. The hospital wasn't wired for cable. Dupuis was unable to watch his favorite stars compete on TNT and SPEED.

Dupuis' intense rehab also caused him to miss a trip to the Pocono 500 in early August. He had won tickets in a prize giveaway at Buster's Garage. He gave the prized passes to friends and focused on finding a way to watch the upcoming race in New Hampshire, the New England 300, set for late July on TNT. As a seriously injured hospital patient who had yet to go home since his accident, this presented a problem. Dupuis was persistent in requesting to be let off hospital grounds. If he could just get out the door, Jody reasoned, he could get down to Buster's. "I put in a request every single day of the week until I got that pass," he said.

Doctors approved the temporary discharge on the condition that Jody not stay outdoors for more than four hours. That was easy—he'd just watch the race from inside the bar instead of his usual spot on the deck looking out on West Broadway. Jody made the trip to Buster's—the first time he had set foot outside of a hospital since his terrible accident.

Dupuis worked as a foreman for Tulley Construction Company and was a member of a local union. He grew up in Boston and has fond memories of New Hampshire Motor Speedway, his home track. He's been a NASCAR fan for more than 20 years, attending races at Homestead-Miami Speedway, Daytona International Speedway for the July race, and Pocono Raceway, 90 minutes west in Pennsylvania.

Like many race fans, Dupuis pulls for a small group of his favorite drivers so long as they drive a Chevy. Dale Earnhardt Sr., Dale Jr., and Jeff Gordon are his all-time preferred wheelmen.

"I just love the cars. I love the speed. I love the technology involved. It's just a really exciting sport," he said. "I've watched this sport transform over the last 20 years and continue to grow every year. I always hoped to be a part of it somehow."

Buster's manager Rusty Schultz was delighted to see his old friend and good customer show up to watch the race. "Not many Manhattan bars show NASCAR, so it's always exciting on race day to see a good crowd coming in from all over the area," Schultz said. "The highlight of the racing season was definitely when Jody came in his wheelchair, happy to partake in the festivities. He's the epitome of a die-hard NASCAR fan."

A stringent rehab schedule kept Dupuis from attending other races that season at Buster's. But as he continued to mend, he kept his sprits up by decorating his room at the Dewitt Rehabilitation Center with NASCAR die-casts, posters, and magazines.

Jody Dupuis got better. Buster's was torn down to make room for condominiums. As the new building went up, construction finally began at the site of the former World Trade Center, roughly 10 blocks south of the former sports bar. Dupuis knew firemen, cops, and EMT personnel who perished when the city was under attack. In a lot of ways, downtown is no longer the place it once was. He doesn't come back often.

PART VI
FAMOUS FACES

Americans love celebrities. Well, it's more of a love/hate relationship. We fawn over the famous while expressing cynicism about their motives. When those blessed with chiseled cheekbones, fame, and fortune show up at a sporting event, surely they're selling their next projects. And they didn't buy their tickets at Stub Hub. At least that's the prevailing belief.

A growing number of A-listers, however, are totally into NASCAR. It's not for show. Their motives are pure. They attend races not for a photo op but because they cherish the same things in NASCAR as everyday fans. They'll come to the race track incognito, hanging in the pits, touring the garage, intoxicated by the same smells of smoke and rubber as the fans who will proceed to turn right when boarding the airplane to go home. Sure, the folks you're about to meet may get a police escort through the infield tunnel, a guaranteed spot on top of a Chase contender's pit box, and a Christmas card from Oprah. But beyond that, they're fans like you and me. They put their Sprint Fan View headsets on one ear at a time. The passion these celebrities have for the NASCAR is worth celebrating, and their stories are worth telling.

Cookin' on the High Side
with Mario Batali and Rachael Ray

I
T's 3 A.M. AT TEXAS MOTOR SPEEDWAY, and Mario Batali's red ponytail is flapping in the breeze. He's gunning a golf cart over an uneven gravel road carved through the track's throbbing shantytown of RVs, trailers, motor homes, and repainted school buses. "We're on a mission to find the real Americana," Batali says, and he's taking his good pal along for the ride. On the back of the zigzagging cart, Rachael Ray laughs and blows kisses to fans shouting, "We love you, Rachael!"

Packed into the infield are thousands of camping and recreational vehicles of varied shapes, sizes, and payment schemes. Some are hitched to huge, cylindrical metal smokers cooking sizzling slabs of choice American beef, which nabs the attention of the super chefs driving past converted old school buses with crushed-velvet sofas bolted onto the roof and sleek new Prevost motor homes that require a jumbo mortgage. The cart's

Super chef Mario Batali, who has been to nearly 50 NASCAR races, introduced his friend Rachael Ray to NASCAR at Texas Motor Speedway. High-speed golf cart rides and hilarity ensued. *Getty Images for NASCAR*

headlights catch the reflection of silver beads hanging from the horns of a wildebeest's head mounted to a school bus painted silver to resemble a 40-foot-long Coors Light can. The beads are everywhere. Fans whooping it up in all directions are awash in them—glittering strands of silver, ruby, pearl, aquamarine, cherry cola, emerald green. Some are the size of marbles, others as big as golf balls. A life-size John Wayne cutout is adorned with several strands. Gold ones for the Duke, who is stranding in front of an ambitious and well-constructed place to entertain friends and view the race: scaffolding three stories high with a maze of ladders leading to a large viewing platform and glowing neon sign proclaiming, "The Redneck Taj Mahal." Across the way, "Sweet Home Alabama," the one tune that from the opening guitar lick can take a juiced-up assemblage of fans into blissed-out nirvana, blasts from a cooler equipped with giant speakers. A dozen young men and women are swirling around the amazing cooler/boom box. They're engaged in a sort of rhythmic tribal dance, slowly windmilling their arms as if swimming leisurely through the smoky, balmy Texas night.

The state of innovation in America may be declining overall, but an impressive spirit of can-do invention is on display this night throughout Texas Motor Speedway. A host of creative contraptions like the spindly erector-set village of scaffolding, the jukebox producing Southern rock and cold beer, and the smokers made from rusty underground propane tanks are helping fans view the track, cook, dance, play music, and dispense adult beverages. The entire infield awaits the day when a fan will invent a device that does all of the above in one contraption you can hook to your Ford F-150 and tow to the races.

At the helm of the golf cart, Batali, a gregarious man with a heavy foot and military-strength radar for locating a good time regardless of the hour, veers down a road doglegging to the left. He drives a few hundred feet and instinctively pulls up to a Western saloon. It's an ingeniously constructed replica of a dusty storefront, the kind of plywood structure you'd see on a Hollywood lot with a hand-painted sign announcing, *Me 'Til Monday Saloon.* "Me maybe till Tuesday," Batali declares. Rachael Ray doesn't hear that because she's off the cart before her good friend and sometimes partner in crime can bring it to a halt. The insanely popular chef, award-winning TV talk show host, magazine publisher, cookware entrepreneur, and best-selling author bursts through swinging saloon-style doors onto an elevated black-and-white-tiled dance floor. In the middle of the floor, the object of everyone's attention, the thing that dominates a scene with plenty of sideshow diversions of eye candy, is a gleaming stripper's pole.

Rachael Ray marvels at the silver pole. It seems to rise improbably from the floor, but after a moment's reflection you can't imagine the *Me 'Til Monday Saloon* or the raceway without it. Rachael eyes the DJ booth, the giddy, beaded, dancing women, and the rough-edged, crewcut boys intent on their affection, and she exclaims in a raspy, whiskey-and-sandpaper voice that's fading fast, "We're in the middle of a race track! These people know how to bring it!"

"Raych, the infield is the heartbeat of NASCAR," Batali shouts. "We happen to be in the geometric center."

THIS COMES FROM EXPERIENCE. Batali has been to nearly 50 NASCAR Sprint Cup Series races since a friend from *The Sporting News* brought him to an event at Dover International Speedway nearly a decade ago. The globally renowned uber-chef, who darts in and out of Greenwich Village traffic on his Vespa, immediately "fell in love" with the speed of the sport, along with the drama-laden cat-and-mouse games drivers and crew chiefs will play to outfox the other teams. Batali has been known to bend the rules—of what a restaurant should serve and how a restauranteur should act. He takes off-putting parts like beef cheeks and squab liver, and from the seemingly inedible cast-offs makes incredibly delicious dishes served in restaurants cranking rock and roll music way too loud. He wears shorts in the winter. At the track in Texas, Mario hobnobs with Jimmie Johnson on pit road at a time when no other fans are seen.

It's no surprise his favorite driver-crew tandem is Johnson and Chad Knaus, the duo in the garage most adept at improvising and adjusting a car on the fly, taking what appeared to be a clunker in the early laps to the front of the pack when it counts. But observing creative wits tinkering with the ingredients at hand to push cars to breathtaking speeds was only part of the sport's appeal to Batali. NASCAR is famous for its multiple-day tailgaters, and the chef—who had recently returned from Spain where he and another famous fabulous New York running mate, Gwyneth Paltrow, shot a highly rated PBS series, *Spain on the Road Again*—naturally wanted to assess the foods of NASCAR and its fans as well.

"I got to Dover and expected hot dogs and hamburgers," he said. "What I saw and tasted was surprising and delicious. The fans were making crab soup, crab cakes, crab stuffing, pasta with crabs, and lasagna with crabs. These were almost luxury food items being made right in the campgrounds. It was a real eye opener."

Batali next went to Pocono Raceway, New Hampshire Motor Speedway, Talladega Superspeedway, and Texas Motor Speedway. He found delightful regional variations and hard-core race fans doubling as "obsessive foodies." He saw each track expressing the region's food. In Pocono, they were cooking venison and quail. At New Hampshire, it was lobster and chowder. In Texas, beef and brisket were all the rage, and at one campsite, he saw an entire steer on a spit, barbecued for 48 hours then carved with a giant sword and served on white bread.

"That, my friend, is impressive, and you see that kind of cooking creativity all over the circuit. I like to say, NASCAR is a microcosm of the James Beard Society. It's like going to a three-day rock concert with great food—Woodstock meets Mad Max meets the Super Bowl meets the Iowa State Fair. I've gone to a lot of sporting events, and I will tell you NASCAR fans are not only having more fun, they're also eating better than fans in other sports."

Batali has seven strong-selling cookbooks, and the NASCAR experience motivated him to write one of them, *Mario Tailgates NASCAR Style*, the first major cookbook attached to the sport. Batali developed recipes like Eggs in Hell, Speedway Guacamole, Restrictor Plate Chili, and Brickyard Barbecued Game Hens to capture the taste, texture, and smells of the racing culture. The second-generation Italian-American boy from Seattle who went to high school in Spain is now as comfortable and familiar with the cuisines of Renaissance Tuscan aristocracy and modern-day Spanish field workers as he is in channeling the cooking styles of NASCAR fans in the campgrounds of races across America.

"I see myself as an interpreter of 3,000 years of cultural and gastronomic history," Batali said. "I'm blessed because I don't have to come up with too much that's new and revolutionary. I'm someone who explains to people how they can make dishes that have been part of other cultures for many, many years."

He happens to be very good at it. Batali's record in *Iron Chef America*, a televised 60-minute cooking competition among the world's top chefs, is an astounding 31 wins and 3 losses. While the taste of food is subjective, and cynics would contend critics can be bought and swayed, that kind of winning record against the titans of the culinary world suggests Batali may be the best chef on the planet.

So when Texas Motor Speedway pitched him on the *Asphalt Chef*, a culinary battle at the race track pairing top chefs with NASCAR drivers, Batali accepted and roped in his friends Rachael Ray and Tim Love, a meat-loving Texan who favors cowboy hats, Western shirts, dusty boots, and Crown Royal whiskey.

Love is no cooking slouch; he grills a mean rattlesnake, has an *Iron Chef America* victory to his credit as well, and is well known in the Lone Star State. But his celebrity Q factor is nowhere close to that of Batali, who has the rare distinction of being able to open a conversation by saying, truthfully, "When I was on Oprah. . . ."

Yet in pop culture awareness, Batali is still a notch below Rachael Ray. Through her food and talk shows, lifestyle magazine, and products now including a personal brand of dog food, Ray exists in the upper echelon of celebrity, able to elicit shrieks and tears from grown men and women by merely showing up in a public place. The dogs probably recognize her too.

The *Asphalt Chef* competition was held next to a large pool in the shape of Texas below the condominiums overlooking Turn Two of the Texas Motor Speedway. Track executives have completely lost their minds, said people who comment on these kinds of things when the announcement was made about new luxury condominiums to be built at the speedway. Today, the condos are worth more than a million dollars each.

While a band played light Texas blues and well-heeled corporate guests and friends of the speedway settled into their chairs at the Lone Star Clubhouse, the cooks were told the secret ingredient—hot chili peppers. A 20-minute time clock was activated, and the teams scrambled for their ingredients, fired up the grills, and began chopping and marinating. Batali was paired with Juan Pablo Montoya, the Formula One superstar who had shocked the motorsports world by jumping to NASCAR. Montoya looked sharp in his chef's smock, though he wasn't smiling, probably because he hates to lose, whether it's the Daytona 500 or tiddlywinks. And who wants to get up in front of a group of rich people, out of your element, not only losing but appearing foolish in the process? Juan's eyes were locked in concentration on a pepper he was slicing.

Batali waved the green flag to start a NASCAR Sprint Cup Series race at Pocono Raceway. *Getty Images for NASCAR*

Rachael Ray was matched with Carl Edwards, who informed his partner he doesn't grill, can barely prepare toast, and pulls the cheese off his pizza as part of a health kick ruling out nearly all foods outside of soup. "Carl tells me all this with a big smile on his face as if it's good for our team," Rachael later explained.

Tim Love, toting a bottle of Crown Royal, cooked with fellow Texan Bobby Labonte. The duo's rib-eye steak marinated in Coca-Cola with shrimp, cannoli beans, basil, and chili peppers drew strong reviews. Bobby earned extra points for working his sponsor (Coke) into the recipe.

The judges swallowed any concerns that blood from a grater-induced cut on Carl's finger might have made it into his team's dish. There had been a catch can at the bottom of the grater Carl didn't see. The driver who does nothing at half speed was grinding the cheese with the intent of a jailed man digging a tunnel to freedom, but nothing came out. The hidden catch can was doing its job. So Carl ground the cheese faster and harder. Carl is one determined dude, and he finally just bore right into his finger. The judges overlooked that and thoroughly enjoyed Carl and Rachael's chili and spicy quesadillas, heavy on the onion and garlic.

But Mario and Juan Pablo ruled the night. Their winning dish was an impressively presented Vietnamese-Colombian surf and turf consisting of a flank steak with red curry and a summer roll featuring Napa cabbage with shrimp, chili peppers, scallions, and cilantro cooked in orange juice.

Batali denied that the dish's fancy presentation and multitude of ingredients contributed to yet another *Iron Chef America* triumph. "Juan Pablo and I won for three simple reasons," he said in accepting a *faux* gold medal for his efforts. "Tim was drinkin', Carl was bleedin', and we were cookin'."

Despite Edwards' cheese-grating mishap, the professional cooks were impressed by the NASCAR drivers' determination and sportsmanship. "These guys are not just danger mavens. They're cool, and they're real people, not like many celebrities today," Batali said. "I don't care where you live or how much money you earn, I judge anyone by two things. First is your attitude toward food—the ability to enjoy and share delicious things. Second is the way you treat busboys. I look at a lot of celebrities, and they don't make the cut by that standard. NASCAR drivers do."

Decency, generosity, and community spirit are traits also shared by the hundreds of NASCAR fans Batali has met. His late-night jaunt with Rachael Ray in Texas reminded him of exploring the infield at Talladega at a time way past most folks' bedtime: "Some fans had created a whole bar scene with a parquet wooden floor and tiki lamps. They'd ring a bell and serve gumbo to anyone who wanted it. Anyone! I love that about these fans everywhere you go on the circuit. They epitomize the essence of good cooking: making something delicious and sharing it with your friends."

Just as a friend introduced Mario to NASCAR, he was able to sell his good friend Rachael Ray on the sport. "I sincerely had the best time of my life at the track," Ray said with the shred of her voice remaining. "I'm just upset it took me 40 years to discover all this. I'll be back."

Mario Batali and Rachael Ray are world-famous figures, wealthy beyond the dreams of most NASCAR fans. Yet, they are celebrities of the people. In the morning, they arrived at the race track in a private helicopter. By nightfall, they were among the fans, passing good jokes and even better bottles of wine, and tearing it up in a golf cart on the way to the most extraordinary Western saloon imaginable. They found the geometric center of the sport and are now proudly part of it.

Tom Cruise's *Days of Thunder*

To be a famous Hollywood actor, a fellow has to have a big head. Not a humongous ego. I'm talking about basic cranial measurements calculated with an old-fashioned tailor's tape measure. Think about it: Bogey, Groucho, Kirk Douglas, Ronald Reagan, Mel Gibson, Burt Reynolds, Russell Crowe, Tom Hanks—all blessed with giant heads that come across larger than life on the big screen.

Of course, equally successful mega-stars like Tom Cruise defy the trend. Cruise's head may be physically smaller than the average Joe's, if you're gonna go crazy in the tape-measure comparisons. But here's the thing that's always struck me about Cruise, whether he's on the red carpet or leaping off a talk show host's couch: *He looks and acts like a modern-day race car driver.*

When actor Tom Cruise hit it big, he wanted to buy only one thing: a fast car. Cruise had always been a daredevil behind the wheel. A film about NASCAR, called *Days of Thunder,* was his idea from the get-go. *Getty Images for NASCAR*

And that, my friends, is a blessed condition to be born into.

Resembling a race car driver is more than having a certain body type. Sure, it helps to be on the small side, taut, rangy, cagey, wiry. More than that, the "look" includes a certain self-possessed, devil-may-care attitude.

Cruise has the full package. He oozes confidence and swagger. He drives too fast. He jumps from airplanes. He's a natural in aviator sunglasses. His electric, larger-than-life presence fills an entire room even when he's physically small enough to slide lithely from a car's window. And then there's that killer grin.

Tom Cruise doesn't just smile. He aggressively *flashes* his teeth in the instinctive way an animal on the range would ward off predators or attract a mate. That special smile brought a lot of new fans to NASCAR in the 1990 film *Days of Thunder*, which Cruise created.

Growing up, he'd always been attracted to muscle cars. In fact, after hitting it big with *Risky Business*, the young actor on the edge of superstardom didn't want to buy an expensive house or fancy clothes. He only wanted a fast car. As Cruise's movie career was taking off in the late 1980s, he landed a big break in working on *The Color of Money* with Paul Newman, a serious professional race car driver who regaled his protégé with romantic racing tales.

"For me as a kid growing up, I always wanted to race cars," Cruise said. "Toward the end of shooting on *The Color of Money*, Paul really got me into car racing, and I ultimately raced on his team. The last time we raced was a few years back. We were trying out different cars at Willow Springs Raceway in California. Per usual, I thought I had him beat . . . but suddenly he comes around the corner. His car is next to mine. Then he flips me off and blisters past. You've gotta love it. It was pure Newman."

Through Newman, Cruise met NASCAR team owner Rick Hendrick. The two drove in the Sports Car Club of America (SCCA) Showroom Stock Series and became good friends. Cruise would spend time at Hendrick's North Carolina lake house and tag along when Hendrick Motorsports drivers tested at different tracks. "We'd pick a track for a test and would ask Tom if he wanted to come play," Hendrick said. "Many times he did."

Sports cars were a panic, but Cruise saw that kind of racing as more a niche for rich guys approaching a proverbial midlife crisis. He wanted a bigger, broader canvas. In NASCAR, he saw a sport tiptoeing out of the Southeast, and he ran to it.

The actor hatched a compelling idea—to make a movie about stock car racing based around a cocky outsider coming in to rile the rank and file. Of course, he'd play the brash young buck turning the sport on its head. His friend Rick Hendrick would be the model for the team owner, and Rick's crew chief, Harry Hyde, the prototype for the young driver's crew chief.

"We were testing at Daytona, and Tom was out there playing around in one of my [NASCAR] Busch Series cars," Hendrick said. "He pulls into the pits, pops out all excited, and says, 'Man, we need to make a movie!'"

Cruise wanted to capture NASCAR's earlier bare-bones, good ol' boys period. "You know it's just America," Cruise said. "It's something about driving in a car. I came up with the idea to make this movie about NASCAR, and these icons in the beginning who created this sport. [Through NASCAR] you just see our history through time, our love affair with the automobile. It's a very unique kind of racing that feels very American. Rubbin's racin', you know."

Days of Thunder was an ideal vehicle for the 28-year-old, whom Newman had dubbed "this generation's biggest film superstar." With his all-American looks and middle-American appeal, young Cruise had already built a reputation as a box-office sensation playing the swaggering overachiever who is knocked down a few pegs and humbled by life lessons. By the time the credits roll, Cruise's characters emerge more likeable than when the house lights went down two hours earlier.

In *Days,* Cruise repeated that formula, playing Cole Trickle, a vainglorious IndyCar Series driver who lost his ride and headed to NASCAR with team owner Tim Daland (Randy Quaid) and salty crew chief Harry Hogge (Robert Duvall). During the Daytona 500, Cole and his nemesis Rowdy Burns tangle in a nasty wreck threatening to end their careers. Rowdy and Cole form a friendship, while Cole comes to grips with his own fears and mortality.

When Tom Cruise sets his mind to do something, he is famous for going all out, whether it involves taking on odd jobs as a kid to help his divorced mother put food on the table or landing his first acting roles in *The Outsiders* and *Taps.* Cruise was so determined to make *Days of Thunder,* the crew dubbed him "laserhead."

Just as he had spent weeks in a wheelchair alongside paraplegic veteran Ron Kovic to get ready for his previous film, *Born on the Fourth of*

July, Cruise immersed himself in NASCAR to learn how drivers spoke in their cars and around the garage. The NASCAR lessons began at the Watkins Glen road course with screenwriter Robert Towne, who had won an Emmy for *Chinatown*. Towne clipped a microphone to his cap with the wire running into his shirt. While the writer recorded racing conversations, the actor, in a floppy sweatshirt and with a ball cap pulled low over his eyes, intently watched the pit stops.

Dr. Jerry Punch, a South Carolina emergency room physician during the week, was announcing for ESPN in the pits on weekends. "I'd talk to Earnhardt and Jeff Gordon and Davey Allison, and Tom would eavesdrop," he said. "It was his first up-close introduction into the culture of NASCAR, and he was absorbing it like a sponge. About halfway through the day, one of our ESPN handheld cameramen recognized Cruise. He spun his camera around and started screaming, 'Tom Cruise is here. We know he's here!' Cruise had to leave at that point. I'm just a pit announcer in an ESPN fire suit, and fans start screaming at me for thinking I'm important enough to be near him. That's when it struck me how big his celebrity was."

The impression Cruise left on Punch, and NASCAR drivers like Rusty Wallace, whose race shop he visited for a tutorial, and Greg Sacks, who in a two-seater at Volusia Speedway taught Cruise the finer points of handling 800-horsepower NASCAR Sprint Cup Series–level stock cars, was that of a perfectionist hell bent on understanding every detail of the sport. "Tom developed a real respect and appreciation for the sport," Dr. Punch said. "What seemed to me to be merely a movie was for him a passion to get it right. He got in the race car and actually drove it. Granted, these cars were pretty much nailed to the ground in their setup, but they still ran some hard laps. He knew the more they let him drive the car, the more realistic the film would be."

It turned out Cruise not only looked like a race car driver, he was performing like one. "Tom could drive a car," Rick Hendrick said. "He's got a lot of talent and absolutely no fear. He'd always drive over his head, whether it was a stock car, a street car, or a boat on the lake. He enjoys speed."

"Oh yeah, Tom likes speed and is very racy," agreed Greg Sacks, who was driving the Slim Fast car for Hendrick in the NASCAR Sprint Cup Series and who in *Days* exclusively drove the City Chevrolet, Exxon, and Super Flow cars. "The first time I met Tom, he jumped into a Corvette and did burnouts right there in the garage. He started racing around the garage looking for any new piece of asphalt he could find, going way too fast."

Valuing the expertise of Hendrick, Punch, and Sacks, the filmmakers made them technical advisors. Sacks became the sounding board and racing conscience for Robert Duvall, whose wrinkled, pitch-perfect character, Harry Hogge, was modeled after the legendary crew chief Harry Hyde. "[Director Tony] Scott would call a wrap, and Duvall would look over at me and say, 'Greg, is it a wrap?' If the shot met my sniff test for how things work in NASCAR, I'd give a thumbs up."

But sometimes he didn't. When Deland says, "Boys, we got ourselves a sponsor," for the first take, he was walking to Victory Lane at Darlington with champagne and paper cups. This wasn't an art gallery opening. Sacks told everyone to lose the cups and spray the champagne around like they meant it.

In Punch's case, after putting in 12 hours in the ER, the doctor would arrive home and field Robert Towne's questions on the telephone deep into the night. Unbeknownst to him, the screenwriter was sketching out scenes. For example, Hogge was involved in a real-life racing episode that seems too outlandish to have actually happened.

"I was working the pits for MRN radio in Pocono, and Benny Parsons lost a lap, and the caution came out," Dr. Punch said. "Benny was on that long 7/10 of a mile backstretch, and he wanted to pit. Harry, who was his crew chief at the time, wouldn't let him. Benny thought it was a race strategy. He cruises by during the caution, looks over at his pit and sees Harry and the entire crew eating ice cream. Not many people know it, but the ice cream scene in the film was a true story."

The mock arrest in which a female cop pulls over Cole Trickle only to disrobe for the young driver actually happened to a real NASCAR driver, as did a much-recalled line of dialogue with Hogge telling Cole, "I want you to go out and hit the pace car because you've hit everything else." Harry Hyde had once sarcastically barked those instructions to an erratic Buddy Baker at Martinsville Speedway.

Many characteristics of the flamboyant, good-looking, and immensely talented driver Tim Richmond fed the development of Cole Trickle. He went by the nickname of "Hollywood," lived on a sleek *Miami Vice*–style boat in Ft. Lauderdale, and wore his long hair and thick, trimmed beard

Twenty years after *Days of Thunder* was finished, Cruise is now introducing his son, Connor, to the sport that continues to inspire him. *Getty Images for NASCAR*

like Barry Gibb of the Bee Gees. No one enjoyed splashing beer and squeezing tight next to Miss Winston in Victory Lane more than Tim, who once said in a TV interview, "I was put on earth to succeed in the fun department."

Like Cruise's character, Richmond, who learned to drive a car under Harry Hyde's tutelage, was a flashy young hotshot long on talent and short on experience. "Tim had no idea what made the car fast and loose," Dr. Punch said. "He could just get in the car and drive it." Richmond was fearless, and a natural behind the wheel. He won the most races in 1986, but Dale Earnhardt had a better all-around season and took the Series title. He got sick with double pneumonia during the off-season, but came back to win several races in the summer of 1987. Richmond got sicker and had to retire. Hendrick said he would certainly have won many races and a few championships had his life not been cut short from AIDS, just as he was coming into his own as a driver.

Dr. Punch's medical background would help Cruise and Towne cast the female lead—an aloof neurosurgeon who'd fall for Cole Trickle . . . and the actor playing the character. "A-list" Hollywood beauties of the day wouldn't cut it as a serious surgical resident. "We wanted an attractive woman, because she'd fall for Tom Cruise, but also someone who had a pasty complexion, because she'd be in the hospital 24/7, and maybe an accent to make her sound especially astute and intelligent," Dr. Punch said.

"When we found Nicole Kidman, who had been a pre-med student at UCLA and didn't have to pretend to be intelligent, the decision was pretty much made right there."

Cruise and Kidman would get married six months after *Days* was released by Paramount. They divorced after 11 years of marriage in 2001.

Days of Thunder exposed the sport of NASCAR to a whole new audience, while those already inside the tent were excited to have "their own" NASCAR movie. Stock car racing had been portrayed in films like *Thunder in Carolina, Stroker Ace*, and *Speedway* with Elvis Presley, but there hadn't been a true big-budget NASCAR flick in a while; certainly, none generating Tom Cruise–proportioned hype and headlines. As Paramount rolled *Days* into thousands of theaters across the country, NASCAR itself was rapidly growing in popularity. Now it was reaching people with no interest in racing who merely wanted to see Tom Cruise. Corporate and ad types who hadn't given a second thought to the sport were rapt in attention watching good ol' boys rubbing fenders on the silver screen. Rick Hendrick said a handful of new sponsors signed on to be part of this big and exciting sport they previously had no clue existed.

No doubt, *Days of Thunder* was entertaining; NASCAR fans would begin an ongoing debate about the film's accuracy and which parts represent the "real" NASCAR. According to driver Kyle Petty, "Well, we both drive cars around tracks . . . and that's about it."

As much as Cruise wanted perfection, his best-laid plans went astray in the editing suite. Dirty cars became clean around the next bend. Cole Trickle jumps into the car wearing black shoes and emerges with white ones. Cars magically switch positions in the running order. Harry Hogge's cap changes logos mid-scene. Most famously, at one point, Nicole Kidman's character turns to Cole and calls him, "Tom."

"That is one of the best continuity errors in film history," said NBC anchor Brian Williams. "I can watch *Days of Thunder* just waiting for Nicole Kidman to call her future husband, 'Tom.'"

On the heels of Cruise and director Tony Scott's runaway success with *Top Gun*, racing purists derisively called the film *Top Car*. They took umbrage at fantastic scenes like race cars built on a dirt floor in a barn in the middle of nowhere, drivers threatening one another over the radio, or when Cole spins out at Daytona but is able to get back to speed and pass other cars in only a few laps.

"A lot of NASCAR fans thought the movie would be like a regular Sunday race with movie stars," Dr. Punch said. "But Hollywood has to make it into a compelling story where boy meets girl. You can't have all racing in that kind of film. And then you had a director [Tony Scott] who had made *Top Gun* and wanted more demolition derby than NASCAR racing as we knew it. But they did the best they could, and it was a step ahead of *Stroker Ace*. For me, it's a loveable campy look at our sport that gets more entertaining every year."

On the track, filmgoers were drawn to a hefty share of fireworks that might not have reflected the real NASCAR each week but were nonetheless revolutionary at the time. The demolition crew put behind the drivers a sawed-off telephone pole attached to a half-stick of dynamite. The explosives would blow the pole into the ground, launching the car into an end-over-end barrel roll. Stunt drivers, who Rick Hendrick calls "absolutely crazy," would hit a switch on the director's command to deploy the bombs, making their cars go airborne. A sticker on the cars' dashboards read: "PRESS BUTTON, TURN LEFT, AND GOOD LUCK".

Most NASCAR fans view *Days,* with its careening barrages of twisting metal and unmistakable NASCAR Sprint Cup Series engine noise, as good old mindless, shut-off-your-brain entertainment. Scott's car-mounted cameras shot the fierce racing action so intimately, fans can practically smell the danger. "My favorite part of the movie is how they got the smoke to look in the corners," said Rusty Wallace, NASCAR's champion the year before *Days* started filming. "Going into the corner after someone's blown an engine, it's a wall of smoke. They captured on screen exactly how that looks to a driver." In theaters, some fans rose from their seats when seeing *Days'* old-school, put-up or shut-up, get-in-your-car-and-drive-the-wheels-off-it racing. Plus, the sound simply rocks; *Days* was nominated for an Oscar for "best sound."

While *Days of Thunder* wasn't the ideal racing movie the NASCAR community wanted, it was closer than what the sport had seen in a long while. There was no riding around in this film—the steel-smacking racing was absolutely fierce. And the relationship between upstart Cole Trickle and veteran Rowdy Burns captured the experiences of an influx of fresh-faced drivers from different parts of the country about to change the sport.

Twenty years later, Greg Sacks still smiles when recalling how Tom Cruise would sneak skydiving jumps into the busy filming schedule. In all, Cruise secretly made dozens of jumps from Deland near Daytona International Speedway. Sacks tried it himself with Cruise and Tony Scott, the trio free-falling from 13,500 feet and landing in the track's infield grass. The money men behind the film, Jerry Bruckheimer and Don Simpson, were not pleased. "We were like three amigos landing in the grass," Sacks said. "Tom had this completely mischievous look in his eyes."

Rusty Wallace, who had a small role in the film playing a NASCAR driver commenting on Cole's on-the-gas driving style, still watches *Days* from time to time to remember the brash, colorful Harry Hyde. With 55 wins of his own, Wallace is one of the sport's greatest drivers. He still appreciates the $5.60 royalty check from his on-screen role, which turns up in his mailbox like clockwork each month.

Tom Cruise would go on to make many more blockbusters, including *A Few Good Men, The Firm, Jerry Maguire, War of the Worlds*, and the *Mission Impossible* franchise. Fifteen years later, he'd return to NASCAR races in Daytona Beach, Atlanta, and Auto Club Speedway outside of LA with his son, Connor, who has become an avid NASCAR fan. He took his daughter Suri to the 2009 road course race in Sonoma. Cruise still hangs out at Rick Hendrick's pit stall and sat at his friend's table at the Waldorf-Astoria when the most successful team owner in NASCAR's history celebrated Jimmie Johnson's third straight championship. Looking back two decades to the NASCAR film he lovingly made, Cruise fondly recalls going hard into the corners and getting to know the very special people who were taking a regional sport into the mainstream.

"My personal Daytona memory is getting up close to 200 miles per hour, personally driving on that track in the car, and meeting those drivers," he said. "Making movies, I love it because I get to enter into a world, and you meet these generous people. It's a great life because I'm interested in life and in engaging in life, and to have those experiences I feel very privileged."

No Fan Is Finer
than Miss North Carolina

A S BEAUTY QUEENS GO, Kristen Dalton, Miss USA 2009, is a quadruple threat.
She can sing, dance, and act. And she's a NASCAR fan. That was proven to
the world when Kristen wore a NASCAR outfit, sponsor logos and all, for
her "national costume" at the Miss Universe pageant in the Bahamas.

When she was considering her "national costume" in the Miss Universe pageant—a
final way for any contestant to stand out—Miss USA Kristen Dalton chose a NASCAR
theme. After all, is there anything more American? *Photo from 2009 MISS UNIVERSE®
Competition courtesy of Miss Universe L.P., LLLP*

Five months earlier on a stage in Las Vegas at the Miss USA contest, Kristen had been judged fairest of them all, thereby fulfilling her childhood dream, though one not exclusively hers if you consider the millions of young girls who have at one time or another tried on a cheap plastic tiara and just imagined. The Beach Boys sung about East Coast girls, and West Coast girls, and, of course, California girls, and this time, it was a North Carolina girl who beat out all the other dazzlingly pretty, well-rounded, and immutably polite women fluent in current events and the general practice of being sweet as sugar during all waking hours as they pursued their own burning lifelong ambition while saddled with the high hopes and dizzying expectations of their respective state populations. (Miss New Jersey has never been crowned Miss USA.) In Vegas, the group of contenders was narrowed to three, and then Miss Arizona and Miss California were banished, and in an open-mouthed blur, Kristen was the last woman standing. She was handed a bouquet of long-stemmed red roses, and against the flashes of cameras, the ruby-encrusted crown atop her head glittered like a kid's sparkler on Independence Day. She projected the quintessential wild-eyed expression of shocked joy as her trembling hand carefully reached to touch the jewels resting on her blonde hair. Yes, this *was* happening.

The celebratory phone calls and text messages had barely died down when the wheels in Kristen's head started turning. This was another step, albeit a huge one, but simply part of the journey. She'd need to get cracking to compete for the title of finest in the entire universe. Venus and Mars wouldn't be sending competitors to the Bahamas, but from our own planet 84 stunning, tanned, toned, multilingual, multitalented young ladies would be there, arriving weeks in advance, and when the cameras rolled during the big show, they'd cause violins to weep, they'd recite pages of esoteric poetry, they'd make a better case for world peace than any smooth-talking politician in a custom suit. Some of these amazing girls seemed a foot taller than Dalton, a petite, blue-eyed stunner from Wilmington, North Carolina, who nevertheless intended to give each a serious run for her money. Heck, Kristen had conquered America in a turquoise evening gown, which verified her unwavering belief that anything is possible if you work hard, go with your gut instincts, and be yourself.

The Miss USA crown was hers, and as Kristen's victory celebration wound down at the Planet Hollywood Resort and Casino, she and her

Spending time with drivers like David Ragan at Lowe's Motor Speedway, Kristen found the stars of NASCAR to be regular guys who were a lot of fun and helped explain the sport's popularity. *Courtesy Ryan Miles, Sage Media Group*

best friend sat in her room, brainstorming a strategy for the Bahamas. Kristen was only 22, but it's hard to imagine how the stakes could get higher at any point during the rest of her life. Miss Universe is the Olympics of pageants—a matter of national pride and, coupled with Miss USA, a serious launching pad for an aspiring motivational speaker like Kristen. More than a billion people would be watching on television. But of greater import, a solid, honorable showing in the Miss Universe pageant was the culmination of that lifelong dream incubating since Kristen was three years old and learned her mom Jennie was Miss North Carolina USA 1982. Here in her hotel room, confident of all the other elements of her repertoire, she realized the most intriguing part, the true wild card, the moment when everything could go wrong or brilliantly come together, would be the national costume.

How do you portray in one garment the country you're so honored to represent?

"Every girl who gets that far to Miss Universe has a good attitude, can speak well in pressure situations, and wears a spectacular evening gown," Kristen said. "The national costume can be one last chance to truly separate yourself. I knew NASCAR was huge in my home state of North Carolina and all over the U.S. As much as the Statue of Liberty is America, so is

Kristen Dalton with Joey Logano before singing the national anthem for the fans in the grandstands at the Coca-Cola 600 and millions watching on television. *Courtesy Ryan Miles, Sage Media Group*

NASCAR. It was one of those ideas where as soon as you say it out loud, you know you've nailed it!"

She had her costume concept. A designer would be brought in to create a bold, red, zip-front, long-sleeved, cut-off unitard, decorated with silver sequins and rhinestones, and bearing the patches of her sponsors: Miss Universe, NBC, Atlantis, Trump, Sam Bass, Diamond Nexus, and others. I may be the worst-dressed guy in PR who once wore two belts to work, but I nevertheless pitched in to design the sleeves, suggesting "Miss USA" and some stars, which were added on, allowing me to tack a very strange line to my professional resume. Complimenting the racy look, Sam Bass, an officially licensed artist of NASCAR, designed a stars-and-stripes helmet that would have made Uncle Sam proud.

Looking like Wonder Woman meets Scott Speed, it was time for Kristen to discover the sport. Her first race was the Coca-Cola 600 at Lowe's Motor Speedway about a month after she won the title of Miss USA 2009 in April 2009. It was her first time home since winning the title, and Kristen's whole family came to the track to support her.

"I definitely appreciated NASCAR from a distance; it was part of the culture of growing up in North Carolina. But honestly, I became a real fan when I got to witness it up close and personal. I never realized the rush of adrenaline each lap around the track causes, the rush of wind from the cars, the overwhelming noise. I found out firsthand NASCAR truly needs to be experienced live to be fully appreciated."

No fan ever forgets her first race, but Kristen had an even bigger reason to remember. For NASCAR's iconic Memorial Day race, a big, history-soaked affair, she sang the national anthem in front of 165,000 fans. "It was a swirl of emotions, and although I didn't drive 600 miles that day, I sure felt like I did."

Before the race, and her chance to sing the anthem, Kristen met many drivers and pit crew members. "They were so genuinely nice it surprised me; most professional athletes do not have that level of approachability. David Ragan and Kasey Kahne really impressed me. They were so down to earth, and I learned they can race with the best of them. And they're also cute. All the drivers felt like real people, guys who the everyday person could be friends with. Seeing them interact with fans, you really understand NASCAR's popularity.

"After you witness NASCAR from such a close perspective, watching on television will never do the sport justice. There is an astounding amount of precision and delicateness that go into these massive cars speeding around at unheard-of speeds. I was able to see that it comes down to the tiniest details in this sport, something I never realized. To be at home, in front of my family, singing the national anthem of the most powerful and honorable country in the world to the most passionate group of fans in the country . . . it's something I will never, ever forget.

"I've been around baseball, basketball, football my whole life in North Carolina, and I can say that NASCAR fans are as dedicated and passionate as they come. There is a true bond between fan and driver, and that, to me, is incredibly special. My introduction to NASCAR was amazing. It's definitely addictive. I plan to go back to the Charlotte race every year."

In the Miss Universe pageant at the Atlantis Paradise Resort on the island of Nassau, Kristen was introduced in her NASCAR costume, and breezed across the ice blue stage proudly holding her Sam Bass helmet and checkered flag. Filled with national pride, oozing confidence, and sizzling in her swimsuit, she made it all the way to the "final 10." As it turned out, Miss Venezuela, Stefania Fernandez, was crowned Miss Universe 2009. But in the hearts and minds of NASCAR fans, in this galaxy or any other, Kristen Dalton will always wear that particular jeweled crown.

Jim Cramer Is Mad about NASCAR

OUNDING THROUGH THE GARAGE at Lowe's Motor Speedway, adoring the kaleidoscope of sponsor logos, Jim Cramer was the proverbial kid in the candy store—if it were located beyond the pearly gates on a gold-paved street in heaven.

"Caterpillar? Home run! Great American manufacturer!"

"DuPont? Has raised its dividend constantly!"

"Aflac? Up 3,000 percent over the last 18 years. The shareholders voted to approve the CEO's pay!"

"USG? Warren Buffett owns it! Is the housing market going to come back? I think so!"

Stock-picking guru Jim Cramer filmed a special for NBC at the track in Charlotte because "NASCAR is a true cross-section of America." Unparalleled access to drivers and the value fans get versus other sporting events help explain NASCAR's success, Cramer said. *Getty Images for NASCAR*

"Target? A beautiful brand! Why not buy when it's at a 52-week low?"

"Ah, Ford! I see a turnaround. The stock is at 6, and I like it!"

"Toyota? One of the foremost companies in the world and one of the largest employers of Americans!"

"Coke? You like the taste? You like the drivers? Do the homework, buy the stock!"

Cramer, the hyperventilating hedge-fund manager turned CNBC stock-picking guru, was on fire, sleeves rolled tight to the elbows, eyeing the freshly waxed team haulers, consuming the race car's colorful paint schemes, running fingers over the smaller stickers near the wheel wells, communing with what he calls NASCAR's "best-in-breed companies" exporting new ideas and best practices to all points of the globe.

"Electronic Arts? Video games are a passion! Do I like them? No. But my kids love them!"

"3M? International company. These guys are inventors!"

"Coors? I like this company. What a merger!"

"Dow Chemicals? One of the largest dividends. Is it safe? I think so!"

The charged-up host of CNBC's popular *Mad Money with Jim Cramer* show was lathered in sweat, frenetic, gesticulating, unleashing rapid-fire commentary summing up the fortunes of the companies making a sport loved by millions possible. He was at the race track shooting a prime-time special, *The American Dream with Jim Cramer*, which would air two months later on NBC. The on-the-road special was the first time General Electric moved Cramer from CNBC to NBC for a program taped at a NASCAR race. On his CNBC show Cramer mentioned he'd be taping at the Coca-Cola 600. Within an hour, he received 400 e-mails requesting tickets. One was from Marcus Smith, executive vice president at Speedway Motorsports Inc., which owns Lowe's Motor Speedway. The executive who runs the track was asking for a ticket to an event on his own pit road. Cramer fans are everywhere.

Now Cramer was flat on his back, beneath the No. 5 Kellogg's Chevrolet. He was completely under the car (you began to wonder if insurance waivers were signed), his glistening bald head peering from under the back bumper.

"I love Kellogg's! Well-run company, fabulous brand!" he shouted. "Even when the market is down, people have to eat!"

All around, sponsor-bedecked cars getting ready for the Coca-Cola 600 were blasting their engines. Over the roaring din, you could still hear the voice of Cramer preaching a gospel of success. His commercial ambition and manic energy were a perfect match for NASCAR—a loud, in-your-face business disguised as a sport.

"I came here because NASCAR is a true cross-section of America," Cramer explained. "Here, you see the real America, the real shape of things. We are in a tough period, but there's optimism here. NASCAR fans don't think the world is going to end."

The market was beginning to crater when Cramer visited NASCAR. As spring warmed, oil prices were on the rise. Costlier gasoline was hitting average Americans hard. The sub-prime mortgage mess had yet to morph into the full-blown credit crisis that would send shock waves around the world, but the economic outlook was worsening by the week. Home prices and consumer confidence were falling. Legendary brokerage Bear Stearns melted like an ice cream cone in the hot sun. The U.S. economy, which had enriched the balance sheets of corporations, created nice lives for most Americans, and propelled NASCAR as a marketing machine and one of most the successful sports in the world, began to feel like a house of cards in a gathering breeze.

The economy would get a lot worse, putting the market into a free fall and pinching the wallets of millions of NASCAR fans. Cramer—who remarked that brokerage Lehman Bros. was on solid ground when in fact it wasn't, and remained bullish well into the market's death dive—would face a humiliating public flogging. Of all places, he took the biggest beating on Comedy Central at the hands of the self-righteous comedian Jon Stewart.

However, in the late spring of 2008, with chin up and chest out, Cramer was still unapologetically pursuing what the poet Walt Whitman once called a "maniacal appetite for wealth." Nothing vulgar about that. Money probably doesn't buy happiness. But most of us would rather be on a yacht when attempting to calculate our net state of bliss. The issue was whether any of the regular folks, the salt-of-the-earth, American-beer-drinkin', Dickies-wearing legions who drive their pickups to the race track, *could* still make money in a confusing stock market that felt more like a random crap shoot than a system guided by the steady-handed control of highly educated people who were supposed to know what they were doing. I was as curious as the fans assembling to hear if his bold optimism in the face of red flags and flashing indicators was merely a well-packaged ruse for

Cramer likens his aggressive, go-for-broke investing style with Kyle Busch's driving technique. *Getty Images for NASCAR*

the airwaves. Off air, isn't Howard Stern a protective, straight-laced father of teenage daughters? Maybe Cramer was all shtick—when the cameras roll, a convincing carnival barker and master of liar's poker, more show-biz bluster than genuine conviction. Or, did Cramer actually believe this confidently expressed "buy buy buy" mantra? Perhaps anxious, paranoid folks like me are the fools, since markets always rebound. Don't they?

A hundred yards from pit road, inside the "green room"—a luxury motor home donated by the motorsports marketing firm, Just Marketing International—Cramer had his laptop fired up. At each break in the taping, he'd make a beeline for the motor home to follow the financial markets. He was punching information into the keyboard, intently whispering as he clicked for answers: *Is the Dow up or down? What's the price of oil doing? How is the Fed going to react?*

I wanted to ask Cramer what he really thought of the economy— serious, no cameras, guy-to-guy. How bad was it? How would the business of NASCAR be affected? After all, sponsorship is the lifeblood of the sport. More than 100 Fortune 500 companies put millions of dollars into NASCAR. These companies invest for good reason. The cars are rolling billboards, and the fans are aware of sponsorship. I've met seven-year-olds who could go through our top 10 and name the sponsor of each driver. Beyond that awareness, the fans are famously brand loyal and vote with their wallets. One woman told me, "I'm a Dale Jr. and Jeff Burton fan. If my husband came home with a Honda, I'd divorce him." She wasn't kidding.

Yet in the disintegrating economy, every spending decision was starting to get scrutinized, particularly multimillion-dollar motorsports commitments. Companies were taking large losses and laying off employees. NASCAR's automaker partners were being challenged like never before. (GM and Dodge would enter into bankruptcy the following season, remaining in the sport but reducing their marketing programs and technical support for teams.) I asked Cramer what he thought of all this. "Time to freshen my resume?" I joked.

Cramer stayed upbeat.

"Listen, are things great right now? Absolutely not," he said. "But now is the time for companies to run *to* NASCAR rather than pull away from the sport. In tough times, companies have to go with the marketing venues that work best. You have to keep marketing. You have to find ways to sell your product, especially in bad times."

There was a lesson for the average investor, he said. "The companies in NASCAR are a great place for any investor to look. These sponsorships are not cheap. The sponsor companies have to have a good balance sheet. They have to be able to put the money up. And if you can do that, it's a sign of financial health."

Cramer switched his damp button-down shirt for a fresh one. He trudged over to a high-tech stage built on pit road. The crowd went wild at first sight of his pink pate. Cramer asked his first guest, driver Carl Edwards, about his own unfolding American Dream. Edwards recounted his early struggles. He'd worked as a substitute schoolteacher and handed out more than a thousand business cards before securing a ride with big-time team owner Jack Roush. "I was hoping to make it in racing, borrowing money from my mother," Edwards recalled. "I told her, 'When I become a millionaire, I'll pay you back.' Of course, I kinda realized I was lying at the time." Carl never gave up on his dream. Now he's one of the sport's brightest stars and has reimbursed his mother.

Another American Dream in progress, up-and-coming NASCAR Nationwide Series driver Brad Keselowski gave Cramer a few hot laps around the 1.5-mile track. The self-professed roller coaster nut, slightly green around the gills when stumbling from the car, was a walking commercial for the Richard Petty Driving Experience, which allows fans to ride along in or drive stock cars at tracks across the country.

"I've been on every great ride in America, but there is nothing better than this 'life-pass-before-your-eyes' experience," Cramer said. "On my show, I say, 'you don't want to hit the retaining wall.' Well Brad was *courting* the wall. I have to say I preferred the straightaways."

Living on the edge is what Cramer does. He grew up near the Poconos and, after graduating from Harvard, covered sports for the *Tallahassee Democrat,* never more than a few steps from the real action. Off the field, he began exercising his knack for making the most of opportunity. When serial killer Ted Bundy began his murderous spree, Cramer was the first reporter on the scene. But being first to expose a madman does not a career make. Cramer struggled for a while. At one time, he lived out of his 1977 Ford Fairmont. "Rags to riches" is not an exaggeration in branding his life story. He got on his feet, worked hard, became a star hedge-fund trader, and ran street.com, where for $5,000 he put the company logo on a car racing in New Jersey. Long before GoDaddy.com and Freecreditreport.com, Cramer may have been the pioneering "dot-com" sponsor in racing.

That experience gave Cramer an early introduction into NASCAR, which he would never forget. "The everyday fan gets shut out in most sports. But not in NASCAR. In this sport, ticket prices haven't gone insane like the NFL, charging what the market will bear because there are enough rich people in the market. You get your money's worth at a NASCAR race."

A notorious Philadelphia Eagles fan, Cramer usually goes to eight football games a year. He enjoys tailgating but won't take his kids. "Pro football is not a family-friendly tailgate. Here, it's different," he said pointing a rolled-up *Wall Street Journal* at the scores of RVs wedged into the track's infield. Cramer's mind didn't take long to veer back to the markets. "Optimism is here. NASCAR fans don't think the world is going to end. But they do need to get educated and plan for retirement."

Cramer likes to create connections. Joining the dots—a consumer need and a company making a product for that customer—is at the heart of his investing philosophy. Similarly, he tries to find connections with those he's interviewing. When chatting with Kyle Busch, who was first in points when Cramer visited Charlotte, he sensed a kindred go-for-broke spirit.

Cramer may be a self-professed roller coaster nut, but when NASCAR driver Brad Keselowski gave the TV star a hot lap at 180 miles per hour, his life flashed before his eyes. *Getty Images for NASCAR*

"Kyle's driving style—putting it on the line every time—reminds me of my investment style. You have to be aggressive to win races and make money."

After two nonstop days of taping, Cramer settled back in the green-room coach and munched on a turkey sandwich made by Pat Lowry, Just Marketing's longtime driver and chef. He stepped outside to take a few photos with Lowry, who watches *Mad Money* religiously. It was a blazing hot late afternoon in May. Cramer wiped his brow and looked around to observe the rows of high-end motor homes in the lot and the scores of NASCAR fans streaming by toting clear plastic bags full of merchandise. He nodded confidently, as if to acknowledge that while American-style capitalism was taking a beating in the markets, the press, and the minds of many concerned investors, the system was still working in places like Lowe's Motor Speedway.

"Of all the venues I've been to, NASCAR is tops," Cramer said. "They treated us the best because that's how they treat the fans. That has to be the root for any business. Find out what your customer wants. Give it to him consistently, at a good value. This sport as a whole really understands how to take care of its base. These fans, the customers of NASCAR, are the true Americans. They represent the best we have to offer. They are the country—resilient and strong, and in the end, they will come up on top. And so will we."

Walking to the Pacific,
George Martin Sees America in NASCAR

Legendary retired NFL lineman George Martin is famous for a 78-yard touchdown sprint after a spectacular one-handed interception. More recently, Martin became known for a 3,003-mile walk—from New York to San Diego—to raise money for 9/11 rescue and recovery workers who are sick and in need of medical help. During the historic trek, he became a NASCAR fan.

Martin's trading card sparkles with illustrious moments: Co-captain of the Giants' 1986 championship team; sacked John Elway for a safety to turn that Super Bowl around; record for most touchdowns by a defensive lineman; and the touchdown interception Coach Parcells called "the greatest football play I've ever seen."

To raise money for the first responders on 9/11 who are now sick, retired football star George Martin walked from New York to California, stopping at Phoenix International Raceway in April 2008 to meet NASCAR fans and become one himself. *Courtesy Lee Reeves*

Martin is less impressed with himself. The Parcells line brings a smile, but he'd rather be known for getting medical attention for real heroes. "Outside of family, this journey was the most important thing I've done in my life," he said. "I've been called a hero for playing a kids' game at a pro level. Nothing I did on the field rises to the level of heroism of those who put their health, careers, and lives in jeopardy."

The Greenville, South Carolina, native was always a leader—a natural take-charge captain sensitive to those in need, ear tuned to the quiet call of the guy who's down. After 9/11, it was a lot of guys and gals. The call was haunting, the clock ticking.

I hoofed the first 13 miles with George when the journey began at the George Washington Bridge in September 2007. Six years earlier, I lived in the shadow of the North Tower. To the world, that's the first plane. I watched that giant building go down, two blocks from my daughter's school, the impossible happening in front of my eyes, a surreal, horrific sight—airborne panes of glittering glass floating high over the city like sparkling, mirrored feathers against the brilliant September sun, gut-wrenching daytime fireworks, the Fourth of July on September 11. On our generation's day of infamy, I found my family, talked my way through the barricades to fetch the dogs, and fled. Strangers were rushing in to save those they'd never met. Our family drove through the eerily deserted Queens Midtown Tunnel onto the Long Island Expressway, which was devoid of all passenger traffic except wailing fire trucks and ambulances headed for Manhattan. We located refuge at the beach on Eastern Long Island. A gorgeous, angry, blood-red sunset filled the sky, a reminder of the carnage left behind. Those defining events were hard to make sense of then, and even now.

Years later, when I heard about George Martin's historic cross-country trek, I wanted to get involved. NASCAR doesn't have a track here in the immediate New York City area, but my gut said NASCAR fans, who former NASCAR president Bill France Jr. called "the kind of Americans who fight and win wars," would embrace George and his cause to help the heroes of 9/11.

First, I wanted to walk a few miles with George. Leaving the George Washington Bridge, "Walking Man" (Martin's nickname) set a blistering pace. Journey volunteers in tow broke into a trot to keep up. The former lineman trained nearly four months for this. His plan was to cover more than 25 miles each day. Like Forrest Gump, he was wearing Nikes.

The procession was a magnet for the men and women protecting our communities. A Teaneck fire truck pulled alongside, and George high-fived the driver. Cops from different towns flipped their sirens and tipped their caps to say "thank you."

Legendary former NYPD detective Richard "Bo" Dietl walked along. Dietl was the most decorated detective in NYPD history, best known for breaking the case on a heinous rape of a nun and for his film role busting Henry Hill in *Goodfellas*. Treading up one particularly steep hill, Bo was sweating like one of his suspects on the run. He clutched his heart. He pawed his pecs. You wondered if we'd indeed get that *New York Post* cover we so badly wanted for George.

As I began to mouth the words, "Bo, should we slow down?" I ankle-rolled on a sidewalk imperfection and went down like a house of cards, tumbling into the gutter, limbs flailing in odd directions, glasses flying off my head, the agony of defeat sans Swiss snow and skis scattering.

Bo scooped me up, got me on my feet. A few minutes earlier, he declared his firm would provide free security all the way to San Francisco. Now you'd have to be out of your mind to take on big George Martin, 56 years old and with arms like columns of concrete. However, should any nutcase have entertained the thought, George was in good hands all the way to California. He completed the coast-to-coast walk in June 2008, with a Journey team member waiving a Sunoco checkered flag.

As George walked across the country—step by step, from sea to shining sea—he became a pied piper for NASCAR fans and partners. Some of the sport's biggest sponsors joined the cause supporting ailing 9/11 rescue and recovery workers.

Best Western was the official hotel of "a Journey for 9/11," providing George, his wife, Dianne, and his security and logistics team with free lodging as they traversed the country. Sprint kept the Journey team well connected with complimentary wireless and data communications—whether they were "walking in Memphis" or across the windy plains of Oklahoma. A Sunoco fuel card kept Martin's Featherlite hauler gassed up to follow the historic trek. Each sponsor I called immediately wanted to help. There was no begging, no haggling, no PowerPoint presentations promising a return on investment. "How can we help?" was the first response.

As he wore through 27 pairs of sneakers and 300 pairs of socks, Martin made two unforgettable pit stops. He served as an honorary race official at

Martin and Michael Waltrip, whose race car promoted "A Journey for 9/11," chatted at the Subway Fresh Fit 500 race about the illnesses affecting 9/11 first responders. *Courtesy Lee Reeves*

the Bank of America 500 in Charlotte in October 2007 and again at the Subway Fresh Fit 500 race weekend at Phoenix International Raceway in April 2008.

In Phoenix, Best Western drivers Michael Waltrip and David Reutimann ran a special "Journey for 9/11" sticker on the No. 99 Best Western Toyota Camry that raced in the NASCAR Nationwide Series race and the No. 55 NAPA Toyota Camry in the NASCAR Sprint Cup Series race.

"George is a cool guy," Waltrip said. "What he did on his Journey was historic and pretty extraordinary—in the dedication it took and the sheer physical feat of covering all those miles on foot. Everyone at Michael Waltrip Racing, including myself and David [Reutimann], were really honored to support George's journey as well as the thousands of Americans who heroically responded to the attacks in New York."

The NASCAR industry's support for the Journey for 9/11 even reached the developmental levels of the sport. When driver Kyle Cattanach made his second career NASCAR Camping World Truck Series East start at Mansfield, Ohio, his Spraker Racing Chevrolet carried the logo for "A Journey for 9/11." The 23-year-old Cattanach, of Redding, California, relocated to Mooresville, North Carolina, and works for Spraker Racing Enterprises. He became interested in the cause through Misty Cary and

Marty Melo. These two, who support Cattanach's racing career, are from Northern California and are both career fire captains.

Along with getting to know Waltrip, and having his cause become a race car paint scheme, Martin counts his 170-mile-per-hour ride-along at Lowe's Motor Speedway as a highlight of a trip in which he encountered rattlesnakes, lost 40 pounds, found $218 in spare change, and was invited into the homes of Americans wanting to feed a hungry man with a few thousand miles to go. When the ride-along was finished and he managed to squeeze his muscular six-foot-five-inch frame though the car's window, Martin asked, "Where's the gift shop? I want to buy one of these."

Another highlight was a surprise visit from his daughter, Teresa, at the Phoenix race. "Teresa is a huge NASCAR fan, so I was skeptical of whether she was coming to see me or her favorite driver, Ryan Newman," Martin joked. "After the race, she quietly murmured to me, 'I *told* you you'd love this.'"

Through his race experiences, Martin realized the importance family holds among NASCAR fans. "During this Journey, I've come to know NASCAR as a terrific sports organization. It's still a family business, and you can feel that. I really admire and enjoy its amazing fan base, which is a sort of extended family. NASCAR fans and the sport's sponsors genuinely recognize and respect police, fire, and rescue workers, who I've learned are a big part of those millions who love NASCAR. Everyone I've met in the sport has been extremely generous and has brought important awareness to the critical medical attention these true heroes of 9/11 deserve. You can safely say I'm now a fan of the sport and also the people who make up the NASCAR community."

George Martin's Journey continues. Anyone can continue to make a donation to the heroic 9/11 rescue and recovery workers through his website, www.ajourney for911.info.

Kevin Costner: Mixing Dreams with NASCAR Gasoline

NASCAR HAS ALWAYS BEEN an object of curiosity and intrigue for Kevin Costner. Growing up in California, he was introduced to the sport by the lyrical voice of Jim McKay on *Wide World of Sports*. After watching the famous Yarborough-Allison brothers fight after the 1979 Daytona 500, his interest grew. "Because I didn't live in the Southeast, I wasn't part of the NASCAR culture," Costner said. "But throughout my life, I kept bumping into the sport. I had to find out what it was about."

Films like *JFK* show Costner is a keen student of history. The two-time Academy Award winner dug into NASCAR's roots. He was moved by the story of a band of strong-willed pioneers who, through sheer guts and determination, created a great American sport.

Kevin Costner cast NASCAR's "King," Richard Petty, for a memorable part in his film *Swing Vote*. He said Petty is "an adored and revered man who walks through life very gracefully." *Getty Images for NASCAR*

"I'm a romantic about the beginnings of big things—the tough and ruthless people who go against the grain and pursue a dream fueled by a passion that won't let them sleep at night," Costner said. "There's a certain compelling thing about genuine mavericks sitting around a kitchen table, making big plans. I imagine it that way, the France family in the kitchen, mapping out those races on the beach."

Costner revels in the hardscrabble narrative of Bill France Sr. packing up his family for a new life in a warmer place. After moving his family from Washington, D.C., to southern Florida in the early 1940s, the young mechanic took his last $50 and bought a new set of tools. Driving down the coast, he'd stop and help disabled motorists, earning back the investment and more. While Miami was the destination, Big Bill wound up in Daytona Beach, where speed demons of the day were racing on the hard-packed sands. He opened a service station that became a favored hangout for the race car drivers. Big Bill began racing himself and promoted the events. He finally put the pieces together and formed a vision to organize and centralize the nascent sport of stock car racing. A great American sport was born.

"Everybody wants to have something as big as this," Costner observed outside his motor home, motioning to the massive crowds starting to fill the expansive grandstands at Lowe's Motor Speedway outside of Charlotte. "But the success of a sport like NASCAR is rooted in the sleepless nights and the hard work of people who found a way to prevail over a few seminal moments, when the whole thing could have come tumbling down. It's the same with young actors looking at my career and asking, 'How did you do it?' They need to see it in reverse—the struggles and the seven years I spent without a SAG card. I look at NASCAR the same way—that mechanic and his $50 worth of new tools, his wife and children in the family sedan on the shoulder while he's under a stranger's hood for a few bucks that will buy dinner. There has to be a roll-the-dice mentality, a real love of the game to succeed at the highest levels, whether it's acting or racing cars."

Costner, who won an Oscar for directing *Dances with Wolves*, scanned the race track with a director's eye. "I enjoy the racing, but the fascination for me is the three days of pageantry preceding the race—the people in their RVs coming to renew friendships in a very communal, nomadic way. You pack up your gear, leave your house, go on the road, and meet up with close

Costner enjoys a break at the track with Martin Truex Jr. Costner says he's an "outsider" to the sport, yet his NASCAR connections in his films and songs, his at-track concerts, and his charity work make him one of the sport's very own. *Getty Images for NASCAR*

friends. You cheer for your guy, you're up late, enjoying your friends in a different environment with tens of thousands of other people doing the same thing in the same place.

"Races are so much more than a bunch of cars going 'round and 'round on the track. The sheer sea of families in their trailers and in the campgrounds, the swing sets they put up, the kiddie pools dotting the campgrounds often with adults in them, the glowing barbecues and smoke pits, it's a whole 'nother world out there. If you put your snobbery aside, these people are having fun in the purest way. Man, there's some Bubbas out there, for sure. And it's *sweet*. They're in a place they love, and no one has to tell them how to have a good time."

Costner, who fronts a country-flavored band, Modern West, wrote a catchy song called "Backyard" as an anthem to guys working on their cars "on the blocks with their borrowed parts . . . mixing fast gasoline with my NASCAR dreams." The cars are clearly discarded clunkers—old Chevys, Fords, and Dodges—but the men "love every one that I get" and toil on to "get them running yet."

Costner said, "The song takes the perspective of an outsider viewing a dream—the everyday guys in the backyard working on cars up on blocks. They're bringing down the property values, and their wives are peering out the kitchen window going crazy, asking 'What *is* he doing?'"

"Backyard" came spilling out, and Costner wondered if the tune was appropriate from someone who had attended a few races but had never built or raced cars. A chance meeting with Billy Joel provided the answer. "Billy had a song about Vietnam ["Goodnight Saigon"]. I told him I loved that song. He became really quiet and reflective. He didn't go to Vietnam and questioned if he had the right to write and sing that song. But those soldiers coming back fed his outsider's perspective, and Billy realized he could write the song respectfully in a way that would move people."

As at tribute to Richard Petty, "Backyard" includes a line, "Dodge's cars, fastest car NASCAR's ever seen, I'll paint it Petty blue, That's what I'll do just like 43." Costner cast Petty in his 2008 film, *Swing Vote*, which features the song. The King appears as himself, showing up when Costner's character Bud Johnson, a likeable drinker whose vote will decide the presidential election, is being wooed by both political parties. Petty lets Bud drive his famous blue No. 43 race car to Air Force One to meet the president.

With Petty's filmed scenes in the can, the King was getting ready to return to North Carolina. Costner sang "Backyard" for him on the set. Even through his ubiquitous dark shades, it was evident Petty was visibly touched. Some of that footage found its way onto the video for the song, which can be found on YouTube.

"Richard Petty is an adored and revered man who walks through life very gracefully," Costner said. "His association with NASCAR has served the sport well, and the sport has served him. He's become a very gracious and grateful ambassador for NASCAR."

NASCAR chairman and CEO Brian France, a fan of Costner, heard "Backyard" and immediately dialed up the West Coast office he'd established to help inject NASCAR into pop culture. He told NASCAR's top entertainment executive, Brad Ball, he wanted to work with Costner in some way. Ball knew Costner from his stint running marketing for Warner Bros., which brought out *Message in a Bottle* and *3,000 Miles to Graceland*, and he set up a meeting between the film star and Brian France. "I felt there was a real race-day feel to the song and wanted to find a way to partner with Kevin," France said. "We thought the best way to establish a relationship was with our philanthropic endeavors." Costner became the 2009 spokesperson for the NASCAR Foundation and the voice and face of its signature event, NASCAR Day, helping to raise nearly $2 million for charity.

In tapping Kevin Costner, Brian France was connecting NASCAR with an artist who's helped define America's pop culture over the last 20 years with films like *Dances with Wolves*, *Bull Durham*, *Tin Cup*, and *JFK*. But most relevant and personal to France is the 1989 classic, *Field of Dreams*. Costner's idealistic Iowa farmer, convinced by ghosts to build a baseball diamond in the middle of a cornfield, reminds him of his grandfather, Bill France Sr.

"People said Kevin's character [Ray Kinsella] was crazy," France said. "But Ray went ahead and built that ball field. The whole notion of his personal dream, embodied in the memorable phrase 'build it and they will come' reminded me of my grandfather's quest. People called him crazy too. And like Ray, nothing was going to stop Bill Sr. When you think about it, the race track he built, Daytona International Speedway, a two-and-a-half-mile venue in the middle of a muddy tract of Florida swampland was an outlandish idea that became a real-life Field of Dreams. He built it, and they are definitely still coming."

Given Costner's appreciation of NASCAR's history, and a personal visit from the grandson of the racing visionary he so admired, he jumped at the chance to narrate the NASCAR film, *The Ride of Their Lives*. The critically acclaimed movie brings to life a half-century of NASCAR racing through the voices of the men and women who lived the dream, including the triumphs celebrated and tragedies endured by families like the Pettys, Earnhardts, and Allisons. Costner's voice brings a rootsy, homespun feel to the film.

Costner may still call himself a NASCAR "outsider," a dedicated student of the sport who comes to the track and trains a filmmaker's eye on the fans' faces and their scenes of friendship and camaraderie. But with his racing-themed songs, videos, and pre-race concerts, his involvement in films preserving the history of the sport, and his hard work promoting its annual fundraiser, he's become one of NASCAR's own. Kevin Costner is on the inside, still curious to learn more.

A Black-and-White Sport
Goes Technicolor

A N UNCONDITIONAL LOVE AFFAIR with NASCAR often starts—and inevitably circles back to—cars. Fast, loud, mean, brutish, intimidating, gorgeous, gleaming, American-made automobiles.

Before this morphs into a Bruce Springsteen song, musing about shut-down strangers and hot-rod angels rumbling to the promised land, let me introduce you to Michael Mauldin, a music impresario known for three decades of hip-hop hits but nevertheless a gentleman whose auto-centered story feels drenched in sepia, like one of the Boss' older rootsy paeans to the redemptive powers of muscle cars that restless young men jump into with their best girl to race toward dreams of something better.

Michael Mauldin is a longtime NASCAR fan who can reminisce for hours about cars and what they've meant to his life. Mauldin became

---

Before he began producing hip-hop hits, Michael Mauldin grew up a car guy, reveling in tales of his dad Lightning, who became a driving legend running in the winding foothills of North Carolina's Smoky Mountains. *Courtesy Michael Mauldin*

the first African-American president of Columbia Records and a leading figure in developing Atlanta as a center of hip-hop. But he started out as a "car guy" in the small town of Murphy, North Carolina, the eldest son of a long-haul trucker named Lightning.

Anyone wondering how a guy driving a truck gets to be called Lightning is onto something. "Lightning"—a brilliant electric flash, then it's gone—described the way the elder Mauldin ran moonshine on Saturday nights in the winding foothills of the Smokey Mountains, headlights out, driving by the glow of the moon and the feel of the road. You heard the car more than you saw it. A flash in the corner of your eye, dominated by a big rumbling sound. Just like lightning.

"My dad viewed himself as 'a driver of moonshine,' not a 'moonshiner,'" Mauldin said. "He saw the difference and took a lot of pride in being a fast, skilled driver. He was legendary—never got caught or incarcerated. The law didn't really want to catch him. They wanted to outrun him. Braggin' rights, you know?"

Lightning was awfully confident in his supremacy for wheeling a car. Heck, he could outrun you backward. And that's what he did, in a fabled bet against the mayor of Murphy, North Carolina. With the wager set, the men lined up their cars, Lightning's Chevy facing the wrong way. Someone fired a gun. To the sound of shooting gravel and squealing wheels, the mayor and the moonshiner gathered speed down a straight back road. Lightning's back bumper handily beat the mayor's front end to the finish line. Lightning proved it. He *could* outrun you backward.

Lightning's son Michael heard stories whispered around town that sounded like outlandish folklore. In reality, they were his dad's own real-life exploits from the previous weekend. How could Michael *not* become a fan of stock car racing? Better yet, he would benefit from his dad's expanding notoriety. When it was his turn to drive, the teen with a genetic yen for speed was frequently stopped and sent on his way with a mere warning. "Growing up, I got a lot of passes from the cops because I was Lightning's son," Mauldin admitted.

Michael was 15 when he got his first ride—a '67 green Ford Mustang he named the "Sex Machine." It said so in fancy script right on the air intake bubble in the center of the 'Stang's mean, black hood. More than 40 years later, when asked about it, Michael was whisked back to sweet

North Carolina summers, mockingbirds singing from the trees. "That car was so hot and so fly: 289, three-speed, full race cam. Suicide steering wheel. Pipes coming out back beside the tires. Pull up to the light, and you're just chuckin' that mean sound, '*gid-took, gid-took, gid-took,*' and everyone's looking at you."

They noticed in a good way, of course. But Michael didn't always want the attention the Sex Machine was guaranteed to draw. When the sun went down and he needed to get away to work his night moves on the lush roads of Cherokee County, he knew better than to chuck that monster gurgle sound. He'd slip from the house, put the Mustang in neutral, and silently roll the car down the hill, starting the engine only when beyond earshot of the Mauldin family.

A part-time job at a local Catholic hospital helped the teen pay for his new car. After his shift one day, looking forward to the drive home, Michael saw a cluster of tape on the side of the hood bubble, covering up the racy car's racy name. The nuns were sending a message.

Mauldin became a NASCAR fan long before grooving the streets in a hot Mustang making good sisters blanch. "We had no choice!" he said. Each Sunday afternoon, the Mauldin family and a few of Lightning's friends would listen to the NASCAR race on AM radio. They'd gather outside, opening the doors of the family sedan and blasting the race on the tinny car radio. "It wasn't something that felt odd or we gave a lot of thought to. On Sunday, you'd just go outside, open the car doors, and turn on the radio. You'd wax and wipe the car while the race was on."

The best races, of course, were ones he attended. He saw Lee Petty race against (and beat) his son Richard at Atlanta Fairgrounds and began following Richard's Plymouth. When he was ten, father and son went to Bristol Motor Speedway to watch NASCAR's daredevils bang around the half-mile track. They drove to Charlotte Motor Speedway to see the World 600 from the infield. "You could close your eyes and tell when Junior Johnson came by. That '63 Chevy sounded different," Mauldin said.

During that race, Lightning became a Junior Johnson fan and Chevy guy. After the race, he stopped at the local dealer and ordered a white 1963 Chevrolet Impala. "Those were the true days of win on Sunday, sell on Monday," Mauldin said. On Saturday nights at local dirt tracks, Michael rooted for his dad, who won some races in Cleveland, Tennessee; in Blue Ridge, Georgia; and at the home track, Tri-County Motor Speedway, which is still around today.

The growing boy was hooked on NASCAR. On schooldays, getting ready for the weekend, he'd grab a cooking pan and drop different-colored marbles in. He'd tilt the pan back and forth so the marbles raced around, bumping and passing one another, just like the rebels of NASCAR on Sunday.

The following year, the whole Mauldin family drove to the Memorial Day race in Charlotte: Lightning and Michael with his younger brother, two sisters, and their mom. They parked outside the track and sat on top of the white Chevy, eating mom's homemade fried chicken. "You could see about half the track, the entire backstretch, the third turn, and the cars coming into the fourth turn," Mauldin remembers. "I'll never forget seeing Fireball Roberts get burned up on the backstretch."

As he grew older, Mauldin was seriously getting into music, most notably as lead singer for the Other Side, one of the area's first integrated bands, which got some TV exposure. The automobile would actually provide an assist in his first big break. In the early 1970s, Michael was trying to make it as a vocalist and drummer, driving what he called a "ghetto super van": a mustard-yellow, 1971 Ford Econoline van with a sofa in the back. A group named Brick was playing a joint in North Atlanta when a band member's car broke down. The band was stuck without a way to haul its equipment. A friend of Mauldin's who was with the group called him. Brick had a new driver, and the band was off to the next gig in Savannah.

Mauldin became Brick's stage manager, then production manager. He went on to work with the funk and soul group L.T.D. and later started a touring company that provided staff and crews for groups like Sister Sledge and the SOS Band. He worked with Roberta Flack, the Atlanta Rhythm Section, Luther Vandross, and Arrested Development.

In 1982, Mauldin promoted a Diana Ross concert at the Omni in Atlanta. Toward the end of the show, Ross invited children in the audience up to the stage to dance with her. His son, Jermaine Dupri, who was not yet 10 but was a talented break-dancer with smooth, funky moves in the style of Michael Jackson, bounded up to the limelight. "Jermaine wound up in the center of the stage by himself and held the attention of the entire arena," Mauldin said. "Diana was like, 'Why you come up here and try to steal my show?'"

Jermaine, who had attended NASCAR races with his dad before music became the focus of his life, would go on to become a super producer and rapper and to found So Def records before he was 20, working on blockbuster hits with Mariah Carey, Usher, and TLC. His dad would become president of the black music division of Columbia Records, where he developed such acts as Lauryn Hill, the Fugees, and Destiny's Child.

These days, Mauldin is focused on his business Artistic Control Group, which markets products to urban audiences, including a motorsports-inspired apparel line. He's trying to build bridges between NASCAR and the African-American youth market.

"The African-American community loves cars. I've always felt this community was under-marketed in motorsports. And I've always lived and worked in an integrated way. My dad's best friends over the years were white, but color really didn't matter. It was about cars—how fast you drove them. If you weren't racing at the tracks, you'd be racing in the streets, every Friday and Saturday night."

Sunday was for NASCAR. Mauldin has had several favorite drivers over his more than four decades of following the sport—Junior Johnson, Richard Petty, Dale Earnhardt Sr., and now Carl Edwards. "Carl's a real racer; he'll challenge anyone," Mauldin said. "He's on a mission to be a [NASCAR Sprint] Cup champion. You know it's coming, and he's destined for it." Since Edwards owns a small independent record label, the two also have a lot to talk about when Mauldin settles into the pit area before races he attends. He's impressed with the diversity of talent Edwards is nurturing. "He's doing it small, not overspending, not saying, 'I'm Carl Edwards, buy this record because of who I am.' It's not about Carl, it's about the artists."

One of the many changes Mauldin has seen in the sport involves the variety of widening interests pursued by drivers outside of wheeling a stock car. Even drivers like Mark Martin are into hip-hop, which is a bona-fide part of the American culture. Mauldin is helping connect this sport to the members of an X-Games-oriented youth culture who might not give stock car racing a second thought. But in the end, it all comes back to the cars.

"Speaking figuratively, the sport has really gone from black and white to color," Mauldin said. "Now, each event is such a spectacle. But I don't think it's changed much in terms of fan excitement. It's not the flyovers or the pre-race concert that matter so much, it's the sound of the motors, watching loose cars go through the turns side by side, the thrills on the track. That's what this sport is always going to be about."

The '67 Mustang is gone. But Michael has an '87 Trans Am in the garage. If you're ever on the blacktop in the southwestern tip of North Carolina, near the Georgia–Tennessee border, and you hear a car chucking a sound that goes something like "*gid-took, gid-took, gid-took*," it just might be Michael Mauldin, son of a driver of moonshine, father of Jermaine Dupri, hip-hop impresario, but really just a regular guy in love with cars, like so many men of different backgrounds all across America.

Getty Images for NASCAR

PART VII
LADIES LOVING NASCAR

With women seen throughout the grandstands and in the garage, it's no surprise nearly half of NASCAR fans are female. Women are serving as officials on pit road and turning wrenches in the race shops. They're competing in greater numbers at the grassroots. So why segregate a few of them in this section? After all, just like men, women enjoy driving fast cars, cooking good food, laughing with close friends, and shopping in diverse retail locations—the basic slate of fun activities in abundance at NASCAR events.

We're roping off a section for remarkable female fans for the edification of those who haven't caught up with the times. A small pocket of folks believe NASCAR's technical aspects are beyond the basic comprehension of women and that the sport's finer points—whether it is winning a race on fuel strategy or using a bumper to muscle a competitor out of the way—are beyond women's range of taste. However, there are female fans who take apart engines and will take you apart if you have a problem with that; who are drawn to the danger and mystery of the sport; who watch races on TV to witness pure passion and unscripted emotion; who love the camaraderie of these family-friendly festivals; who feel the nervous anxiety of the lip-biting wives atop the pit boxes. And there was one who told me, "Uh, have you *seen* these guys? They are young, good-looking, and drive fast cars for a living. You're seriously asking why I like NASCAR?"

The more ladies in NASCAR garb you chat with, the more you realize they're fans just like the guys. Political commentator S. E. Cupp may have said it best: "All I want to do is watch my driver win. And maybe see a colorful fight or two afterward."

For whom is that not a perfect Sunday?

NASCAR fans are basically the same, regardless of gender. But I give you this section anyway because women deserve to be loved and honored. And because they have pretty good stories.

Good Vibrations

TAVA MIYATA STANFORD'S FIRST childhood memory takes place on a California drag strip in 1968. She was at the track with her dad, Wayne Miyata, an intense, quietly confident man, living in the moment, then off to the next adventure. When Wayne wasn't riding the big, curling waves off Hermosa Beach or hand-crafting the colorful surfboards he'd become famous for, he raced on the local drag strips. Wayne was also a fifth-degree black belt in karate—not to be messed with—but he was a pussycat with his daughter Tava, who was daddy's little girl in every sense. Wayne enjoyed bringing little Tava and her mom to the track, especially when testing his car.

Before one particular practice session, while Wayne waited for his window on the drag strip, his wife went to the ladies room. Moments after she left, the track became his. Wayne was paying for the time. The Miyatas weren't rich, and the clock was ticking. Wayne glanced impatiently toward the bathroom for his wife to reappear. He looked at the empty track and

When she was two years old, Tava Miyata was strapped into a race car by her dad, Wayne, creating a lifelong race fan and unbreakable father-daughter bond. They attended races at Auto Club Speedway in Fontana, California. *Courtesy Tava Miyata*

down in the stroller at his two-year-old daughter. He checked his watch again, calculated the cost of each minute, and made a practical decision. He found an extra race helmet, way too big for his little daughter's head but a good, sturdy helmet nonetheless. This would work. He placed the helmet on Tava's head and strapped the girl into the front seat of the car. Father and daughter blasted down the drag strip.

"I couldn't see a thing; I was so little, and the helmet fell over my eyes," Tava said. "I remember it was loud, very loud, and I felt the vibrations."

In the years to come, Wayne cut back on his drag racing. It wasn't because he feared a catastrophic blow out or lost interest in the sport; racing just became too expensive. The ocean, however, was wide open and free. Wayne satisfied his competitive thrills riding waves in the Pacific Ocean and was even featured in the cult surfing film *Endless Summer*. He was a man who carried himself with dignity and authority and had a fluid, cat-like grace, giving him a powerful physical presence that belied his slight stature. It made this intriguing surfer from Hawaii someone you couldn't help but notice. The film's director started observing Wayne on the beach and in the water. He wanted to catch Wayne conquering the biggest possible wave. When the director finally approached Wayne, he'd already been in the ocean for three hours. Surfing for a movie was an intriguing proposition. But there would be a cost. The surfer talked the director into giving him a free lunch and a case of beer. Wayne went back in the water and became one of the first surfers ever filmed successfully riding through a tube wave, completely disappearing behind the curling wall of water and then triumphantly bursting out atop his surfboard.

As his daughter grew older, Wayne built a business making trendy custom surfboards with signature "rising sun" patterns. Cars still bound father and daughter together. As he tinkered with the family autos, Tava was often at his side. She helped change the oil and spark plugs on his Datsun 240Z and big Lincoln Continental Mark IV. Whenever possible, he and Tava would watch NASCAR and all forms of televised racing. If they weren't together during races, they'd talk on the phone. "It was just a special bond we shared," Tava said. "My mother was never into it, so it was just our thing."

In 1997, Roger Penske built Auto Club Speedway, a spanking-new, clean track that brought NASCAR to the Los Angeles area. Tava decided to give her dad a big surprise. She combined his birthday, Father's Day, and Christmas presents into one gift: season tickets at the new race track. The best part of the present was that father and daughter would attend the races together.

For several years, they rented a motor home and claimed a spot in the infield at Fontana to watch the NASCAR and open-wheel events at the two-mile track. Wayne was always a Ford man. He loved that big Lincoln Continental, and father and daughter cheered loudest for Mark Martin. Friendships formed, sometimes in the most mundane of circumstances. When the power in Wayne's RV went down, he asked Jeff Dash of Long Beach, one row away in a rental RV, if he knew anything about generators. Jeff fixed it, and the Dashes and Miyatas would be friends for life. Members of their crowd, in the second row near Turn Three, share barbecues, cocktails, stories, laughs, even the floors of their RVs for sleepy kids who want a change of pace that night. "Remember, we are here at the track for five days," Dash said. "You have breakfast together. You run out of water, need ice, wood for the fire, whatever, you go next door. It's a happy feeling, everyone helping one another. We're fans at a race, but it's like you are true neighbors in every sense."

Jeff and his wife—yeah, they met at the track—now travel up to the Bay Area to visit Tava and her family. "The friends we made would do anything for us, and we'd do anything for them," Tava said. "The Speedway asked if we wanted to move closer to the track, to the first row, but we turned it down. We couldn't leave the neighborhood!"

The Dashes would play poker with the Miyatas, watching Wayne grow uncharacteristically animated as the pots increased in size. "Wayne's pretty reserved, except when his money is at stake," Dash joked. They loved to hear Wayne's old surfing stories. The girls would do lemon-drop shots "like a bridal party at the track," Dash said. Wayne was the one guy allowed in on the fun.

Then Wayne Miyata got sick—a fast-spreading cancer of the esophagus. "My dad got out of the hospital in February 2002 and was basically going home to die," Tava remembered. "I decided we were going to the race. At first, dad wasn't up to it and didn't want to make the trip. I basically dragged him there, feeding tubes and all. As soon as we got there, he became very happy and had a really good time. All our neighbors came by and said their goodbyes."

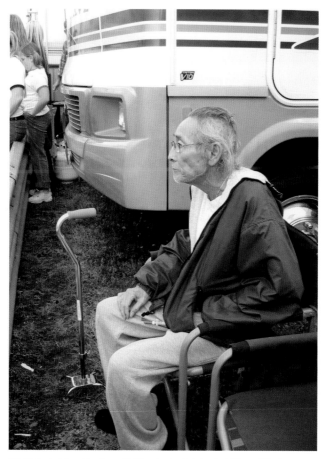

He once raced on Southern California drag strips, but Wayne Miyata was
best known as the first surfer caught on film riding through a tube wave.
Shortly before he passed away in 2005, Wayne attended the NASCAR
Sprint Cup Series race at Auto Club Speedway and said goodbye to many
close friends. *Courtesy Tava Miyata*

First thing each morning, Wayne would unhook his IV and walk outside the camper. He'd sit with his Hawaiian coffee and tell stories. "He
could barely talk, but he wanted to spend time with his friends," Jeff Dash
said. "We told him we loved him and he'd be in our hearts forever."

A month later, Wayne Miyata passed away. He was 63 years old.
Tributes from those he touched all over the world poured in to Tava. On
Hermosa Beach, more than 100 surfers joined hands in a circle to say aloha

to their mentor and friend. On the north shore of Oahu, the last place her dad had surfed, Tava walked out on the rocks, tossed some plumerias in the water, and then threw in her dad's ashes. "Gosh darn, they blew all over my legs," she said. "Dad was up there laughing. I just knew it."

She wanted to keep hearing that wonderful laugh. She held onto the RV spot at the track. It keeps her close to her dad and the memories fresh. After Wayne's passing, the Dashes and the Miyatas drew tighter than ever. The families made a pact: as long as NASCAR keeps putting on races at Auto Club Speedway, they'll be there. Nothing would prevent Tava from making the poignant twice-yearly pilgrimages to the race track.

That promise would be put to the test when Mother Nature and impending motherhood presented a double-barreled challenge. During the speedway's Labor Day event in 2007, Tava was expecting twins while oppressive heat baked the inland valley. The scorching weather triggered fires in the mountains and a blackout in LA. Forty miles east, inside the speedway, Tava was trudging around in 114-degree Labor Day weekend heat. Around the track 1,000 fans were being treated for heat exhaustion. Jeff Dash was running heat-stressed fans to the infirmary in a golf cart. Following her big belly, Tava walked through the roasting infield to see qualifying and then hiked over to Apex, the track's new high-end restaurant.

"Up at Apex, there is a nice fountain of glass, and women were rubbing their boobs up against the frosted glass to cool off," she said. "My husband started slapping $20 bills against the glass. It was hot, but we managed to have a pretty good time." Following the race, Tava checked into the hospital and went into early labor.

Her twins, Lucille and Canter, haven't missed a single race when the NASCAR Sprint Cup Series makes its westward swing. At 13 weeks old, they slept in the RV's closets. "The doors were open!" Tava was sure to point out. When the babies reached 9 months old, they slept at the opposite ends of the bottom bunk.

Who knows, when Lucille and Carter hit the ripe age of two, Tava may channel a little bit of Wayne Miyata, buckling them into a fast car to get a decent run on the hot pavement and feel those good vibrations, like all those years ago.

NASCAR is a Thing of
Beauty in a Boise Salon

TALKING NASCAR WHILE GETTING a haircut and a shave is about as old as the sport itself.

Talking NASCAR during highlights and blow dries is a much newer phenomenon.

One of the places the new NASCAR conversation echoes is at a high-end beauty salon in Boise, Idaho. At Mystique Salon, owner Julie Catalano vividly recaps the previous weekend's NASCAR Sprint Cup Series race to all her customers in earshot. She does so in front of a Carl Edwards cardboard cutout at her workstation. Another Edwards life-size replica stands in the reception area. When Edwards wins a race on Sunday, Julie runs a special on Monday, like a free manicure or pedicure.

Inspired by her Carl Edwards life-size stand-up, Julie Catalano talks racing while doing hair and nails at her beauty salon in Boise, Idaho. She has converted many customers into fans, who join in and talk track smack. *Courtesy Edelman Public Relations*

Julie appreciates the physical challenge of driving a race car and boasts that her driver, Carl Edwards, is the sport's most physically fit. When Carl wins on Sunday, on Monday Julie offers a free special, like a free pedicure or manicure. *Courtesy Action Sports Photography*

Before he gets to Victory Lane, Edwards is famous for climbing on top of his car and doing an acrobatic back flip. You could say Julie has, in turn, flipped for Carl.

Catalano, who opened Mystique Salon in 2000, can't help herself. She's an incorrigible NASCAR evangelist, a prolific ambassador who can analyze a four-tire, 13-second pit stop while performing equally impressive wonders of speed and dexterity with sharp scissors and a bottle of peroxide.

A captive customer can spend serious time in the chair, especially when going for extensions and a coloring. A few of the ladies genuinely enjoy chatting about all things NASCAR. Take Sandy Steward, a fellow Roush Fenway Racing fan with family employed by Ford and a husband who has at least one chamber of his heart reserved for Mark Martin. Sandy has been coming to Mystique for five years for hair, nails, the occasional massage, and of course the NASCAR low-down. Usually, when she sees Julie, four or five races have gone by since her last visit to Mystique. There's serious ground to make up.

"Julie and I talk about the last race, how the Roush Fenway drivers have done, especially Carl. We'll discuss the major happenings in the garage like Dale Junior leaving his stepmom's team and Tony Stewart

As the "Official Small Business of NASCAR," Mystique's logo—stiletto and all—was emblazoned on Carl Edwards' Ford for a NASCAR Sprint Cup Series race. *Courtesy Action Sports Photography*

forming his own race team. The conversation tracks whatever's happening in the sport."

By nature, those who cut and style hair for a living enjoy the art of discussion. They're like bartenders with better hours or therapists forced to stand and unable to write a script. For the customer getting the work done, well, it's like going to the dentist, without the pain, mouthful of latex, and gum-pinching apparatus. Looking up at Julie, even the recalcitrant few find themselves chatting a blue streak. The salon stylist-client situation is a hothouse for bubbling discussion covering everything and nothing. Julie feels pride in "making someone feel better about themselves in a half day" while expounding on the finer points of Carl Edwards' ascendancy to superstardom. From NASCAR's perspective, this talented hair stylist and successful entrepreneur who proselytizes the sport like she's a shareholder staked in the enterprise is the best volunteer employee the sanctioning body could imagine.

A few customers "razz" Catalano for being a vocal, 24/7 NASCAR fan who watches SPEED channel every day and won't miss an episode of ESPN's daily show, *NASCAR Now*. Some clients wonder if she takes this NASCAR fanaticism to peculiar extremes. Julie has noticed an eye roll or two over the eight years she's run Mystique like an outpost of the Official

At work, she does her business next to a cardboard Carl. But at the track, Julie met the driver in the flesh at the unveiling of his race car bearing her own logo. *Courtesy Action Sports Photography*

NASCAR Members Club. That only fires her engine. The uninitiated are missing out, and she can fill a void. She's discovered something—part sport, part entertainment, part business, part soap opera—worth sharing. She knows it and will try her darnedest to make sure her customers do too.

"I tell them this sport is a lot more than go fast and turn left. There's the physical challenge of driving a race car, the strategy unfolding during a race, the fascinating movement in the garages and back at the shops, all happening behind the scenes. Anyone of any age can relate to NASCAR. You can choose a driver because you like his personality, his sponsor, his car color, or even his number. I know one thing. If you start watching, you'll get hooked."

Catalano's energetic explanations about the intricacies of the sport have created a few Boise-area fans. She's planning to add a new TV to Mystique. When it's glued to SPEED, roaring stock car engines and chattering Southern-twanged commentary will compete with the gentle mood music floating through the salon. Those sounds appear to be harshly incongruent—Johnny Thunder cars versus John Tesh's harp—but they make sense to those in Boise who have had makeovers while arguing whether restrictor-plate tracks produce better races or not.

It's hard to imagine how this busy entrepreneur who added a second floor to her spa and now manages 13 employees could find extra room in her life to become more enthused about NASCAR. Yet Julie's passion grew when she finally attended her first race. Mystique Salon was chosen as the fourth annual "Official Small Business of NASCAR, Courtesy of Office Depot." As the winner of one of the most successful sponsor promotions in NASCAR, Catalano had her company's name and logo—a leopard-print stiletto—on Carl Edwards' Office Depot Ford. The official NASCAR logo is stamped on her stationery and used in promotions. Best of all, she and her husband, son, and daughter were treated by Office Depot to a VIP weekend at Kansas Speedway.

Even though Julie is absolutely enamored with Carl—who her husband jokingly refers to around the house as "mama's boyfriend"—she was cool and collected when meeting the driver at the track. "It's really great to meet you, Carl," she said, offering her hand for a no-nonsense, business-like shake. "Are you gonna win on Sunday?"

Edwards, a genuine good guy who gives away the race trophy to a different sick child after each win, was proud to be associated with a successful businesswoman so knowledgeable and passionate about the sport. He liked his new logo too. "I have to say, a leopard stiletto on the back of my car is pretty cool," Edwards said.

Edwards, who owns an independent record label called Back 40 Records, supporting artists from his hometown of Columbia, Missouri, was eager to support a feisty small business. He understands the time and effort that goes into building a business from scratch, then attracting and retaining customers. Getting to know Catalano over dinner with her family, he appreciated how Julie has created a loyal cadre of customers who, after they've moved away, will time their haircuts for return trips to Boise. While the salon evokes a relaxed, serene feel, underscored by its earth-tone walls, soothing music, and the rhythm of cascading waterfalls, some of Julie's best customers are a group of men usually scheduled in a single afternoon.

Hey, the hairstyles are first rate. And the conversation is an equal draw.

"It's a blast going in to talk NASCAR," said Byron Ferrin, a 15-year client whose dad was a crew member for Cale Yarborough—Julie's favorite driver as a kid. Ferrin's dad tested tires for Goodrich at the Indy 500 a half-century ago and raced on local dirt tracks all over the country. He once spent two months in the hospital followed by many more in rehab after barrel-rolling his car down the front stretch of a track in Kentucky. All that racing history in the DNA of Byron Ferrin finds an outlet, of all places, in a Boise beauty salon.

"I'm a big Junior fan, and if Carl Edwards had a particularly good race, Julie will ask, 'Where'd your boy wind up last week?'" Ferrin said. "It's not often you meet a woman who styles your hair and knows more about NASCAR than you do."

"Office Depot really couldn't have picked a better person to represent them," said friend and customer Sandy Steward. "She's a very determined, very positive, very successful person. She's going to give the sport some incredible exposure. And she's absolutely going to have the time of her life at her first race."

As Mystique Salon enjoys the distinction of being the Official Small Business of NASCAR, Catalano has the unique opportunity of getting the level of mass-market exposure reserved exclusively for large companies with behemoth marketing budgets crunched by MBAs analyzing NASCAR for its deep reach among fans that purchase a sponsor's product. The reams of positive data and color-coded charts paint a picture of a big and healthy sport, leading many executives to write large checks representing support and faith in NASCAR. The money coming from the Fortune 500 companies literally fuels the sport. These big companies deserve the strong value they pay for. But it seems pure and proper, a correct reflection of a higher order, for a die-hard fan like Julie Catalano to have the logo of her business, a symbol of her own blood, sweat, and tears, emblazoned on her favorite driver's race car.

Cold Steel, Cow Farts, and the Science of Speed

ATCHING A NASCAR RACE with Dr. Diandra Leslie-Pelecky is an experience I'd imagine to be like sitting in the stands with Albert Einstein. The professor of physics at the University of Texas in Dallas is a human kaleidoscope of mathematical explanations, colorful observations, and travelogue commentary shedding light on the fascinating science behind every aspect of stock car racing.

At a race, Diandra is the proverbial kid in the candy store, if the owner had turned over the keys to the kids and bolted town. NASCAR races are a large, loud science experiment, and the eagle-eyed, sharp-as-a-tack professor has the run of the lab.

Diandra and I are walking through the garage toward pit road at Texas Motor Speedway before the Dickies 500 NASCAR Sprint Cup Series

While channel-surfing the TV dial, Dr. Diandra Leslie-Pelecky saw a NASCAR wreck. She wondered why only one car darted up into the wall. To get the correct answer, she spent a year asking questions, attending races, and hanging out in the garage. She then wrote a book about the science of NASCAR. *Getty Images for NASCAR*

race. Teams are lining up sponsor-decorated cars on pit road, getting ready to qualify for the race. The colorful cars are tethered to large metal boxes on wheels. "Those generators are heating the oil before the grid rolls," Diandra explains. "Teams warm the oil for qualifying, since viscosity decreases as oil gets hotter. Thinner and lighter oil is better for lubricating the engine's nooks and crannies. It's the same idea as microwaving your pancake syrup to get it to pour more easily."

OK, I had never understood the effects of viscosity on lubrication. But now that she is talking flapjacks and Aunt Jemima, I finally get it.

Diandra looks up at the blue Texas sky. "During the pre-race flyover the planes are never where you expect them to be because light waves travel about a million times faster than sound waves," she says.

We touch a stack of Goodyear tires. "Right-side tires are bigger than left-side tires," she notes. "It's like a marching band turning a corner. The players on the outside have to take bigger steps. Similarly, the car's outer wheels travel a greater distance than the inner wheels; larger outside wheels help the car turn."

This is my seventh season in the sport. I still don't know a dipstick from a dipshit. Walking the track with Diandra, I am learning interesting new things. She explains that over-the-wall crew members who frenetically change four tires in less than 14 seconds paint their lug nuts florescent pink because that's the most jarring color to the human eye. "Pink is the best color to choose when you have a fraction of a second to connect a heavy air gun over the center of each nut," she says.

We move closer to the cars. "NASCAR windshields are made from the same plastic as your iPod screen," she notes.

We pass the Sunoco station where race cars get their fuel, and Diandra has calculations to share. "NASCAR really doesn't use that much fuel. One weekend in the NASCAR Sprint Cup Series consumes the equivalent amount of *two seconds* of America's total gasoline consumption," she explains.

In my free time, I watch brainless TV reality shows in which a group of unbalanced strangers sharing a house drink too much while attempting to find a life mate. Diandra, in her free time, is tabbing how much gas a field of race cars burns.

She explains that America and its politicians can learn a lot from these race cars, which are more efficient than those in the parking lot at the local Walmart. "Lance Armstrong on his bike can produce one horsepower.

These race cars generate 800 horsepower. Compared to a passenger car, they're more efficient. A NASCAR Sprint Cup car consumes 28 times more fuel than a passenger car but produces 32 times more horsepower for that fuel. It's because race cars have advanced valve coatings."

If you're asking why they don't put better valves in the cars the so-called "average American" drives, Diandra says it's all about cost, which she has already calculated. "Using that kind of valves in the car you drive would drive the price of each valve from $6 to $200."

I am still wondering about Lance Armstrong and his measly one horsepower, but drivers were firing their engines, producing a Godzilla-takes-on-King Kong roar loud enough to tickle your ear drums. "A quiet car is a slow car," Diandra shouts. "A muffler actually bounces the exhaust around, which slows the engine down. Engineers call it back pressure. You want to remove the air from the engine as fast as possible."

We head up to the NASCAR skybox above the grandstands. Two track employees on a pickup truck slowly circling the track are shooting balled-up t-shirts into the grandstands from an air gun. "There's projectile motion at work!" Diandra exclaims. She can see physics and materials science everywhere, even in the glass insulating the luxury suite. The green glass is sloped inward. Looking from the inside of the box toward the track, the top of the glass is closer to the track than the bottom. "I wonder why that is?" she asks herself aloud. "It may have to do with the reflective properties of light?" She will find out when she gets home.

The world is an ocean of questions, washing over her all day long. She grew up in Milwaukee, her father a lawyer with a physics degree, her mother a mathematician. She inherited their brains but not their patience. She was bored and unchallenged, sought and found mischief for stimulation, and then dropped out of high school. A college dean saw a beautiful mind with limitless potential and welcomed the 16-year-old to the University of North Texas. She earned degrees in physics and philosophy, went to Michigan State University for grad school, then taught at the University of Nebraska. She worked with Dr. Dean Sicking, who won the National Medal of Technology, the highest scientific honor for a civilian in the United States, for creating the "SAFER" barriers in NASCAR—track walls that disburse the energy in a crash and save lives. She asserts NASCAR is a test tube for society; principles developed in the sport now make America's highways safer.

In addition to her NASCAR passion, she does have a day job—serious, cutting-edge science attempting to improve chemotherapy. "Cancer drugs work by killing the cells that divide the fastest," she explains to me. "The problem: the second-fastest dividing cells are hair follicles. That's why people wind up wearing wigs after a few chemo treatments. White blood cells are also fast dividers, so chemo takes a serious toll on the body's immune system."

Diandra's team at the University of Texas is asking, what if you can make chemotherapy drugs magnetic? What if your doctor held a magnet over the tumor, confining and directing the drugs specifically to eradicate the cancer? Magnetic treatments would vastly improve the cancer-busting effectiveness of chemotherapy while eliminating side effects.

Solving the problem of getting nano-particles to deliver a drug to the cancer cells keeps her up at night. "When you're a scientist, you feel if you work on something long enough, and work hard enough, you will figure it out," she says. She hasn't figured it out yet. She'll keep working.

You get the sense Diandra will bore through a brick wall with her teeth to figure this one out, channeling an inner pit bull gene for finding answers to questions that keep coming. It's a good gene to have when your obsession is trying to cure cancer.

She paraphrases Isaac Asimov by saying: "The moment of discovery is not punctuated by 'Eureka,' it's punctuated by 'Hmm, that's odd.'" She works 70-hour weeks, in labs with rats, trying to coax a "hmm, that's odd" moment. She finds time, however, to go online every day for NASCAR news and on the road to evangelize the science of speed at schools in places like Kansas City, St. Louis, and the Bronx.

She tells me schools today do a pretty good job at turning kids away from science, but NASCAR can change that. It's fun to freeze liquid nitrogen and smash it against the table, but that gets old. The NASCAR garage offers more interesting material. There, she became an expert in rubber, which is awfully complex and never explained or taught well in schools. The momentum transfer of bump drafting fascinates her too. Driver Brian Vickers told her he's been hit so hard from behind in the bump draft, he gets headaches. Vickers sees a driver in his rearview mirror and remembers to press his skull against the headrest. On Valentine's Day in Daytona, she asked Vickers to take her bump drafting. "I know, I know; most women want candy and flowers," Diandra admitted.

She structures her travel to catch NASCAR in airport bars. "The shorter [NASCAR Camping World] Truck Series races are the most fun because drivers don't have time to wait in the back to see how their truck is doing, and most of them genuinely don't like each other," she says.

Up in the suite, the Aflac commercial with the duck at the wheel driving Carl Edwards' car appears on the TV, and she notes that during Carl's trademark backflip off the car after a win, his center of gravity moves in the shape of a parabola.

Students who cheat insult her intelligence. Check that. The student who cheats without creatively trying to outthink her, *that* insults her intelligence. This explains her begrudging respect for the way Jimmie Johnson's crew chief Chad Knaus operates.

She believes science is not about learning facts. It's about asking questions. She tells me a really good question should produce more questions. Those kids you knew when you were growing up who asked a million questions? She was one of them.

One Memorial Day weekend, during rare moments when Diandra wasn't trying to cure cancer, she was watching TV. Just mindless channel surfing. A pack of race cars circled the track. One darted up and crashed into the wall. The others kept their lines. She asked, "Why?" The answer would come in seconds, she thought. There was no easy answer. A million variables are at play in how a race car is built and set up, changing tire and track temperatures, the wind coming off the other cars, a hot dog wrapper that sticks to the grille and ruins a $200,000 race car. Each question prompted another. The sport had amazing, fascinating complexity. It had multimillion-dollar engine dynos and computational fluid dynamics juxtaposed with simple carburetors from 1958.

She spent a whole year asking questions, befriended a NASCAR team, and started writing a book called *The Physics of NASCAR*. "Why did that car go into the wall?" consumed a year of her life. The final answer still eludes her. If she could precisely figure out the sport, exhaust all the questions with correct answers, build the fastest car with four tires equally gripping the track and engines on the brink but not blowing, she'd be working on a NASCAR team making a lot more money.

Her schooling is in materials science, and the hardest thing to understand about NASCAR was aerodynamics. She was no aero expert. She became one. She spent three exhausting months asking questions about air coming off the back spoiler, air rushing around the car, air that easily turns a highly skilled, time-tested race-car driver into the fence. She thinks bump drafting on the freeway would theoretically work. "But first do the math on how quickly you'd have to decide to brake when the truck in front begins to stop. It's a virtually assured probability you'll be embedded in his rear end."

A collection of NASCAR team members in the garage—some eating lunch with a sandwich in one hand and a tool in the other, some with advanced mechanical degrees who work behind the glass at a high-speed computer—are her good friends. She has special affection for driver Elliott Sadler and his No. 19 team, who granted her hours in the pit box many Sundays. With a scientist's dispassionate eye and a fan's breaking heart, she has watched the No. 19 team lose many battles in the endless war of achieving the optimal balance in tire pressure, chassis adjustments, and aerodynamics.

When she's not at the airport bar but home on a Sunday, she turns the TV sound down and logs onto NASCAR.com to hear Sadler in his Virginia drawl cussing out his crew chief.

She brought Halloween candy to the No. 9 team because they like sweets the most. She has experience-based knowledge of who makes the best coffee in the garage.

When walking into a race shop, she loves the overwhelming smell, a mixture of brake cleaner and gear oil. She says it smells like cow farts when teams paint the race cars due to the unique chemical found in automotive paints.

Watching the race, her mind always wanders to figuring out how to attach multiple cancer drugs successfully onto a magnetic nano-particle, eradicating the negative effects of chemo. She has yet to calculate the affect on the wig industry. If all goes right, she forecasts great consternation among the toupee people in five to ten years.

Tires, twisted sheet metal, springs, shocks, and front-end splitters clutter her office. The dean strolls in for a chat but can never pay full attention to what she's saying. His eyes divert to all the NASCAR parts. The elephant in the room is an Eagle from Goodyear.

Her burning desire is to get this country back to producing brilliant scientists by bringing NASCAR into the classroom. At the track, she is about to interview the driver Vickers, the reluctant bump drafter who reads science magazines and is a blogging Mac geek who hangs out in the Apple store in SoHo. The on-camera discussion will be slotted into National Science Foundation curriculum using NASCAR to teach science in schools.

She asks, "What can't you get enough of in a race car?"

Vickers says, "Grip, grip, grip; you always want more grip on one end of the car or the other. You're never really satisfied with how the car sticks to the track. If the front of the car is gripping and the rear isn't, you are loose. If the back is gripping but the front isn't, you're tight. A NASCAR race is four hours pursuing more and better grip."

"Perfect," Diandra says. "That's just what we need." She calls it a wrap.

She has attended dinner parties with Nobel Prize recipients. They speak at science conventions and thank their patrons and donors. She thanks "my sponsors," just like a NASCAR driver.

"The people who fund science projects don't get NASCAR," she says. "They don't believe NASCAR fans understand science, and they are wrong." She believes the scientists who control the budgets and don't get NASCAR should be like the Amish—before you want to commit to a way of life or a profession, go out into the real world to learn how real people speak and act and work. Then decide if it's right for you.

When she says she wants to do something, she does it. A dozen five-minute NSF modules featuring NASCAR drivers, crew chiefs, and engineers illustrating friction, heat, drag, down force, conservation of energy, ideal gas law, centrifugal force, and the internal combustion engine are now available to teachers and students everywhere for free at www.science360.gov.

She sees science everywhere in the sport and explains it very well. She knows science is a liberating force for our children's minds because if you don't question things, how can you be free?

She keeps asking questions. Someday, someone will ask enough of the right questions in the proper order to wind up curing cancer. If Diandra Leslie-Pelecky keeps at it, maybe that person will be a NASCAR fan.

A NASCAR Alien in New York

T HE COLUMBIA UNIVERSITY HISTORIAN Jacques Barzun once famously claimed, "Whoever wants to know the heart and mind of America had better learn baseball."

Sarah Elizabeth Cupp, a rising political commentator better known as "S. E.," wondered if this reliable saw had outlived its relevance. It's not that Cupp had anything against baseball. She's a boisterous New York Mets fan who appreciates "America's pastime," especially when it includes a ballpark hot dog and large cups of draft beer. But she had also been hearing about a new generation of boys of summer commanding full-throated Detroit muscle at gigantic race tracks all over the country. S. E. thought that perhaps a better way to understand the country's heart and soul was to turn her attention away from her beloved National Leaguers running around grass fields in uniforms that looked like pajamas. She would examine the modern-day rebels driving stock cars over seared asphalt and try to understand why such enormously

To really get to know America, political commentator S. E. Cupp decided she'd need to learn about NASCAR. She picked "badass" Tony Stewart as her driver and easily got lost in the sport's drama, swiftly changing storylines, and thrilling door-to-door racing. Watching from Tony's pit box wasn't so bad, either. *Courtesy Keith Payne/S.E. Cupp*

large crowds were pouring into the grandstands each weekend to follow the thunderous spectacle.

The problem was, having grown up near Boston and gotten degrees at Cornell and NYU, Cupp had never been to a NASCAR race and didn't know a single fan. "NASCAR Nation was the 'house-cleaning husband' of sports to me," she said. "I was assured it existed, but I'd never seen it for myself. In my mid-20s, I was no longer content in my NASCAR agnosticism. My curiosity got the better of me, and I definitely needed to find out more."

She started by watching a race on TV. As she was being introduced to this new world, she made a list of a few things she had to know:

- Who was this fabled "Junior" character, and did he have an actual name?
- What is "bump drafting" exactly? Can one do it on the dance floor? Does it hurt?
- What is the "wicker" on the car, and can I sit in it and read a book?
- Is "the restrictor plate" a Weight Watchers offering? Does it come with a health-wise dessert?
- Does the "commitment cone" have anything to do with all the people getting married at the track?
- Who is on the pole, and will they use it to vault anything?
- How can the field be "frozen" in the middle of July?

And so on. . . .

S. E. is intelligent, inquisitive, and funny. We had lunch, and cappuccino came out of my nose. She's one of those people who'll say the darnedest things to make you laugh, but she has a very serious side as well. S. E. questions things, dives into the subject matter, and whips the answers into wry political columns in publications like the *Washington Post* and *New York Daily News*, as well as during her frequent TV appearances on Fox News. With NASCAR, as the mainstream media flirted with their "NASCAR Dads" stories that pop up at election time like gophers in a whack-a-mole carnival game, Cupp was determined to penetrate what she expected to be a "greasy underbelly" of this wildly popular national pastime. Unable to chuck everything and rent a Winnebago to follow the circuit, she did the next best thing—picking a driver and following intently for a year. "I figured if I watched every race and read all the analysis, at the end of the season, I'd at least have an informed opinion about NASCAR and would learn a lot about a big part of the U.S. population. If you find out what moves people and why, you can better understand them."

Cupp shared these plans with her Manhattan friends, whom she describes as "blue-blooded, Northeastern bankers, lawyers, and writers, the kind of folks who clamor over U.S. Open tennis tickets and cashmere socks at a Barney's sale." She boldly announced 2005 would be the "Year of NASCAR." Jaws stayed locked, and there was no delirium in the air.

These friends had seen the urbane TV star slip into her coal miner's daughter persona before. A few years earlier, S. E. had gotten into fishing, hunting, and shooting. She may be the only resident of her hip Chelsea neighborhood with a 12-gauge shotgun. "My friends shrugged their shoulders and generally agreed I had officially become a redneck." To further irk them, Cupp would turn up for cocktails at swanky New York City hotspots wearing camouflage pants.

This 20-something woman full of fascinating contradictions who delights in raising eyebrows selected Tony Stewart as her driver. "I knew nothing of his racing career—only that Tony was a badass and loose cannon [who] had difficulty staying out of trouble. I figured, at the very least, he'd make the season interesting. And, much to the horror of my male friends, I found him to be very, very good-looking, which always helped hold my attention through the seasons of other sports. Thank you, Mike Piazza, Robin Ventura, Brett Favre, and Drew Bledsoe."

Cupp figured she'd need an entire season to understand the appeal of NASCAR. Yet the attraction was instantaneous. Standing behind the pit boxes in Charlotte, the sport had her at "Gentlemen, start your. . . ."

"The flyovers and overt patriotism, the rugged drivers with their crews lined up for the national anthem, the sound of race cars and the television commentators imploring me to 'crank up' the volume, the complexities of drafting and car setups—it was all fascinating and utterly compelling," she said.

That first season served up a cascading series of fantastic storylines. "Tony wins at the Brickyard and four other races, he starts climbing fences, has a run-in with Brian Vickers, gets fined and placed on

Following Tony Stewart's wins, the conservative author and commentator wears her prized No. 14 hat on TV shows like *Red Eye. Courtesy Bill Schulz/S.E. Cupp*

probation—and of course goes on to win his second championship. It was like the season was tailor-made for my experiment in fandom."

And it only got better. That summer Cupp had been busy working on her book, a political tome knocking down right-wing stereotypes. She was eager to include a chapter on NASCAR. In debunking falsehoods like "Republicans Are Racist," "Republicans Hate the Planet," and "Republicans Are Bad in Bed," the addition of a myth-busting chapter on NASCAR ("Republicans Are NASCAR-loving Rednecks") made perfect sense. "The main point was Republicans are not necessarily what you'd expect them to be. They don't all behave, talk, and think alike. And I think it's the same for NASCAR—its fans are not who you'd expect them to be, either. Fans come from all backgrounds and walks of life. The sport has grown to the point of touching every aspect of American life, urban or rural, rich or poor."

Confident that Cupp would reject the cartoon characterization of two types of NASCAR fans—the bearded, Skoal-dipping mechanic and her husband—NASCAR invited her to the Champion's Lunch at the 21 Club in New York City. She sat with Greg Zipadelli, who was Tony's crew chief, and race team boss J. D. Gibbs. During dessert, she was introduced to Stewart.

"Needless to say, it was memorable. I will never forget Tony telling me, 'I'm like Burger King. You can have it your way.' I wasn't sure if he was plugging his sponsor or wanted a date. In person, Tony was everything I thought he'd be." S. E. would eventually watch Stewart race at Lowe's Motor Speedway from Joe Gibbs Racing's pit box and interview him for *Why You're Wrong About the Right*.

Cupp may have picked Stewart as "her driver" for his rebellious attitude and smoldering looks. Yet during the book interview when Tony discussed his fan base, she found a surprisingly clear and resonant intellect. The urban conservative commentator had linked up with a rural conservative athlete who knew exactly where his sport fit in the national political landscape. When Cupp heard Stewart had previously spoken at the National Press Club, it all made sense. He debated nearly as well as he drove.

"Tony made a convincing case that NASCAR's fan base was too broad and diverse to be defined by simplistic snapshots served up by mainstream media. He encouraged me to look at all the places he races—California, Las Vegas, Phoenix, Michigan, Kansas, and Illinois. He challenged me to see NASCAR through the lens of those geographies while reminding me the sport's weekly 'all-star event' pulled in a diverse patchwork of fans from all over the country. He was right. When I went to the races, I saw South Carolina factory workers and Wall Street investment bankers, heavy machinery mechanics and the board of directors of the heavy machine manufacturers. It was chicken wings and beer, sushi and champagne; trailers down in the infield and luxury boxes high above the race track. I thought about my friends' perceptions and noticed a lot of places at the track where they would have fit in just fine."

Checking out the racing scene would be no momentary dalliance. Cupp's NASCAR experience became a lead chapter, but she also turned into a full-fledged race fan, sticking with the driver who drew her in. "Four seasons later—years marked by a little turbulence, some weight loss and gain, and changes in team, car, and crew—Tony is still the guy I want to watch," Cupp said. "And NASCAR is every bit as rewarding now as it was that first season. I've even managed to turn some of my friends into fans, though my father still insists on chiding me with questions like, 'Who won the Hubcaps-Make-Great-Wind-Chimes 500?'"

Cupp proudly displays a picture of Stewart meeting President Bush at the White House on the wall of her Manhattan office. "My colleagues think I'm an alien. But occasionally someone from another floor will walk past my desk and ask, 'You're a NASCAR fan too?' We'll speak our secret language and giddily reminisce about the highs and lows of 2005—my experimental Year of NASCAR—and what's happening today in a sport that's been very, very good to me. I only hope to return the favor."

S. E. is already doing that. Following Stewart's 2009 win at Pocono Raceway, she appeared on the Fox News show *Red Eye* to discuss executive pay caps and the censuring of Miss California for her views on gay marriage. Cupp got into a NASCAR frame of mind, pulling on a No. 14 Tony Stewart hat. As usual, the hosts, Bill Schulz and Greg Gutfeld, eyed her like a creature with green skin and three eyes. "Whenever I bring up NASCAR, it's like I've just landed from outer space. But that's OK. I get a ton of email from appreciative NASCAR fans. One day, I'll get Bill and Greg to a race. They'll immediately understand, and back in the studio you'll see all of us wearing our NASCAR hats."

Chris Trotman/Getty Images

PART VIII

CHASING A RACING DREAM

NASCAR driver Kyle Petty once said NASCAR is like the family business, no different, for those born into it, than a profession like farming. You're brought up in the racing life. Stock car racing was what your father did, and his father did, and it's what your own kids will do. Most of the time, it's a high-profile and glamorous life. But it's still the family business with the long hours, worries, and challenges that come with running pressure-filled, for-profit enterprise.

Drivers like Kyle Petty, Michael Waltrip, Steven Wallace, and Dale Earnhardt Jr. pursue their dreams within the family business. Our next set of fans grew up outside of racing. More than anything else, they wanted to be part of the sport. They've worked hard and made big sacrifices to break into NASCAR, whether it's a position behind the wheel or behind the microphone. Some are further along than others in making it to the top of the sport. In having the guts and courage to do what they love and to chase a racing dream, you could say all of them are already living that dream.

Brad Daugherty
Measures His Own Success

BRAD DAUGHERTY, FORMER NO. I NBA DRAFT PICK, one of the all-time great college basketball centers and now a NASCAR team owner and analyst on ESPN, was in the garage at Homestead-Miami Speedway where teams were tweaking their cars in preparation for the season's final race. Unlike other sports, with their secretive X's and O's discussed at hush-hush private team practices surreptitiously captured by opposing team spies aiming long telephoto lenses from hotel rooms across the highway, NASCAR's "locker room" is open to fans and media. They have the full run of the place and can freely stroll about, watching the NASCAR Sprint Cup Series teams work on their machines. Fans can literally bump into drivers. These athletes about to strap in to put it on the line will take

He was picked first in the NBA draft, but Brad Daugherty says NASCAR has always been his first love. To honor Richard Petty, Daugherty wore the No. 43 basketball jersey throughout his illustrious career. *Getty Images for NASCAR*

a moment to pose for a photo and sign an autograph. Broadcasters like Daugherty "work the garage" for fresh perspective and the highly sought after scoop to bring to viewers.

The team haulers were parked in a symmetrical, angled row, about four feet apart. The drivers on the track get all the credit for their skills, but equally amazing is how the pilots of these big, boxy haulers expertly wedge in their huge machines like giant, evenly spaced dominos. Near the center of the line of haulers, the dense crowd was bunched up, signaling a popular destination. Wherever the sport races, a pulsating knot forms in front of one hauler—the No. 88 of Dale Earnhardt Jr. A throng of buzzing fans holding cameras aloft and waving hero cards pressed in, hoping for an encounter with "Junior." The fans were excited but respectful. Their driver was speaking with his crew chief. The fans knew this conversation could bring an insight that would add a little speed to the car, help it stick in a corner, maybe find a faster line on the track. The fans tiptoed closer, but no one wanted to interfere.

Standing seven feet tall, Daugherty is an imposing physical presence and still nimble on his feet. He was able to slide through this impromptu province of Junior Nation setting up temporary residence in the presence of His Greatness and maneuver through the cameras and extended Sharpies alongside the object of everyone's gaze. The day before, the driver whose every word reverberates throughout NASCAR media and blogosphere, had suggested the sport shorten its exhausting 10-month season. With the schedule clearly on his mind, Junior asked Daugherty, who scored more than 10,000 points over an illustrious career with the Cleveland Cavaliers, how he managed to play so many games at a high level over the course of a grueling campaign. Daugherty, who dealt with the rigors of life on the road pretty well—he was the Cavs' all-time leading scorer until LeBron James came along, although he's quick to point out James took more shots—had his own concern. Brad drives too—a late-model car with a special seat. Once he's able to bend his jumbo frame like Gumby into the cramped cockpit, he's a surprisingly proficient race car driver at short tracks in places like Myrtle Beach, South Carolina, and New Smyrna, Florida. Daugherty's NBA career ended after 10 terrific seasons (5 as an all-star) due to an injured back, which was acting up today, and he wanted Earnhardt's view on a new hybrid neck device designed to help drivers avoid serious injury in bad crashes.

The megastar driver and round-ball-legend-turned-announcer wrapped up their conversation. Junior pulled on his helmet and jack-knifed into his race car. The engine roared, the crowd parted, and the No. 88 Chevy squealed off for a practice lap. Daugherty was wearing the expression of a guy just told to take a vacation so the company could renovate his new, bigger office, oh and by the way, enjoy the big raise and new car when you get back. A similar blissful look occupied his face when NASCAR visited Talladega. ESPN set up on the front stretch, and he could barely do the TV show because he was swiveling in his chair like a human dreidel to catch every car in the pack roaring off the final turn and down the front stretch.

"I am a huge fan of Dale Junior and all of these drivers, these modern-day gladiators," he said. "When I played pro ball, fans couldn't get near us. After the game, we'd walk through a petitioned-off tunnel. I just love being near these drivers. And the thing is, you *can* get near them. I hear the cars and still get excited. I'm drawn to the power, speed, smells, and violence of this sport—man versus machine versus man. I'm a racing nut. Always have been, always will be."

As a boy growing up in Black Mountain, North Carolina, Brad Daugherty's first love was auto racing, even before basketball. Until he was a junior in high school, he could not have cared less about hoops. Shooting a ball into a basket was mundane. Getting an engine to rev at its peak without blowing up, now that was a fun challenge.

Daugherty realized that the extraordinarily large body God gave him could enrich his mind by paying for college. Basketball was a utilitarian means to a first-rate education at the University of North Carolina. No one had guessed he'd turn into such a fine ball player, an All-American, one of the greatest to take to the hard court for a storied school. After Daugherty averaged 20 points a game his senior year, Tar Heels coach Dean Smith called him into his office and announced he'd be drafted first or second in the 1986 NBA draft. "That's great, at least I'll be picked," Daugherty jokingly said to the coach he so admired.

Basketball was never the ultimate goal. It would provide fame and fortune and a lifestyle most folks in the hills of North Carolina don't dare dream about. Basketball turned out to be Daugherty's golden ticket. But motorsports were always his true passion. On every team for which Brad played, he asked for the number *43* and was reminded of his hero, Richard

LIVE

Jeter: .489 BA, 4 HR, 9 RBI, 9 R last 11 games

Daugherty is blazing trails as an African-American commentator for NASCAR on ESPN and a team owner at the sport's elite level. In August 2009, he interviewed President Barak Obama when *NASCAR Now* went live from the White House lawn. *Courtesy ESPN*

Petty, whenever he pulled on that jersey. His father Roy and Uncle Buster built hot rods and dragsters. Racing conversations with these "total gear heads" would bond the young man to the older men who would be enduring role models, encouraging him to work hard, carry himself with dignity, and live life as if he were equal to everyone else.

Those words left a mark on Daugherty, as did the power and explosiveness of the street rods his uncle built and memories like chatting with Richard Petty at Daytona in 1977 and watching the 1979 Daytona 500 live on TV with his dad. That now-famous telecast was the first time the "Great American Race" would be broadcast in full on network television. Before that, NASCAR was seen mostly on ABC's *Wide World of Sports*, sandwiched between cliff diving and Ping-Pong. For the inaugural "flag-to-flag" broadcast, the elder Daugherty was in front of the TV in his favorite chair, one hand dipping into the ever-present hard candy dish, the other cradling a Winston. His lanky 14-year-old son squirmed uncomfortably on a sticky sofa. "My mom would not take the plastic off that furniture. I was sweating like a pig, stuck to the couch. My dad was fiddling with the TV, adjusting the rabbit ears, up and down, up and down. Dad was a real big man, six seven, 300 pounds. Every time he got back in the chair, you'd hear a huge thud."

Daugherty will never forget this particular living room scene because that Sunday's race would include one of the most talked-about finishes in

NASCAR history, an electrifying duel with extracurricular activities that put stock car racing on the national sports map.

Bobby Allison, his brother Donnie, and Cale Yarborough all wrecked in the early going of the 1979 Daytona 500. But Donnie and Cale rallied to run 1-2 in the closing laps. Yarborough, a muscular bruiser who grew up on a tobacco farm in South Carolina and lied about his age as a teenager so he could race at nearby Darlington Raceway, had a faster car and set up to slingshot Allison in the last lap. Cale could have gone on and passed Allison's Chevy and won the race handily. But he wanted to make a show out of it, and what a show it became. Running wide open on the high banks of Daytona, the drivers thumped and bumped and banged and finally wrecked each other into the Turn Three wall on the final lap, allowing Richard Petty to zip by for the checkered flag. Bobby Allison pulled over in the infield to check on his little brother. Words were exchanged between Bobby and Cale before all hell broke loose live on national TV. As Bobby would later say, "Cale hit my fist with his helmet."

To the Daughertys, it was just a few good ol' boys settling matters right then and there, mano y mano. They watched a great race and got a boxing match to boot. "Besides racing, my dad's other love was professional wrestling. After that wild finish, the fight was like Christmas morning for him," Daugherty said. It was like that for young Brad too, watching Petty capture his sixth Daytona 500.

Yarborough later commented, "Not a very fair fight—one Yarborough against two Allisons, but that's the way it ended up. We were friends the next day, and we've been friends ever since."

Daugherty's best friend was Robert Pressley, whose dad was a short-track racing legend at Asheville, just down the mountain from the boys. Pressley and Daugherty rooted for Richard Petty, David Pearson, and Jack Ingram, and started building cars and racing motorcycles and four-wheelers. When Pressley began racing seriously, Daugherty, then an NBA star, funded his friend's ride in the NASCAR Nationwide Series. Running a car with this friend/sponsor's logo—"The Brad Daugherty Basketball Camp"—Pressley even won a race in NASCAR's number-two series. Daugherty is now part owner of JTG/Daugherty Racing, which competes in the NASCAR Sprint Cup Series.

While racing was part of the fabric of growing up in North Carolina, Daugherty didn't attend many races. "The culture was different then," he

Brad Daugherty races stock cars and ran well in a promotional race at Bristol Motor Speedway in 2009 against NASCAR legends such as Junior Johnson, Cale Yarborough, and Harry Gant. *Courtesy Bristol Motor Speedway*

explained to me in the ESPN booth at Homestead-Miami Speedway, just weeks after Barack Obama was elected president. "Racing as a career for me wasn't an option. It wasn't feasible for my dad to say, 'You can be a [NASCAR] Winston Cup driver.' He wanted me to work hard and be respectable. He told me, 'Live your life as if you are equal.' I've always remembered those words. If you want to be treated equally, you need to live up to a certain standard."

When Daugherty, a journalism major at UNC, took the ESPN announcing job to become the first African-American in the TV booth calling a NASCAR race, he expected to raise eyebrows. "We live in the freest, greatest country in the world," he said. "Inevitably, a small segment of any group of people won't like you because you are you. I accepted that. I also realized no African American would have the same opportunity as me. I decided to do this well, be responsible, and represent myself to the best of my ability."

Sometimes, life feels like you walk two steps, get knocked down, pick yourself up, then walk a few more. It's the getting up and moving forward that counts. As Daugherty helps tell NASCAR's story on television each week, hundreds of African Americans have told him they've now become fans of the sport. "Coach Smith told me, 'Always measure your own success.'

That's so true. None of us should live up to others' standards. We should set our goals, make sure they are high enough, and aspire to those goals."

As a boy, Daugherty wanted simply to get a decent education that his dad, a career military man, couldn't afford for him. NASCAR was a dream but not a goal. And now, decades later, he put on his necktie, about to step in front of hot lights and join former NASCAR champion Rusty Wallace in discussing whether Jimmie Johnson would, 400 miles from now, win his third championship in succession. Like those few blessed to make a living doing what their hearts have always desired, Brad is living the dream.

"I wish my dad were alive to be here today to enjoy the sport the way I do," he said. "He'd be tickled to come to a place like this, walk into the pits, same as any other man, lay his hands on a race car. You know, once he told me I could be president of the United States if I wanted. It wasn't very realistic in that different era, but he meant it. And look at us today. He was right. We have all come such a long way."

Daugherty grew silent. Showtime was approaching. He knotted the tie tight against his neck and slid behind the console next to Wallace. A producer counted down from 10. The camera light went red, and Brad Daugherty, a seven-foot-tall black man, was on network television comparing Jimmie Johnson's historic quest for a third consecutive title to the extraordinary athletic feats of Tiger Woods. It was not hard to imagine a kid somewhere in America, could be in a ramshackle farm house or a big-city high-rise apartment, sticking to a plastic couch and dreaming big, because this is the freest and greatest country in the world, where dreams are not exclusively for those asleep.

This Girl Wants to Be
Jeff Gordon in a Skirt

W ITH A DAD WHO OWNS a Chevy dealership in Fargo, North Dakota,
Natalie Sather has enjoyed some fantastic NASCAR perks, particularly for a young lady moving up in the ranks as a race car driver. One
of her great thrills was riding in the pace car with Jeff Gordon at the 2004
Daytona 500.

At such giddy moments on a grand stage before a marquee event, a
star-struck fan will usually lob the driver a mundane softball like, "Are you

Natalie Sather is intense, determined, tough, and hotly competitive, and she likes
to shop, get dolled up, and bake chocolate-chip cookies. Just your typical, up-and-
coming, young NASCAR driver. *NASCAR Media Group/Scott Hunter*

going to win today?" Natalie was typically forthright and direct, searching for an angle to help her career. She asked her racing hero how it feels when fans boo him.

"Jeff said, 'As long as they're making noise and know you're there, that's all that matters,'" Natalie remembered. "That answer has stayed with me to this day."

There was a reason for her blunt question. Natalie, then 18, had in her earlier teenage years blazed trails in the Midwest in sprint cars—those small, powerful, open-wheel vehicles seen at local short tracks around the country. She was now cutting her teeth in stock car racing and had received several hostile e-mails questioning why a nice young lady would want to drive a stock car on Saturday nights when she should be gussying herself up for an evening on the town with a nice local boy.

"These women were telling me I need to drop my dream and become a child-bearing housewife," Natalie explained. "I don't get these comments every day, but when I do, I remember Jeff's words. He made me realize people are recognizing what I'm doing and paying attention. That's all that matters. Then I try to kill 'em with kindness, thanking them for contacting me and letting them know how hard I'm working at my goal. It was important to get this advice because I grew up admiring Jeff Gordon. He was told so many times he'd never make it. Now look at what he's done. That's so inspiring to me."

Whenever teachers, relatives, or friends asked Natalie what she wanted to be when she grew up, her response was always the same: "I want to be the next girl Jeff Gordon." Now that she's grown up, she says with a sparkling smile, "I'm gonna sign autographs like Jeff Gordon in a skirt."

"If Natalie had not been such a big fan of Gordon and the sport, we probably wouldn't be striving so hard to meet this goal of making it into NASCAR's diversity program to further her racing career," Natalie's mom, Tessa, said.

Nothing about her daughter's unique career choice has surprised Tessa. She sensed Natalie was special in her intensity and determination right there in the maternity ward. "She's tough and ultra-competitive but in a confident rather than an insecure way. You could say she's a different breed of cat."

As a young girl in kindergarten, Natalie would bring toy cars to "show and tell." She changed high schools in order to take shop class. She loves to hunt and fish. Without a hint of self-consciousness, Natalie will show

After a wreck, doctors said Natalie might never race again. She was back in her car in a few months. Here, she gets some advice from Drive for Diversity initiative mentor Wendell Scott Jr. *NASCAR Media Group/Scott Hunter*

you a 10-inch scar running up her right shin, the product of a bad racing accident. She was 17 years old and running well in her fifth race in sprint cars. She tried to pass a driver on the outside. He wasn't about to be shown up by a pretty little girl thinking she could come in and take over the track, and he promptly steered her, nose first, into the wall. It was a hard hit, but Natalie was OK. She had never been wrecked before, but she got through it, or so she thought. Her car was immobile on the track, next to the outside concrete barrier. Unfortunately, the caution flag was slow to come out. The leader, who happened to be a friend and also sponsored by her father's car dealership, came roaring around Turn Four, went high on the track, and slammed into her at 120 miles per hour.

It was the type of accident drivers fear the most, to be a sitting duck, rammed hard on the driver's side. Natalie had been violently T-boned with such force that the cars went airborne. When the race car drivers stopped spinning, Natalie looked down and saw her foot jutting from her leg at a grotesque, unnatural angle. Her lower leg was badly broken in three places. As the emergency crews removed Natalie from the car, she kept asking, "Can I race? Can I race?"

With strong finishes and a 2009 win in the NASCAR Whelen All-American Series, Natalie Sather is taking steps towards the sport's elite divisions. *NASCAR Media Group/Scott Hunter*

The high school senior was told she might never race again. At a minimum, she'd need to wait a year. Doctors inserted a metal rod running from her knee to her ankle to hold together her fibula. Natalie is not a big girl, and screws were sticking out of the skin. She developed a golf-ball-sized infection in her leg. She couldn't wait to get back in the car. Less than four months after the scary wreck, she was racing again, wearing a special leg brace in case she took a hard lick. She posted two top-10 finishes the same season of her accident and surgeries.

"She broke the leg in May and was in the car September 1," Tessa proudly declared. "Yeah, we got in a little trouble with the doctor on that one."

"I knew I shouldn't have been racing," Natalie acknowledged. "But there was nothing that could have kept me off the track. Even with the brace on my leg, I knew if I got in a pretty bad wreck, maybe I'd never be able to walk again. I weighed my options. This is my big dream, what I want to do. Up to that point, I'd worked so long and so hard to be a successful race car driver. I wasn't going to give up just because of three breaks, three screws, a rod, and seven surgeries. I decided it was worth it. Go big or go home, right?"

The special brace wasn't really needed, the leg healed, and the mother-daughter tandem began fearlessly barnstorming racing events across the country like Thelma and Louise. Mother and daughter have a difficult-tocategorize desire to achieve their racing dream. They've found a way to cackle in the face of danger, kick fear in the teeth, slingshot past challenges, leave it all on the race track, you name the racing cliché to describe the competitive fires burning in this defiant, determined, dynamic duo, and it will fit.

One time, at a track outside Dallas, Natalie was wrecked from another hard hit. The plan after the race was to drive home to Fargo—a long 16-hour haul. Once on the road, Natalie didn't look so good.

"We went to a hospital in Denton, Texas, to get a CAT scan," Tessa said. "We figured we had to stop. What if we kept going and she went into convulsions in the middle of Kansas? We didn't need that in my car!"

The scan revealed a concussion but nothing more serious. Still, the doctors didn't want Natalie to sleep yet. With the help of Starbucks and mom nudging Natalie every few hours as she dozed off, she'd be fine.

The young race car driver's dad, who owns Gateway Chevrolet in Fargo, had to spend a few years of his business career in Chicago just as Natalie started racing go-karts at nine years old. Tessa, who is as industrious as she is stubborn, became Natalie's crew chief. Tessa isn't mechanical by nature. She learned the inner workings of a car by asking lots of questions. "I had the company that made the go-kart motors on speed dial," she says.

Through sheer relentlessness and a desire not to fail, she became a mechanic. Picture Erin Brokovich brandishing a wrench instead of water company memos. At night, Natalie would bring her homework into the garage while mom was scaling the go-kart. The two would show up at the track and catch peculiar looks. They took it in stride, even relished the attention. "There's only one thing worse than being beaten by a girl. And that's when the mom's the wrench," Natalie said.

For the boys, there may be another thing worse than being beaten by a girl—and that's when the girl is a looker who's not afraid to show her feminine side. "I'm the girliest tomboy you'd ever meet," Natalie said. She bakes scrumptious chocolate-chip cookies, likes to shop, and was the captain of her high school cheerleading squad. To show how a girl can be feminine while competing in a male-dominated sport like racing, she entered and nearly won the Miss Teen North Dakota beauty pageant, even with a slight limp in heels from the sprint car wreck. (With her dark hair, dark eyes, and smoky looks, some might say she bears a strong resemblance to the most famous modern-day female race car driver, Danica

Patrick, but that would short-change Sather, who has softer features and a gentler effect.)

Natalie's easy smile and outgoing manner should fool no competitor. She is not on the track to develop friends who'll receive that next batch of cookies. She truly hates losing, and her driving style reflects that attitude. It's a long, unforgiving, treacherous road to the select few spots at the top of the sport, but she's passed the early tests. After winning a national go-kart title, Natalie became the first woman to win a major sprint car championship, taking the American Sprint Car Series (ASCS) Midwest points championship in 2007. In 2008, she was rookie of the year at Knoxville Raceway in Iowa. In 2009, in heavier stock cars, she ran in the NASCAR Whelen All-American Series at Evergreen Speedway in Monroe, Washington, for Total Velocity Motorsports.

While Natalie Sather tries to make her mark in NASCAR, mother and daughter still watch Gordon and the stars of NASCAR whenever they can. Their racing trailer is equipped with TVs on each end to follow the races when working on the race car in the back or tending to sponsorship paperwork up front. The trailer has become home. Natalie is lucky if she's back in Fargo a few times a month. She's a "seasonal friend" to the girls closest to her back home. She's okay with that. The racing dream beckons. "I wouldn't trade any of this—the scars, the pain, being in a hot sweaty car all the time, for anything," Natalie said.

Even though she's part of NASCAR's next generation, Natalie has an old-school understanding of the importance of the sport's fans. She deeply appreciates her followers' support—to her and the entire sport. She reckons it's a commitment that sometimes goes above and beyond the call of duty, like at Eagle Raceway, a small dust bowl of a track in Eagle, Nebraska. The cars kick up so much dirt, fans closest to the track wear eye protection.

"After the race, they take off their goggles, and their faces are black except for these raccoon eyes," Natalie said with a laugh. "They're thanking me for racing, holding up a dirty beer, and I'm thanking them for sitting in the wake of dirt my car's kicking up. I come out of the car cleaner than the fans watching us race. I mean, who's the crazy one?"

Gunning for the NASCAR
Sprint Cup Series … with a Little
Help from His Friends

P AULIE HARRAKA HAS A HEAVY FOOT and a silver tongue. His ability to talk and drive is a formidable one-two combination. It's brought a kid from New Jersey multiple racing championships, a mentor in retired NASCAR legend Ricky Rudd, and a great education at Duke University. Paulie is just getting started.

Take this example of driving, then talking, then driving. When he was 15, Paulie was practicing for a go-kart championship race in New York State. He'd qualified second and had every intention of winning the race and another title. It started raining. Conditions in the pre-race morning

New Jersey native Paulie Harraka is balancing a double major at Duke University with winning races in the NASCAR Camping World Series, a stepping stone to his ultimate goal: the starting grid at the Daytona 500. *Courtesy Roger Morris, Two Rock Media, Inc.*

practice got bad. A tie rod in Paulie's kart broke, and it veered off the track. Harraka skidded across the wet grass, and his head smashed into a tree.

"I thought he was dead," said his dad, Paul Sr.

The hyperventilating dad rushed to the accident scene and found his son groggy and disoriented. After he'd regained consciousness, Paulie's head hurt like the devil. He knew he was in New York but couldn't name the other 49 states. Aside from that, the kid *was* talking (though, if Paulie had a pulse, you knew he'd be yammering away).

Paulie was strapped onto a stretcher and taken to the hospital. The entire ride he was urging the ambulance driver to "step on it, I've got to get back to the track in time for the feature race." He told the doctors to hurry the CAT scan. The next race was in four hours. The doctors said the kid was nuts. He had a concussion. No physical activity for one week–minimum.

Harraka would have none of that. The cobwebs in his head had cleared, and wheels were turning. He was intent on solving two problems: getting out of the hospital pronto and fixing a kart with only three wheels touching the ground after hitting the tree. He had every intention of running and winning the race.

Paul Sr. would rather watch his son career around a track than anything else in life. But he didn't think this was such a good idea. Yet, his son has that way with words, and the dad was weighing pros and cons, and beginning to like the pros. Like many battle-tested fathers about to take part in something questionable while anticipating potential harsh repercussions of assuming sole responsibility, Paul Sr. made the inevitable decision.

"Ask your mother," he said.

If Paulie could convince his mom he was fine to compete, he could enter the championship race.

When his mother arrived at the hospital, Paulie explained the crash in terms so mundane she almost yawned. "The doctor says there's no bleeding in the brain, isn't that great news," Paulie informed her. He conveniently neglected to mention the severity of the concussion and a throbbing skull that felt like AC/DC was practicing inside.

With mom's sign-off in the bag, Paulie sped back to the track. He found the heaviest guy at the track to jump up and down on the kart to bend it back into shape. Paulie started in last place and passed 17 karts for a fourth-place finish. He was pissed off he didn't win.

Forget the young man's immense sense of desire and motivation. If Paulie continues consistently to drive as fast and smooth as he talks, the kid may have a long and prosperous future as a race car driver.

In high school, he was the New Jersey state champion of the Future Business Leaders of America . . . while managing to win a track championship in California as part of NASCAR's Drive for Diversity program.

Each of those accomplishments is extraordinary on its own. To earn them 2,600 miles apart—excelling in high school on the East Coast while commuting cross-country to become the top NASCAR late-model driver at All-American Speedway in Roseville, California—nearly defies belief. To do it as a 17-year-old makes Harraka something of a teenage superhero, in a mild-mannered-honor-student-turns-into-a-fierce-race-car-driver sort of way. The super-motivated teen had logged more than 150,000 frequent flier miles during his senior year in high school. Overall, in four years of high school in New Jersey and North Carolina, Paulie missed 152 days of school, meaning he basically violated every truancy law on the books. But Paulie skipped school to go racing with the full cooperation of local authorities. The tireless young man with the gift of gab cut a deal with his New Jersey high school principal: if he got straight A's, he could miss school, fly the red eye, and continue racing. If his grades slipped, he'd be subjected to standard no-tolerance absentee rules and would have to give up racing. Paulie got the grades and the track title.

When applying to Duke University, his serial truancy was positioned as a positive. The dean of students was impressed anyone could miss so much school and do so well academically. Paulie convinced him it could be done in college, even at the "Harvard of the South." Duke extended early admission to Paulie and treats him like an honest-to-goodness student athlete. The school is working to ensure Paulie has every chance to succeed as both a student and a race car driver. He's allowed to schedule tests around his busy race schedule and submit class work when he's back in town.

Aside from hitting the tree in New York, Paulie was injured only one other time, but it was a lot worse. In Ohio, he flipped his kart four times and suffered a collapsed lung. He was hospitalized for two days. "Quitting was never a consideration," Paulie said. "In fact, I thought the opposite. You never want to dwell on it. I didn't. I just wanted to get back out there in the car."

"Am I afraid one day he'll get hurt?" Paul Sr. asks. "What I really fear is some day Paulie will be sitting on his couch saying, 'I could have been a NASCAR champion if I had been given the chance.' Now he can say he's getting his chance. How many people have the opportunity to pursue something they truly love and are really good at? How could he possibly be deprived of that?"

"Good at it" is an understatement. Harraka has won 13 national karting championships and 6 world championships. After starting at NASCAR's lowest level—the NASCAR Whelen All-American Series, where he grabbed 11 wins and the 2008 track championship by beating a well-funded 42-year-old veteran who wasn't afraid to use his bumper to move Paulie out of the way—the young driver has moved up a notch to the NASCAR Camping World West Series. The ultimate goal is the pinnacle of American racing, the NASCAR Sprint Cup Series.

He'll need no introductions on the way there. NASCAR brass already knows Paulie Harraka. Once, in the NASCAR scoring tower at Daytona International Speedway, which has tighter security than the Vatican, NASCAR president Mike Helton turned around, and there was young Harraka, watching the race. He'd talked his way into a place few race car drivers ever visit, let alone a teenager at the bottom rung of the sport.

"You don't have to worry about that kid," Mike Helton said. "If he doesn't make it in racing, he could be president of the United States some day, and I'd vote for him."

If the consummate networker runs for office, it won't be from lack of trying to make it in racing first. Paulie got into the seat as a five-year-old when Paul Sr., who had built race cars with his brother in New Jersey for more than two decades, bought his son a go-kart. "I knew from the first minute in the kart he was good," Paul Sr. said. "He wasn't nervous at all. He was cool and focused, intelligent behind the wheel. You can almost see him thinking inside his helmet during the race."

When Paulie was seven, he attended the 1996 Daytona 500, where he met many drivers in the pit area. Paulie stood next to the stage and got a few dozen autographs on a hat he still has. The youngster was glued to his scanner, listening to the driver–crew chief conversations. "It was very cool to see a pack of 43 cars, running three by three by three down the line," he said. "It's something I'll never forget. It was then I really got interested in racing and said to myself, 'Hey, I may want to do this.'" Paulie was so taken by the racing he begged his dad to take him to other races, and they traveled to Bristol, Charlotte, and Talladega.

To take care of his sponsor, Harraka brought a Simpson banner to the Roman Coliseum. Harraka is as adept with the media as he is barreling into a corner at 180 miles per hour. *Courtesy Paul Harraka*

Before he was eight, Paulie began racing competitively. First time out, he won the feature race at Flemington Speedway in New Jersey. He won 10 of the next 12 kart races and took the state championship against kids three years older. In 1998, he won 28 of 32 races and earned the state championship. Each time he progressed a level, he won the title. In 1999, he moved up to the World Karting Association (WKA), a pipeline for NASCAR Sprint Cup Series drivers like Brian Vickers and Jamie McMurray that holds events in many states across the country. The nine-year-old rookie won the WKA championship, becoming the series' youngest-ever champion. The next year, he made history by copping the coveted World Karting Triple Crown by winning four National Championships in one year on different types and series of karts. It's a feat that had never been accomplished before and hasn't been duplicated since.

Father and son drove across the United States, putting 400,000 miles on their Ford Expedition, the kart jammed in the back, luggage on the roof. Paulie raced in 32 states, Canada, even Italy. They slept in the back of the Ford to save money for tires for the kart races. At 15 years old, in his first Senior Division start, Paulie won the World Championship at the track where he'd seen his first NASCAR race—Daytona International Speedway. In Victory Lane, Paulie told a reporter, "Winning at Daytona is like getting a chance to play baseball in Yankee Stadium." It made the front page of the sports section of the *Daytona Beach News Journal*.

Paulie was shining on the track and also developing his corporate skills, most notably turning on the charm for Bill Simpson, who ran a company that made race helmets, fire suits, and shoes. When he was barely nine years old, the precocious kid made the case Simpson needed a youthful spokesperson. He landed a deal to endorse Simpson safety equipment. Ever since, Harraka has had a full-blown Simpson deal, getting free equipment each year. Some NASCAR Sprint Cup Series drivers don't have that type of lucrative arrangement. In fact, outside NASCAR's top series, only one driver has a Simpson deal—the kid from Jersey with the lead foot and silver tongue.

Many drivers can go fast. Simpson sensed this kid also talked the talk and would go the extra mile for his sponsor. Paulie did that in Europe during the by-invitation-only World Karting Championship. He had envisioned a special opportunity for his sponsor, asking his dad to stop at the Roman Coliseum. He'd brought along a Simpson banner, which he wrapped around a few columns of the fabled stadium. The Italian police have had happier moments. They marched over and ordered the banner to be cut down but not before Paulie had snapped off a few pictures. He asked gladiators outside the Coliseum to carry the banner. Back in the Unites States with the coveted photos, he told Bill Simpson, "Even Roman Gladiators know who to trust for safety equipment."

Through this kind of bold and confident approach to life, Paulie landed a job as a 16-year-old with Gillett Evernham Motorsports (now Richard Petty Motorsports) in Charlotte and a friend in retired NASCAR Sprint Cup Series driver Ricky Rudd. Rudd, who had raced karts 30 years earlier before a long career in NASCAR, wanted to experience competing in a modern-day kart. He teamed with young Paulie to run a three-and-a-half-hour endurance race at New Castle Motorsports Park outside of Indianapolis. Paulie drove more than three quarters of the race against 85 professional karting teams, leading the Harraka-Rudd tandem to a dominating win over open-wheel luminaries like Scott Dixon, Thomas Schecter, Dan Wheldon, and Sarah Fisher.

Rudd, who has seen many young drivers come along during 32 years of racing at NASCAR's top level, believes Paulie is special. "The kid stands out, not only with his driving ability, but also as an intelligent, respectful, hard-working young man. His determination seems to know no bounds. On a Friday night, Paulie and his dad would drive all the way down to Florida to race, then all night Saturday back to my shop in Huntersville, where they'd pick up a tool and work all day Sunday. At 7 p.m., they'd get back in the car to drive all night to New Jersey for Paulie to make it to school Monday morning. The kid did that five weekends in a row. He never complained once. The whole time, he was maintaining a straight-A average. I don't know how he did it, except that he's a truly gifted, talented, and determined young man."

Rudd knows about athletic determination. He set a legendary example in all sports for a hard-headed will to compete. In 1984, Rudd was involved in a bad wreck at the Busch Clash exhibition race in Daytona. His eyes were swollen shut. Unable to see, it would be impossible to compete in the following week's Daytona 500. Rudd wouldn't accept sitting out the biggest race of the year. He simply taped his eyes open with duct tape and soldiered on to finish seventh. The next week, still sore and swollen, Rudd won the Pontiac 400 at Richmond.

An iron-willed mentor like that doesn't have to say much to make an impact. The advice Rudd gives is a bonus. As Harraka runs in the NASCAR Camping World West Series, his sights trained on the sport's premier national series, he still calls Rudd for counsel—especially before taking on a challenging road course, where Rudd excelled, winning six NASCAR Sprint Cup Series races. Paulie also draws on the sage experience of Wally Brown, Carl Edwards' former crew chief and current research and development lead engineer at Joe Gibbs Racing. Brown was Paulie's boss when he worked at JGR, pointing out the intricate mechanics of the car. He took time to explain how subtle changes in shock absorbers and the angle of the upper control arms in the chassis can make the car faster through the turns. Paulie traveled with Wally to car tests, serving as his tire specialist. His job was to measure the tires, monitor their wear and tire pressure, keep them in sets, and communicate all of the information he gathered back to the engineer. "Learning about tires in that kind of detail has helped me a lot when I'm racing," Harraka said.

Another one of Harraka's bosses, Elton Sawyer, former NASCAR Nationwide Series driver and current competition director at Red Bull Racing, also continues to guide the young driver. Paulie was 15 when he went to work for Elton on the Gillett Evernham Motorsports NASCAR Nationwide Series team. He started out cleaning cars and eventually worked his way into small assembly. Elton is a constant sounding board and takes time to spot for the driver. He'll give advice like when to brake getting into a corner or which tracks Paulie can use the apron on if necessary. "Since Elton has so much experience, having him as a spotter is a huge help. He can tell you the best place to pass a car and offer suggestions for changing your line."

Beyond the mutual respect race car drivers and engineers develop in the garage, Brown, Rudd, and others who know Paulie appreciate the man he is becoming—a kind person with a good heart. One Christmas season Paulie walked into the house, night after night, with a new gift. There were two girl's bikes and two pairs of roller skates, clothes and toys. Paulie had been taking names from the Salvation Army and buying gifts for the needy kids.

The frenetic networking that's brought Paulie notice throughout NASCAR and helped secure a spot at Duke is a key skill for building a racing career today. Paulie posts a blog after each race and personally e-mails reporters, which has resulted in glowing profiles in such publications as the *New York Times*, *Charlotte Observer*, and *Newark Star Ledger* and frequent appearances on Sirius XM radio. No other driver at Paulie's level is a regular on NASCAR Channel 128. But Paulie is like no other driver.

His penchant for building relationships and keeping them fresh has brought speaking engagements as well. In 2006, for NASCAR Day, the sport's annual fundraiser, he appeared at Lincoln Elementary School near Charlotte. Paulie's confidence, poise, and machine-gun bursts of words splayed into neat, coherent paragraphs of expression had everyone believing he was a lot older than 16. A few months after the talk, a check arrived from NASCAR to pay for the talk. Paulie felt more comfortable with the money staying within the NASCAR Foundation. The check was sent back.

In the context of a changing sport, the Harrakas' background—100 percent Syrian—is noteworthy. Paulie's grandparents on both sides came to the United States in the early 1900s to escape religious persecution as

Christians in an overwhelmingly Muslim country. Paulie acknowledges the Syrian culture is a big part of his background. "It's where I'm from and an important part of who I am," he said. But he doesn't like to dwell on his ancestry, and he tactfully brushed aside my attempts to coax him into claiming he's a torch-bearer for diversity in NASCAR. The kid is looking ahead, not behind him.

It's well established that America is a land of opportunity. The country has endured hard times of late. Some claim we've lost part of the stature and respect we've enjoyed for many years. But make no mistake, this nation remains a shining beacon of hope, a place where anything is possible. Whether or not you care for his politics and policies, the election of an African American, Barack Obama, to the office of president demonstrates the United States of America is—and will always be—the land of the possible.

To declare that NASCAR is a microcosm of the hope and promise and possibility making this country great can sound like a grand stretch, a proclamation diminishing a noble idea with sugary hyperbole from a PR guy buffing the veneer of a sport that's been pretty good at wrapping itself in the American flag. Maybe I do go over the top here with equal parts enthusiasm and naiveté. But consider this. Hard work, the willingness to put others first and sacrifice for the team, to lay your guts on the line, to prepare and persevere and perform, and to be rewarded for all that, well, those are the wondrous ingredients of the American Dream. And those are the requirements for success in this sport of NASCAR.

Paulie Harraka, a determined, honest, likeable kid whose ancestors checked in at Ellis Island to escape hate and intolerance, a young man quietly carrying his Bible in his backpack, falling asleep while writing term papers on the airplane heading for his next race, is seeking that dream. Paulie's goal happens to be a place on the starting grid at the Daytona 500. Will he attain the dream in full, run the race, finish well, laminate the press clippings, spread them on the dining room table one day for adoring grandchildren? Realistically, it's a long shot. Simple math—thousands of would-be drivers vying for 43 slots—computes to daunting odds. But the better question is: does it really matter? Winding up at the destination you've always dreamed about is one way to measure success. In the grander scheme, though, isn't it the way you approach the journey that counts the most?

Miss Sprint Cup

Anne Marie Rhodes, a.k.a., Miss Sprint Cup, is one of those coltish, charming and courteous girls of Southern stock seemingly bred for a life in NASCAR. Her Uncle Bobby won races in street stocks. Her cousin Rodney Price was the North Carolina state karting champion. Her brother Ryan, helped by Uncle Charles in the pits, would become rookie of the year at Southern National Speedway.

"I've been a race fan since I started breathing," Anne Marie said. "As a child, I can't remember a Sunday when the race wasn't on. Wherever we were, at home or in the car, it was just normal to hear the race. My mom would always make her famous biscuits, or we'd grill out. So now when I'm walking into the track and I smell all the fires and grills, I want to walk over and watch the race with them. That's the way to go—arrive early, set up the RV, grill out, and watch some racing."

Anne Marie's dad and Uncle Charles, the ringleader who scored the tickets and arranged everything, have brought her to NASCAR races for as long as she can remember. But one race stands out. The 1998 Daytona

The moment she spotted Miss Winston in Victory Lane, Anne Marie Rhodes wanted her job. Anne Marie's dream came true when she became Miss Sprint Cup in the 2007 season. *Getty Images for NASCAR*

500, a triumph for the entire sport and a day etched into the memories of millions of NASCAR fans, foreshadowed the future for this talkative girl who loved to sing and dance.

When Dale Earnhardt won the Great American Race after 20 years of futility and heartbreak, "the grandstands just exploded," Rhodes remembered. "I'd never heard anything so loud. Every crew member went out on pit road and saluted Dale. It was incredibly emotional, and the whole track was electric."

As Earnhardt drove his famous black No. 3 Chevy into Victory Lane, Rhodes was there observing the delirious victory celebration The 17-year-old in a Tide racing t-shirt wasn't just watching Earnhardt, even though the members of the Rhodes family were so dedicated to NASCAR, they felt as if a brother were finally enjoying a cruelly elusive career milestone. While relieved fans were soaking in Dale's every expression, amid the Victory Lane scene of unconstrained joy, Anne Marie's eyes were following Miss Winston. With her dazzling smile, bright red uniform, and sleek white boots, the trophy presenter was first to greet the new race champion. As the celebration unfolded, Miss Winston seemed to be enjoying the moment as much as Dale and his team. She was glamorous . . . even drenched with beer. Most important, she was *there* on NASCAR's grandest stage, for the entire world to see.

Anne Marie thought, "Wow! I want to be in there. I want to do that."

And as fate would have it, she would.

Ironically, Miss Winston would be instrumental in Anne Marie's journey to become Miss Sprint Cup. At 15, she was a tall, gangly girl who idolized Dolly Parton and pored through fashion magazines dreaming of a fabulous globe-trotting modeling career. Anne Marie was introduced to Marilyn Green, the proprietor of a nearby modeling agency. Green had been chosen the first Miss Winston when marketing-savvy tobacco company RJ Reynolds became title sponsor to NASCAR's premier series in 1971. The vivacious blonde from a small North Carolina farm went to the local tobacco company's audition as a lark and wound up inventing one of the most recognizable off-the-field icons in professional sports. After a few seasons on the NASCAR Sprint Cup Series circuit, Green left RJ Reynolds and opened her own agency. She met Rhodes and became an instant fan.

"Anne Marie came to the agency when she was 15, and we were taken with her even then," Green said. "A lot of beautiful young women

Back in the day, Anne Marie was a big Darrell Waltrip fan, as evident by her t-shirt at the 1990 Daytona 500. *Courtesy Anne Marie Rhodes*

come to us. Every once in a while we are fortunate to run into special gals. She's one of them."

Anne Marie had braces, but Green knew those weren't forever. She observed an outgoing and determined young girl who'd work hard and make herself a success. Green made an exception and for the first time hired a model whose smile sparkled with dental hardware.

It was the right decision. Anne Marie could befriend a brick wall and was wildly popular with clients. Modeling gigs for Wrangler, High Point–area furniture companies, and sports clients like the PGA tour and the NHRA followed. Anne Marie moved to Los Angeles to continue her career, but a phone call from her "second mother" would beckon her to return to the East Coast. Green served up heart-pumping news. The cell-phone company Sprint, which had replaced Winston as NASCAR's title sponsor, was seeking two young ladies to represent the company to fans.

"Sprint wanted girls who were smart, dependable, honest, and hard working," Green said. Dozens of beautiful young women from all over the country auditioned. Sprint chose two from North Carolina—Anne Marie and Monica Palumbo. "It wasn't about the location in the heart of NASCAR; Sprint just loved their personalities," she said.

The role would be different from the voluptuous Miss Winston persona Green created in an earlier era, embracing beauty queens best remembered for kissing the winning driver in Victory Lane. Today, if Miss Sprint planted a juicy one on a driver, OSHA regulations would likely require precautionary hepatitis shots and a mandatory sexual harassment seminar for anyone in the general vicinity of Victory Lane.

NASCAR's top sponsor has elevated the age-old concept of perky trophy girl greeting the grimy, sweat-stained race winner. Sprint has found a way to place attractive young ladies in Victory Lane as modern brand ambassadors promoting positive messages for young girls and boys. Anne

Marie Rhodes and Monica Palumbo are striking. But physical attributes are the icing, not the cake.

On top of that, Marilyn Green, the first Miss Winston, calls Anne Marie "a real class act—organized, dependable, honest, and hard working. A lot of girls are beautiful but, after their flight is cancelled, wouldn't rent a car and drive hundreds of miles to make the appearance, which is something Anne Marie did."

While most fans recognize Miss Sprint Cup from those raucous, beer-soaked Victory Lane celebrations seen on TV, fans at the track meet an ambassador for Sprint and the entire sport. During race weekend, Rhodes chats with race fans and corporate customers, interviews drivers in the Sprint Experience fan attraction, and provides entertainment at special events. She is a well-versed proponent of Sprint's latest phones and applications. "I like to show off Sprint Cup Mobile, which gives you all the NASCAR information you need right when you need it. If you're unable to watch the race at home, you can have all the stats and the radio broadcast on your handset. I really like that you can also personalize it to your favorite driver. It's such an innovative way for race fans to always stay tuned to their favorite sport. What a cool idea, huh?"

Each race weekend, Miss Sprint Cup will routinely field a few marriage proposals, declining with grace and humor. "Some of it is liquid courage and some I'm not sure!" Rhodes said. (Palumbo joked if she ever seriously considered a proposal, the suitor would have to agree to become "Mr. Sprint.")

Indeed, at the track, love is in the air as much as the smell of burning rubber. At Daytona, a couple showed up unannounced at the Sprint Experience, asking to be married on the stage. Rhodes quickly became a bridesmaid. "One minute I'm onstage throwing out hats, the next I'm in a wedding ceremony," she said.

Some fans come with a heavier heart, and Anne Marie serves more as a psychotherapist and spiritual advisor than Sprint ambassador. At Dover, she spent a half hour with a race fan who had recently lost his wife. "There was no agenda; he just wanted to meet and talk. We spent a half hour together."

A returning solider from Iraq offered her a gold ring and necklace. She initially refused the over-the-top gift. The soldier insisted. Anne Marie was honored to accept his generous offering. Another fan from the

For the best part of Anne Marie's job, she gets to be the first person to greet the winning driver and see the utter jubilation on his face. Here she celebrates with Monica Palumbo and Tony Stewart after Smoke won a cool $1 million at the NASCAR Sprint All-Star Race. *Courtesy Jeff Pohlman*

military, U.S. Army Corporal John Hyland, who was confined to a wheelchair, recounted being badly injured in Iraq by a roadside bomb. "He was saved by a great medic. Four days later, the medic and three of his friends were killed. I listen to these stories of heartbreak and devastation just amazed these heroes want to come to me and share them. It's an honor and really inspiring to meet people like that." (Anne Marie struck up a lasting friendship with Corporal Hyland; she introduced Hyland to me through Facebook, and his story starts on page 49 of this book.)

"I look at my job as a connection between the fans and NASCAR," Rhodes said. "This sport has always been known for having kind-hearted people, and I know the fans appreciate my time. The fans make the sport; they always have and always will. I'm fulfilled to know that for a brief moment I can make someone's day in some small but meaningful way. It's a great way for them to get closer to their favorite sport, and it's great for me because I've always loved meeting new people."

While Miss Winston could have stepped into a photo shoot for a tool calendar, Miss Sprint Cup sports a more sensible black-and-gold driver's suit. The sleek, custom-made uniforms draw a big reaction. "I love the response that we get for the uniforms," Rhodes said. "Everyone loves how bright and beautiful they are. The uniforms are one of a kind for us, so they aren't for sale, although I've pitched the idea. For now, though, just come visit us at the Sprint Experience, and we'll be more than pleased to take a picture with you."

Today, there are more opportunities for NASCAR fans to interact with Miss Sprint compared to Miss Winston. Shannon Wiseman, the final Miss Winston, said, "We got to do some glamorous things like dinners and charity events, but make no mistake, my purpose was to give out cigarettes to drivers and their crews. You could say I closed an era of *smokin'* hot trophy girls."

Even though she gets closer to NASCAR drivers than any fan, Anne Marie is impartial to any individual driver. "I would have to root for Richard Petty, of course, if he ever got back in a car," she joked. "I get butterflies every time I see him. But overall, I'm a fan of the sport. I want to see tough, exciting racing with drivers trading paint."

In a world fraught with doubt and disorder, the track is a familiar, comforting respite for Rhodes. "When my little brother started racing, Uncle Charles was always in the pits helping out. I don't think he ever missed a race of Ryan's. The last time I saw my uncle before he passed away was at a race, wearing the team's No. 83 hat. When I walk down pit road, thoughts flood through me of my childhood, sitting in the stands with my family—everyone cutting up, laughing, and having a good time. Racing just brought us all together. It was some of the best memories of my life with family all together."

Mostly, she loves being where she first saw Miss Winston—in Victory Lane. "You get to see people who have worked their whole lives for that moment. You're looking at their faces at the very moment a dream has become reality. I'll never forget Jimmie Johnson's face when he was holding his third championship trophy, or seeing Dale Jr's smile after winning at Michigan on Father's Day. He was so happy. Nobody was left in the stands. They were going absolutely nuts."

It was just like the day Dale's father finally won the Daytona 500, when Anne Marie Rhodes peered wistfully through an iron gate and wondered what it would be like to have the world's coolest job, in Victory Lane, hosting the best party in the world, scheduled after a long drive every Sunday afternoon, guaranteed.

Author photo

PART IX
I'M A FAN TOO

Most fans can pinpoint the moment of their NASCAR conversion: at their first race, they were baptized in the sights and smells of the track and surrendered to the sport when the pack of cars thundered past the green flag.

I became a fan at the track too, but there wasn't a car in sight. It was the day of my job interview. I'd flown into Daytona Beach and caught this amazing sight, right across the street, a sports shrine I last saw as a kid spanning the globe with ABC's *Wide World of Sports*. I had to see Daytona International Speedway. The interview wasn't for a few hours. I jumped from the rental car and trotted across the grass. It was a weekday afternoon, all quiet. I'll sneak in, I figured. Well, it can get awfully marshy in Central Florida. I looked down and, oh crap, my suit pants were covered with mud.

I ran back to the rental car completely freaking out. I wanted the PR job, but more importantly, I didn't want to look like an idiot. I worked frantically, using tissues, spit, and the floor rugs and upholstery to clean my suit pants and wing tips.

Of course, after I cleaned up and drove away, just around the bend was a giant welcoming sign that said, "TRACK TOURS—ALL DAY TODAY."

After the official tour, the one you get without having to jump a fence, I stepped into the interview. Must have been an important one because two top NASCAR execs were there. They really liked my resume. One of them said, "We're not gonna waste anyone's time going over your past experience. We just need to know one thing: *Do you have the passion to do what it takes to succeed in NASCAR?*"

I looked down at my soiled slacks and crusty shoes, and I said, "Gentlemen, let me tell you the story of a man who flew to Daytona and just had to see the track."

Whether or not I would get this job, it was then I realized I was a fan too. Here are a few of my stories including more wardrobe malfunctions.

My Doctors Only
Want to Talk NASCAR

THE NASCAR SEASON is a traveling circus from February through November. For 10 months, a dedicated group of people pull off a Super Bowl on steroids just about every weekend. Even after the champagne flies to crown a new champion in Miami around Thanksgiving, there will be scant rest for the weary. Each series has awards banquets, and Daytona is looming over everyone's head like a safe dangling on piano wire. Following the longest season in professional sports, the only real vacation for thousands in the NASCAR industry is around Christmas. After that, we all prepare to launch a new season. For my family each year, a late-December respite in Vermont is the much-needed, so-called battery charge.

One particular off-season ski trip was my chance to move beyond "intermediate" skiing. Out on the slopes, the sun was disappearing behind

During an accident-prone, physically trying period, the author's New York doctors weren't interested in discussing jaw-bone grafts, broken collarbones, or ankles. They only wanted to talk about NASCAR. *Courtesy Viviane Giangola*

the formidable mountain. Closing out day one, I'd have four more to distinguish myself and improve my technique.

For the proverbial last run of the day, Viviane and I come across a black diamond called "Superstar." Just seeing that name gets my adrenaline pumping: strong and confident notions of red-white-and-blue achievement, Superman, Wonder Woman, and Mark Spitz and Michael Phelps in their USA Speedos. If my run were televised, Jim McKay would be in a canary yellow blazer describing it.

Viviane is smooth and light on her skis. She describes my style as Jean-Claude Killy on the green bunny runs and Jerry Lewis on the blacks. Today, Jerry is a no-show. I haven't gone down once. The legs feel good. It is time to master the elements, blast past the fat part of the bell curve, and enter the rarified realm of the expert skier. I am a superstar.

I point a pole to the beckoning trail sign. Viviane nods, and a bad idea builds momentum with the trail's steep decline and wind-blown moguls. (Are the scary bumps called "moguls" because they mimic Donald Trump's hair?)

My wife is out in front, finding her way down the difficult slope. I pick up too much speed and try to cut back in a groove between slick moguls, a move that would have looked good on the chalkboard. Too bad we weren't in a classroom but were sliding down an iceberg. My skis hit a rut and pull to the side. My top-heavy body surges in the other direction as if launched from a circus cannon, except my arms aren't stoic at my sides. This is a flailing, out-of-control, agony-of-defeat cartwheel.

Athletes view life at a different speed. NASCAR drivers see crashes happening in slow motion. Wayne Gretzky once explained when he scored a goal, time slowed, and the puck appeared the size of a pizza pie, the goal as wide as the Hoover Dam. None of that here. It is an instantaneous, oh-snap blur, white canvas screaming toward my face. Greg Louganis couldn't have hit the surface at a more precise 90-degree angle. It sounds like chomping a mouthful of Cap'n Crunch. I bounce like a Super Ball. On the second revolution, my head smacks the rock-hard mountain like a bowling ball dropped from a roof. Finally, silence.

It is a sad reflection of our YouTube culture that lying there, thankfully breathing (albeit stunned) and reassured my skull was not split like a rotten pumpkin, I am wondering if anyone on the chair lift captured my spastic circus-act flop. *Please tell me no one camera-phoned this.* I am destined to be an Internet laughingstock. Without royalties.

There were no cameras or giggling. I am alone, in one piece. It can't be that bad. The morning papers said a Manhattan window washer survived a 47-story fall.

All my digits are moving. But as the commercial says, I've fallen, and I can't get up.

That initial crunch wasn't the give of snow. It was something in my shoulder breaking.

My wife kept her wits and balance, and she had pulled to a stop below. The grade is too steep for her to come up. All was OK, no worries, I reassure her with a lefty superstar-like thumbs-up. The covenant of marriage allows making claims to your life partner that you do not believe. She tells passing skiers following her gaze up the mountain, "Oh, he's fine. He's just catching his breath."

All I can do is flash a dumb crooked smile and that thumbs-up with the one working arm.

"Baby, just put your skis on and ski on down!" she urges.

Maybe an expert skier could do that. I'm an eternal intermediate, forever checking that middle box on the rental line, a reckless overachiever who flirted with bragging rights for superstardom beyond his proficiency and paid the price. The run couldn't have been named "Devil's Emergency Room" to scare me away? I try to stand, but the shoulder is shot. I slide on my bottom across the slippery surface, faster and faster down the steep hill. This is not going to end well. I dig boot heels into the ice and lurch to a stop.

The mountain is quiet, save my gasping. I lean on my good shoulder and crawl, inches at a time, across the mountain, toward the woods. Isn't that where animals go to die?

Someone, it's a ski instructor, is waving his poles and shouting down from the lift. "Do you need me to radio for help?"

Up there, I've looked down at the meek humiliation of the daring and the clumsy, those unfortunate injured skiers who are strapped in and carted away on the Red Cross sled. Yeah, call it in. Now I will know how it feels to be present for your own funeral procession. Like driving a stock car at the track in Charlotte, which had a different ending of hearty slaps on the back and a framed photo on fake marble, I can check off another bucket-list experience.

Viviane says they closed Superstar after my crash. Too treacherous; an out-of-control intermediate from the city was nearly killed. My fast-fading manhood was revived. Yes, it was the ferocious mountain, not me. Mother Nature won today's battle, but the war is mine. I am a superstar . . . until I find out Viviane is conjuring a well-meaning fib, something the covenant of marriage allows a married woman with noble intentions to do, but something that contains nary a shred of truth.

The doctor examining me says he'll take x-rays but it looks like a broken collarbone. "What do you do for a living?" he asks rotely, not at all interested.

"I'm with NASCAR." He smiles, makes eye contact for the first time, and asks if Jimmie Johnson is going to win a third championship.

In the mirror, I basically have no right shoulder. The disappearance of a frequently used body part is sickening. My arm is dangling low like an ape's, the shoulder having apparently said, *hasta la vista*. The surrounding skin is already yellowish green. I want to puke.

"This looks pretty bad. Do I need surgery?"

"I don't think so. I want to know this. Earnhardt moving to Hendrick: is that going to change the competitive balance in the sport? I mean, Dale Jr., Gordon, Johnson—that's like a Murderers Row or the Purple People Eaters. What a lineup! They're gonna dominate!"

I start to shiver, slipping into shock maybe. The dull pain is spreading to my chest. I wonder if they'll screw rods into my body like some of the drivers I've talked to, or if I'll be limping around like the Hunchback of NASCAR in New York.

"Do I have to stay in the hospital?"

"We'll fix you up here, and you'll be out in just a few minutes. There's quite a separation in the bone break. You must have hit pretty hard. Hey, I've seen some hard hits in NASCAR this year. I couldn't believe Gordon walked away from that lick in Pocono. How about those HANS devices and new softer walls? They're really making NASCAR much safer."

"This hurts a lot. How long will the pain last?"

"Oh, it's like any bone break. We'll give you some strong medication. Did you know Dale Senior broke his collarbone at Talladega, the car just flipping like crazy, and then he drove the next week with that broken collarbone?"

"Yes, he actually won the pole and the race. Watkins Glen. Road course. Toughest course to drive, I'd imagine, with a painful injury like that. Doctor, I'm on the first day of a five-day vacation. Do I have to go home? We can get back to New York in about five hours."

"It's up to you. Frankly, you'll at first be uncomfortable wherever you are. You can stay in the lodge. Hey, speaking of New York, that track NASCAR was building is not going to happen?"

This dance goes on until the doc gives me a sling and bottle of horse pills. He tells me to see an orthopedic surgeon back in New York. "I'd bet that doctor will want to operate. If I were you, I'd avoid surgery. You could place one end of your collarbone on one side of the room and the other end on the other side, and the bones will find each other. The collarbone is a truly amazing thing. You should be OK in a few months."

HE WAS RIGHT. I GOT BETTER. (The collarbone *can* find anything; too bad it can't go work for the CIA and find Osama bin Laden.) I got back into tip-top shape. But then I gruesomely rolled an ankle at Texas Motor Speedway. What used to be a jutting ankle bone at the bottom of my skinny chicken leg soon resembles the kind of plump tomato my grandmother would have proudly thrown in the pot for Sunday's sauce. You hit 40, and you become spastic. Your body grows hair in odd places and progressively falls apart. TV commercials offer electronic devices to alert the authorities when you become incapacitated. I can accept that. Harder to deal with is how I used to view those who get hurt on business trips as losers. I'm in that club too. Not exactly on the bucket list.

Each NASCAR track has a well-staffed mini-hospital in the infield. It's meant for drivers, not clumsy, aging, accident-prone PR people. I hobble to the infield care center for an ace bandage and a tape job. I am hosting CNBC and the *New York Daily News*, will be on the ankle all day, and need to stabilize it. The Speedway doctor won't tape me without taking x-rays. Sure enough, the tip of the fibia is broken. The doc shows me the film—a chunk the shape of India floating beneath the shin bone. The kind, gentle, and efficient folks at the Texas Motor Speedway Infield Care Center strap on a metal boot, hand me crutches, and suggest I see an orthopedic special-ist back home. "I know," I say. "I bet they'll want to operate."

The busted ankle brings out the best in the service companies. Avis fetches my car at the hotel, no charge. Continental bumps me to first class with curb-to-gate wheelchair service. I make a mental note to fake an injury before future trips. In light of recent events, pretending won't be necessary.

I return to New York to see another doctor. You can guess what happens when he hears I got hurt at a NASCAR race. The orthopedic surgeon at St. Vincent's Hospital in Greenwich Village secretly wishes he were Tony Stewart's jackman:

Clumsy PR Guy: So, it's broken. Bummer. But there's no ligament damage, right?

Doctor: No, none. What amazes me is how fast those drivers go when they are so close to one another. Extraordinary, isn't it.

Clumsy PR Guy: What about the tendons?

Doctor: The tendons are fine. You don't have to worry about that. They say it's the roar of the cars and the whole massive feel of it. You go to a race, and you are just blown away and hooked.

Clumsy PR Guy: I have been elevating the leg and keeping ice on the ankle. How long should I do that?

Doctor: As long as needed. I hear NASCAR is still looking at building a track in the New York area. Jersey? Near the Meadowlands? Out on the Island? No, no, Staten Island. Yes, that's it. Is it true? That would be great. That sport really needs to be here in New York.

Clumsy PR Guy: Unfortunately, there's not enough political support, and that's not gonna work out. Listen, getting back to me and the ankle, I imagine there's some sort of physical therapy ahead?

Doctor: You will absolutely need rehab. We can make a recommendation—plenty of good places. It really seems to be a sport that has caught on like wildfire. I have a friend at ABC who was a big skeptic but is now completely sold on it. They show your races, right?

Clumsy PR Guy: Yes, ABC is a partner, and NASCAR is very popular. I sit at a computer all day. My main exercise is hitting the send button on email. So I like to run at night. When will I be jogging again?

Doctor: Should be a few months. Just between you and me, it gets pretty wild at some of those tracks, huh? What's it like?

Clumsy PR Guy: It's fun. The fans are a riot. I'm writing a book on them. There's a nurse who took the NASCAR flag to the top of Mt. Everest. Another guy walks around at the track naked except for a Goodyear tire and ratty Tom Sawyer straw hat. Come to think of it, he walks a lot, and I'll be walking a lot. I can do that with the cast you'll give me? No crutches?

Doctor: Yes, of course. I don't understand Staten Island. Why didn't they just go buy the land at Grumman airport out on the Island? It's totally available.

This is a top ankle and knee guy in *New York* magazine's list of the city's best doctors. He was in demand and hard to reach. I was able to see him instantly. You see, his assistant was a Sprint phone-carrying NASCAR fan. She saw "NASCAR" on my email requesting an appointment. I was promptly slotted in. Getting my first preference for follow-up appointments was a snap. I just had to answer a few questions about what Dale Jr. was like, and does he really have a girlfriend?

Who says they don't love NASCAR in New York?

Wardrobe Malfunctions

IT'S GRATIFYING TO WORK IN NASCAR, a sport I've grown to love, and still live in New York, the pulsating city I adore and where our corporate marketing office is located.

What I like most about New York is you can order Chinese food at 4 a.m. and have it delivered to your apartment. Not that I've ever ordered General Tsao's Chicken shortly before dawn. But it's important to know I can.

The food always comes on a bicycle. The point being, this is not a city known for its "car culture." Therefore, some have asked, "Why does NASCAR have an office in New York?" The truth is, our Big Apple operations are a vital part of NASCAR. We're on Park Avenue along with the other leagues—the NFL, the NBA, and Major League Baseball. Being stationed in New York means I can't benefit from hallway conversations

---

American icon Richard Petty and author Andrew Giangola before the King threw out the first pitch at Yankee Stadium. *Courtesy Philip Welp*

in Daytona Beach that are a lifeline to what's really going on in the sport. However, from time to time, I do enjoy exposure to our top executives, though it's not always pretty.

Here's what I mean.

Once, I was to accompany NASCAR chairman and CEO Brian France for his induction into the Broadcasting & Cable Hall of Fame. This was a big, deserved honor for Brian—a distinction reserved for the likes of Bob Hope and Uncle Milty.

The role of yours truly was . . . well, I'm not sure. To appear and be present, perhaps. Woody Allen said 90 percent of success in life is showing up, and I have that down cold. Call it Descartian PR: I show up, therefore I am. My job is to appear in my tux and be available and vigilant, to make sure no reporter accosts our chairman with a dopey question. If they do, I'll heroically throw my body in front of the microcassette recorder like a Secret Service agent.

Of course, Brian is a complete pro with the press. He understands there are millions of fans with an insatiable appetite for information, especially how and why decisions are made by him and his leadership team, and he will take the time to explain it to reporters for the benefit of the fans. I would be diving in front of no one.

Actually, I am pretty excited about this prestigious event at Cipriani on 42nd, a splendid, soaring space that feels like a joint from the Gilded Age. They don't build 'em like this any more. The morning of the Hall of Fame induction, I grab my formal wear from the closet, stuff the tux in a garment bag, sling the bag over my shoulder, and head for the subway.

At the office, I hang the bag on the door and start emailing my brains out, which is how each day begins. I spend many hours at the computer, bopping up and down like Billy Preston on the keyboard, madly sending messages as if the balance of world peace and the existence of the planet hinges on my notes. Lunch is usually partaken in front of the screen, crumbs and sauces and dollops of tuna and assorted toppings and condiments inevitably dropping from my mouth because I'm not even tasting the sandwich when ripping off a forceful e-mail. If a member of the night cleaning crew ever turned over the keyboard, enough food would fall out to feed a family of four. I send so many notes (like Pavlov's dog as if he could text, each push of the send button triggering a bath of pleasure-producing dopamine from the brain), you might mistakenly believe I'm paid by the keystroke. It has apparently never dawned on me that the more e-mails sent, the less attention people pay. Of course, as the chairman heads to New York, I am cranking out e-mails at a feverish pace. I lose myself in the digital fervor and wait until the very last minute to put on the formal wear.

I zip open the garment bag and slip on the pants. There is a definite coolness in the room.

Oh, goodness.

The slacks are Swiss cheese.

A moth—or, probably, a large family of moths, moths who didn't watch the video in health class and have reproduced at a fantastic rate—have apparently been feasting on the wool trousers all year long.

Numerous holes aerate the pants, mostly around the crotch. The openings in the fabric range from pinpricks to the size of an Indian-head nickel. There is an additional gash the size of a Susan B. Anthony dollar halfway down the inside of my left thigh. My, oh my. Lordie lord. This would not do.

Brian had landed, and his car had probably left Teterboro, heading for the river tolls right then. You hate to delay the Chairman, but I secretly hoped the driver didn't have an Easy Pass, which would buy me 10 more minutes. As it was, I was supposed to meet Mr. France in 15 outside of Cipriani. It wasn't like I could run to Barney's or even the Men's Wearhouse and pick up formal wear, 42R, at 6:15 p.m. What to do?

Marketing people love to solve problems on the white board—which is like a chalkboard except you feel less grammar schoolteacher-ish and more important by using markers that can be wiped clean with a damp Bounty. The downside is you can't drag your fingernails across the white board to make that stomach-turning screeching sound so much fun for startling guests passing through the hallway. I've never accomplished a single thing with a white board. I ordered one for my office to telegraph professional dedication, an ample workload, and large thoughts. Anyone with a white board must have complicated, important, strategic thoughts. I reckon President Obama has masterful penmanship at the white board.

Aside from impressing people, the white board has never really come in handy. Until now. With my holey pants screaming for a solution, I notice the small metal tray attached to the bottom of the board. A large, fat magic marker is calling, *yoo-hoo, Andrew!* I close the office door, drop my drawers, and madly color my pale, pasty, mid-winter legs a gorgeous shade of black.

The room smells like a printing press—a piercing, oily stench that produces an instant headache. It's an odor that takes men my age back to the printing segment of high school shop class. I pull the pants on. Presto, you can't see the holes.

I walk briskly downtown, passing the Maserati dealership on Park where they are having another cocktail party I wasn't invited to. On the wide sidewalk, folks bark into their cell phones. Others power on, heads down, New Yorkers on a mission rushing to trains, dinners, mistresses, psychotherapy, wherever. Indifferent to me, that's for sure and that is wonderful. My paranoia is slowly diffusing like air leaking from an old tire. No one notices this curly-haired gent dressed like a four-star waiter except for ridiculous Swiss cheese pants barely covering industrial-ink-slathered legs. Maybe in younger days, when my wife claimed I looked like Richard Gere, before the ravages of time and gravity and pepperoni pizza and bus fumes and city living and the toxic lower Manhattan post-9/11 air slowly began decimating me, someone might have glanced at my crotch, where the holes are biggest. Those days are gone. That's good tonight, depressing beyond.

Before Brian arrives, I make it to Cipriani, the marvelous high-ceilinged, Italian Renaissance-inspired, Roman-columned former bank. We meet up and find our numbered table, which is a huge relief because I never can manage that very well. Brian is formally entered into the Hall of Fame and, without any notes, gives a very nice, humble speech, acknowledging his granddad, who founded the sport, and then his dad, who took over for more than 30 years before passing the torch to him. The reporters leave us alone. The table wine is even decent, which may explain why the media is at bay. I am in holey pants at a high-class event, hobnobbing with captains of industry. There is a rank smell of freshly printed newspaper in the air, but no one seems to notice.

Except, the next morning when I wake up in my tighty whities.

Hal, our Pomeranian, spots me. He peers at my big, black legs. The fur above his eyes lift quizzically. He tilts his head in unmistakable canine body language, saying, *ARE YOU FRIGGIN' KIDDING ME?* Hal starts barking like the chuck wagon just zipped by. He just goes bonkers. I try to quiet and soothe the crazy Pomeranian. My efforts yield no results. There is just no stopping a young dog who has seen something this utterly disturbing.

When not wearing formal wear doubling as dinner for the moths, I'm usually in a NASCAR-logoed shirt, which makes me the butt of office jokes but speeds each morning's clothes-selection process while kick-starting conversations about the sport among strangers on the way to work. New York is not known for its closet space, but there are more closet fans than you can imagine here.

One occasion when I wasn't wearing the NASCAR shirt was Halloween, and Viviane and I were about to go for a drive. I had to retrieve the car parked a few miles uptown at the only lot we can afford. It was quite warm for that time of year, just a beautiful, balmy late-October day. It was the kind of day where you don't feel the weather—neither hot nor cold, just your skin and the air, blending in harmony. Quiet anticipation was growing as the city got ready for the famed Halloween parade in Greenwich Village. I decided I wanted to run to the car and would pass through the Village to see how the preparations were faring.

I couldn't find anything "summery" to wear except tight, silky shorts. Hadn't worn them in a while. Short shorts, maybe once in style in the 1970s. They were small. Bobby Brady could have fit in them. Actually, I'm not sure when exactly they'd have been in style.

I wanted to get moving, and the tiny, shiny, satiny shorts were in my drawer. I put them on with, for unknown reasons, tube socks. Wore those tube socks nice and high. Found a tank top, too tight as well. My hair was really bushy at the time.

Sixth Avenue was closed. New Yorkers were three deep behind the police horse barricades, waiting for the famed Halloween parade. I decided to run up Sixth—an infrequent chance to jog an empty Manhattan avenue during daylight.

As I was running past the crowds, hogging open pavement usually clogged by vehicles, checking out the costumes, enjoying life, a young girl from behind the barricades squealed, "OH MI-GOD! LOOK! HE'S GOING AS RICHARD SIMMONS!"

A Fact Check with Peter Jennings

WHEN DID HUMANS START ASKING neighbors what they did for a living? Thousands of years ago, that question must have led to a pretty boring conversation. *Homo erectus* all had the same job—hunter-gathers. They must have had awfully dull cocktail parties before the invention of movies and the stock market, nothing to grunt about except how tough things were in the hunter-gatherer business.

I don't go to many cocktail parties, but I still get the "what do you do?" question, whether in line at the DMV or the dry cleaners.

Those hearing I'm with NASCAR (if they don't already make the connection in seeing the ubiquitous logo'd shirt) automatically assume an expansive knowledge of automobiles. I catch them glancing at my fingernails, as if checking for grease from Dale Jr.'s car. They ask how to get better fuel mileage. Take the subway, I say.

I'm a New Yorker who in the morning rummages for his MetroCard rather than his car keys. This places me at a slight disadvantage for a job in racing. I'm about as familiar with the inner workings of an automobile as you are with the engine room of a nuclear submarine. Working at a gas station during college, I pumped fuel into a truck's oil intake. In

Getty Images for NASCAR

290

those days, I thought a Volvo was part of the female anatomy. I got a flat heading outbound on the Throgs Neck Bridge. I feverishly changed the tire, and the new one went down before we got to the Bronx. I'd put the spare on *backward*.

Seriously, frighteningly, laughably clueless about cars, I joined NASCAR midway through the 2003 season. My first race weekend was Talladega. I heard that was the best place to catch the draft, so I brought a blazer. News you can use: Don't walk the infield in a blazer and loafers. Let's just say you won't fit in, and the fans will have a lot of fun letting you know. The next day, I ditched the blazer for black Dockers and a black shirt. From atop his converted bus, a fan dressed in nothing but jean shorts shouted at me, "When are the aliens landing?"

You know things are way off kilter when guys in jorts (that's "jean shorts" to those yet to attend a race in the summer) are loudly criticizing your clothes.

At Talladega and other tracks, I learned not to go as the "man in black" and gleaned other pointers for avoiding unnecessary ridicule. For my first visit to the infield of Michigan International Speedway, I happily donned my "rookie stripe." Just as rookie NASCAR Sprint Cup Series drivers have a yellow stripe on their back bumpers, "First Timers" in the infield are required to affix bright-yellow police-line tape to their bodies. Wearing this tape that screams "CAUTION" puts other fans on alert. For me, it mostly meant I had to run errands for the infield veterans. It was an interesting experience, and I performed my duties with haste and good humor when summoned by the repeated shouts of "Hey rookie, get me a beer!" from the roofs of many a hauler. Not once did I secretly shake the can before tossing it to the thirsty fan above. I swear.

Joining the sport midseason, I still hadn't been to "the granddaddy of racing," the Daytona 500. As my first series-opener approached, I remained a fish out of water, a city boy taking the subway to a glass skyscraper where I'd incongruously promote stock car racing. I couldn't describe the difference between "loose" and "tight," two oft-used terms characterizing the car's on-track grip. Given the heavy, cakey food in the tracks' media centers—picture a *Top Chef* cook off with the signature ingredients of chili, wings, and Crisco—I recognized one thing that was tight rather than loose: the pants around my expanding waist. Another thing I observed growing bigger and bigger: this sport.

Case in point: *ABC World News Tonight* was preparing a story on NASCAR fans' reaction to "The Chase," the sport's new playoff system. You gotta love the broadcast guys, learning something new every 15 minutes, from starvation in Africa to a dirty bomb scare in New York, then on to NASCAR Nation. All in 22 short minutes with a few words from our sponsor, followed by *Access Hollywood*, *Desperate Housewives*, and your local news.

My memory usually stinks. I blame it on all the glue inhaled as a kid. (It was legitimate, Testor's glue; I was making model airplanes.) But I so clearly remember this impromptu conference call with ABC and the NASCAR research team in Charlotte. On the fly, we were trying to educate time-pressed network news guys on the sport's growth. *Yep, more than 70 million fans supporting the sponsors, voting with their wallets, that's one in three American adults who are fans, 40 percent women, do the math, about 30 million female fans, and the number-two sport on TV to boot . . . oh yeah, a higher regular-season rating than baseball, good sport, slept in Mets pajamas as a kid, lotta heartbreak that makes you stronger, too bad about all the juiced players nowadays, not a problem for us (knock on wood), steroids don't help anyone go any faster in a stock car. . . .*

On we went, modern-day carnival barkers hawking viewership numbers instead of bearded dwarfs.

Then, a familiar baritone voice boomed over the speakerphone, and I glanced over my shoulder to see if the TV was on.

"Hi, it's Peter Jennings," the voice jumped from the box.

He'd been eavesdropping. Decent man, that Jennings, identifying himself instead of playing with us and *then* revealing himself to be the ABC anchor.

"I wanted to see if NASCAR PR is shaking off the rust," he said. "You did great in snowing my producers with those fictitious stats. Seriously, you guys are on your game, which is impressive before your season has even started."

Those accolades felt good, coming from the smooth and sophisticated anchor that had reported from the rice fields of Vietnam and talked America through the *Challenger* explosion and, later, the terrorist attacks on New York. In an instant, my feelings toward Jennings warmed. You see, in the suspicious days following 9/11, aware of his left-of-center reports critical of the "you're with us or against us stance" taken by the good old

U.S. of A., I was aggressively watching *ABC News* with fists clenched in the blind patriotic rage of a father whose first grader was walking to school two blocks from where the first plane hit and whose apartment building roof in lower Manhattan had been checked for body parts after the attacks. I wasn't a big fan of the Canadian anchor being so hard on a country wantonly attacked in, get this, the name of religion. But now, hearing Jennings talk racing, his skepticism about U.S. policies was forgiven. Time had tempered my rage, and for all I cared Peter could have been wearing an "I ♥ the Blind Sheik" tee under his blue blazer, so long as he stayed fascinated with our sport's growth, and said so on air—and isn't it truly amazing how big this NASCAR phenomena has become, he was telling us.

I'd actually met Jennings years before in the 1980s, as a naïve young radio magazine editor attending a rubber chicken lunch at a New York hotel. It was a forgettable awards ceremony in one of those grand ballrooms filled with ancient, stooped, hairy-eared waiters who've been gruffly shoveling chicken breasts and asparagus spears onto heavy plates for decades. The chicken looked like you could play kickball with it, so I wandered backstage, and there, made for his suit, was Peter Jennings, big anchor on campus, part news man, part 007 agent, drinking liquor on ice and sucking a cigarette before hitting the panel. I sat next to Jennings and ordered a bloody mary.

That was 20 years ago when a cocktail at lunch was considered part of an honest day's work. No way to bring up that lunch on the phone, but I did mention that NASCAR's weekly series was racing in his native Canada. Jennings was aware and happy to see the sanctioning body investing in stock car racing north of the border. "They're just as passionate for fast cars up in Canada as in the Carolinas," he said. I was impressed Jennings correctly called NASCAR a "sanctioning body."

We talked aimlessly about motorsports for a few more minutes, and as abruptly as he had appeared, Peter Jennings dropped from the call, and, you could say, our lives. There were breaking details on the dirty bomb scare in New York. Beyond our crowded, anxious island, it had been a week of deadly insurgent bombings, and the wires were reporting the explosion of another roadside device in Iraq. I reckon talking racing was a very nice break for Peter Jennings, legendary newsman and NASCAR sophisticate, before he went back to chronicling a world wobbling on its axis, the center no longer holding quite so steady.

EPILOGUE
A MATTER OF LIFE AND DEATH

MAYBE IT'S THE MANY HOURS they spend huddled around campfires. Or maybe it's because so many of them enjoy fishing, and we know how fishermen exaggerate. The wealth of priceless raw material available—the daily soap opera in the garage, the late-night revelry in the campgrounds—certainly contributes to it. Whatever the reasons, NASCAR fans have amazing stories to tell about other fans. Though there are some bona-fide whoppers.

In sifting through tales of out-of-the-ordinary NASCAR fandom, it's difficult to separate historical truth from possible urban—or, in this case, shall we say "rural"—legend. It's fitting the most fantastic story I've come across, which several high-placed industry sources confirm to be true, originates at Talladega Superspeedway, the track known for the highest speeds, most spectacular wrecks, and biggest, rowdiest fan parties.

Talladega is NASCAR's largest track, a 2.66-mile tri-oval ringing a large, raucous infield. Tens of thousands of fans come to 'Dega in RVs, campers and converted school buses, often arriving at the track days before the race and, once there, flying their flags proudly. In fact, when fans set up camp in the infield, the first task is to mark their turf and announce an allegiance by raising their NASCAR flags.

At one NASCAR Sprint Cup Series race at Talladega not too many years ago, a fan was raising the banners of Dale Earnhardt Jr. and, of course, his dad, the late, great Dale Sr.—the ubiquitous menacing black No. 3, a flapping pennant seen at this track and wherever the circuit visits, then and always. This particular fan happened to be performing this flag-raising ritual during one of the fierce storms that will, with little warning, tear across the Alabama countryside. This time, the rain and winds were no surprise. The fan saw the sky darken and greenish-black clouds gathering wrath in the distance, low, fast, and fierce like the flyover to come on Sunday. He'd be damned if a little weather was going to prevent the flags of the Earnhardts, NASCAR, and America from going up before the cars hit the track for qualifying. In the driving rain, the fan was securing his metal flagpole. An apocalyptic crack of thunder, as loud as if the sky had split apart, erupted. It came with a brilliant flash of blue-white light. The searing bolt of electricity beamed into the flagpole.

Even a mild lightning strike generates nearly a billion volts of juice. This unlucky fellow holding the pole was instantly fried to death by the sizzling laser. His buddies inside the camper heard the thunderclap and a thud—the body hitting the ground. They ran outside to discover their burnt and lifeless friend. They waited out the storm, and following a brief discussion featuring mild dissent quickly dismissed, the group made an improbable decision: to dig a shallow grave there in the infield and continue their race weekend plans. After all, "it's what he would have wanted," they agreed. One may have mumbled a joke about it being the NASCAR version of the movie, *Weekend at Bernie's*. Since none of the crew had any special religious convictions, did it really harm anyone, including the deceased fellow's family, to delay a funeral anyway? Their friend was horribly, tragically, irreversibly dead. Nothing would change that. You can book a church and call in flowers and cold cuts anytime in modern-day America. After the race, they'd take care of grim details no one wanted to think about just yet. Until then, a race was to be run.

The weather cleared. A southern belle proudly belted out the national anthem with fans proudly at attention, hands over hearts and then lifted to the sky cheering military jets screeching past. Gentlemen started their engines. The pack of 43 cars freight-trained around the track. There was the requisite big wreck. And one happy driver surged first to the checkered flag.

And then, after the last bottle of champagne was sprayed in a banshee Victory Lane celebration, a few hundred yards away, the boys dug up and cleaned off their friend. They solemnly reported the death to local authorities. Not many questions were asked. An open-and-shut case of death by lightning strike. No one's ever charged Mother Nature with murder. Tough to prosecute that one. The boys lowered their flags and drove home with a little more room in the pickup truck than when they arrived a few days earlier.

AFTERWORD
BY KYLE BUSCH

RALPH WALDO EMERSON ONCE SAID, "A man is what he thinks about all day long."

I'll be honest, like some fans you've read about, I think about racing just about every minute of the day. My own concerns are: How can I make my car faster? What could I have done different

Courtesy M&Ms

in last week's race? What will I do in a certain situation next week?

I'm a race car driver, plain and simple. In 2008, NASCAR conducted 96 races in its top three divisions. I competed in 84 of them, meaning I drove in nearly 88 percent of the races in the NASCAR Sprint Cup, NASCAR Nationwide, and NASCAR Camping World Truck Series. And believe me, if I could have raced in the other dozen on the schedule, I would have.

Why do I do it? Well, I like competition, and I like winning trophies.

But one other reason stands out more than any other. Racing is fun. The thrill of driving a car (or truck) nearly 200 miles per hour against some of the best drivers in the world is a blast. You never know what's going to happen from one second to the next, and every race, every track, and every series presents a different challenge.

When I'm fortunate enough to win, there's no better feeling than hearing the cheers from the grandstand, pulling into Victory Lane, getting showered with confetti, and accepting that trophy. It's the ultimate high—not only for me but for my crew and my sponsors.

Some fans may not know my racing isn't limited to large race tracks or NASCAR's top three divisions. I have a blast racing my dune buggies in the Nevada desert, racing radio-controlled cars against my friends, or running for the Late Model team that I own.

And you know what? I'm just as competitive in the desert or on a computer as at a place like Bristol Motor Speedway with over 150,000 fans watching. I hate losing in any type of racing. When I don't win, I spend a lot of time thinking about what I did wrong and how to correct it for next time.

Finishing fifth in a "10th-place car" doesn't frustrate me nearly as much as finishing second in a car I know could have been first. If I lead 90 percent of the laps in a race but don't get the trophy, that's as frustrating as it gets. Everyone can see it eats at me. I don't hide those emotions very well, but that's what fans can see in our sport that they don't get anywhere else.

Racing is an extremely emotional sport, and I try to remind myself it's supposed to be fun. Not just for me but for the crew, the sponsors, and, most importantly, the fans. While there's nothing personally more gratifying than winning, it's very important for me to know the fans are having fun. I don't care if you're cheering for me or booing me—and I do get my share of so-called Bronx cheers—I want you to have a great time at the track or wherever you're watching. Fans deserve it: sacrificing so much, spending your hard-earned money, braving the elements, and letting me know in your own special way how much you pull for me. Sure, some have a different way of signaling to me I'm number one, but at the end of the day, I appreciate them too.

The fans really make my job enjoyable. Just play back in your head Carl Edwards and me battling for the win in the 2008 August Bristol race. But instead of over 150,000 people in the stands, there are 16. I can assure you, Carl and I would have been driving just as hard, but it wouldn't be nearly as much fun without the fans cheering (and booing). I wasn't a happy camper after that race, but that's why fans watch, to see what's going to happen next, especially in a classic duel like that.

There aren't a lot of secrets in NASCAR. The media coverage is intense, and fans assume they know all the drivers pretty well. But I believe a lot of fans don't know this about me: You and I are similar in a lot of ways.

NASCAR fans love to sit around and talk about past races, debate about who the best driver of all time is, or who was at fault for an accident. Well, my friends and I do the same thing.

NASCAR fans work all week long and can't wait for the green flag to drop on Sunday afternoon. I'm the same way, working with my crew all week, eager for the green flag to drop on Sunday afternoon. The only difference is, I've got a steering wheel in my hands.

Fans follow NASCAR for the competition and excitement, but they follow most of all because it's a heck of a good time. (Yeah, it's definitely true, "the weekend starts on Wednesday.") I'm in the sport for the exact same reasons—the competition and the excitement, but most of all because it's fun.

Some of us are in the grandstands and others are in the driver's seat, but we are all having the time of our lives.

And isn't that what's most important?

—Kyle Busch
Hackettstown, New Jersey
August 2009

Acknowledgments

NASCAR FAN JUDY BARR said to me, "If I had your job, I'd be all black and blue from pinching myself to see if I was dreaming." Another fan, Mike Wright, sends post-race emails addressing me, "Dear Lucky Dog."

Indeed, I am fortunate to be part of an organization run by smart and dedicated people not afraid to take chances. I don't know of another sport that has told the stories of its fans . . . or has let one of its employees do so in his own voice. I want to thank NASCAR executives Brian France, Jim Hunter, Paul Brooks, Steve Phelps, Paula Miller, Jim O'Connell, Brad Ball, Jay Abraham, Ramsey Poston, and Norris Scott for supporting this unique endeavor.

When I first suggested a book celebrating NASCAR fans to Jim Hunter—who runs public relations for NASCAR with equal measures of plain-spoken counsel and country wit—without hesitation, he said, "An-*droooo*, that's the kind of book Bill Junior would love!" Jim, I hope Mr. France would have been proud of these pages.

As part of my "new hire" orientation, I went to the scoring tower and heard the cars referred to as "the number 24" and "the number 17" rather than "the cars being driven by Jeff Gordon and Matt Kenseth." To be impartial, NASCAR sees inanimate numbers, not individual drivers. NASCAR employees, I learned, are supposed to treat the drivers the same way . . . as you'd act toward your own children, in a manner of speaking, equally and without prejudice. However, Tony Stewart, I must say you stand out as one special dude, even when opposite the sanctioning body on a hot issue. Your candid swagger is a virtue, and your driving is a joy to watch. Thank you for all you do for the sport and especially for contributing the foreword for this book.

Equally, Kyle Busch brings so much to NASCAR, including headlines and highlights, which all of us, particularly those in PR, greatly appreciate. Kyle also voiced a terrific afterword. No boos here. Thank you very much, Kyle.

I am grateful to my agent Amanda Mecke, who believed in me and these stories from the get-go and made many valuable suggestions while providing rock-solid support during a path to publication that in its twists and turns resembled Infineon Raceway. I also want to thank Catherine McNeill of NASCAR Licensing for her support and good cheer throughout the publishing process and John Farrell for his eagle-eye fact check.

My even-keeled editor, Chris Endres at Motorbooks International (MBI), grasped the potential of this unique project from our first conversation and spent considerable time giving spot-on advice and helping shape it into the product in your hands. In addition to Chris, I also benefited from a solid team behind me at MBI, including Zack Miller, Kevin Hamric, and Nichole Schiele, who took a chance on a quiet, humble (ahem), first-time author and put in a lot of time and effort to support him.

I am indebted to Lou Garate, F.L.G., of NASCAR's New York office who on a lark spouted the words that became this book's title and reminds me of the incident regularly. *Gracias, mi amigo.* In this same office, Matt Shulman, Mike Kozak, Matt Moran, Leah Workneh, Virginia Foxton, Dana Lent, Genelle Drayton Lisa Banbury, Sean Downes, and Kyra Safronoff provided a slew of creative marketing ideas and have my gratitude.

Many individuals with teams, tracks, sponsors, agencies, the media, and NASCAR provided terrific leads and valued support for compiling these stories, including: Nicole Anastasi, Taylor; Judy Barr, the University of South Carolina; Dick Berggren; Tim Black, Alison Public Relations; Zak Brown and Evan Frankel, Just Marketing International; Rob Bronfeld, Dana Landry, and Andy Burch at Catalyst Public Relations; Paul Corliss, Phoenix International Raceway; Roger Curtis and Sammie Lukaskiewicz, Michigan International Speedway; Michael Drucker, Delusions International; fans/unofficial editors Molly Choi and Mary Jane Renza; Det. Bill Martino, NYPD; Scott Cooper, Lowe's Motor Speedway; Matt Crossman, the Sporting News; Judy Diethelm, Blu Moon Group; Diane Driscoll and Janet Risner, NASCAR; Jesse Essex, Hendrick Motor Sports; Jerry Gleason, Weber Shandwick; Phil Grieco and Ryan Bowling,

Mars, Inc.; Andy Hall, ESPN; Paul Harraka Sr.; Jake Harris, Darlington Raceway; Bill Janitz, TrueSpeed Communications; Erica Johnson, Crown Royal; Heather Kincel, Elevation Motorsports; Rob Kinker, Bulldawg Marketing; Mindy Kramer, Heidi Fuchs, and Jeff Owen, Office Depot; Melissa Ludlum, NBC; Kimberly Meesters, Sprint; Debby Robinson, Victory Management; Lenny Santiago, ISC; Max Siegel, the 909 Group; David Sartory, Paramount; Kevin Triplett and Lori Worley, Bristol Motor Speedway; Mike Zizzo, Texas Motor Speedway; and Gillian Zucker, Auto Club Speedway.

Special thanks to Dave Nesi, Lee Reeves, Ryan Miles, and Jeff Pohlman for your quality photographs, and to sportswriter and space nut Rick Houston for graciously sharing your interview with Lt. Col. Doug Hurley, maximizing our time as Doug got ready to blast toward the heavens on the Space Shuttle *Endeavour*.

I want to extend my appreciation to NASCAR's Brad Klein for his fast and efficient daily support, always with a positive attitude. You rock, Brad.

They say, "You never hear of people on their death beds regretting not working more during their lives." Unfortunately, at that time, I'll probably be on my Blackberry. My family deserves special recognition during this project. To my wife, Viviane, you continue to awaken me. Thank you for your bottomless well of patience and good cheer in enduring the life of a writer's widow on many nights and weekends with our dear daughter, Gaby. And G, I can't tell you how much I appreciate your refreshing, bracing humor, like when I returned from a week in Daytona Beach, poked my head in your room, and asked, "How were things while I was away?" and you responded, "You were gone?" I know your first book will be a better read than mine, and I'm completely OK with that.

Each and every fan profiled in these pages has my heartfelt gratitude. You welcomed me into your busy lives, cheerfully answering oddball questions, allowing me to be the proverbial fly on the wall in your kitchens and campers, and never swatting me away. Most of all, thank you for your friendship and your continuing support of NASCAR.

You truly make the sport go.

Index

12 Hours of Sebring, 83

All-American Speedway, 263
Allison
  Bobby, 10, 19, 29, 33, 47,
    252
  Davey, 186, 209
  Donnie, 252
Arning, Mike, 106
Auto Club Speedway, 33,
  124–126, 128, 191,
  222–225

Baja 500, 83
Baker, Buddy, 187
Ball, Brad, 212
Bank of America 500, 207
Barr, Judy, 141
Barzun, Jacques, 240
Batali, Mario, 176–182
Belleville High Banks, 99
Benson, Johnny, 117
Bickford, Carol, 116
Bodine, Todd, 57
Bonnett, Neil, 31, 32
Bookie, John, 161–163
Botts, Julie and Rob, 90
Bradley, Connie and Jordyn,
  129–133
Bradley, Ron, 129, 130
Bristol Motor Speedway, 34,
  39, 48, 69, 87, 110, 132,
  133, 216, 253, 297
Brown, Wally, 267
Bruckheimer, Jerry, 191
Burton, Jeff, 81, 84, 92–94, 201
Burton, Ward, 130
Busch, Kyle, 9, 15, 24, 78,
  79–82, 85, 86, 88, 89, 103,
  200, 202, 203, 296–298
Byron, Red, 19

Cary, Misty, 207
Catalano, Julie, 227–232
Cattanach, Kyle, 207, 208
Champion Motor Speedway,
  99, 101
Charlotte Motor Speedway, 39,
  74, 88, 141, 216
Chevy Rock and Roll 400, 105
Chicagoland Speedway, 84, 143
Childress, Richard, 95
Chili Bowl, 100
Chitwood, Joie, 57
Citrano, Steve, 69
Coca-Cola 600, 31, 39, 54,
  195, 198
Collier, Ron, 22
Conway, Danny, 171
Cooley, Jack, 94, 95
Cooley, Kathryn, 92–95
Costner, Kevin, 13, 209–213
Cramer, Jim, 197–203
Cruise, Connor, 188, 191
Cruise, Tom, 13, 19, 20,
  183–191
Cupp, S. E., 221, 240–245
Curtis, Roger, 131, 133,
  158–160

Dalton, Kristen, 192–196
Damron, Mike, 48
Dan Lowry 400, 74, 75
Darlington Raceway, 30, 33,
  36–39, 141, 187, 252
Dash, Jeff, 224–226
Daugherty, Brad, 248–254
Davis, Sherri, 171
Daytona 500, 18–25, 28, 33,
  34, 42–44, 46, 58, 59, 100,
  113, 130, 133, 144, 165,
  167, 180, 185, 209, 251,
  252, 255, 261, 264, 267,

269–273, 275, 291
Daytona International
  Speedway, 18, 20, 22, 44,
  68, 69, 93, 95, 169, 173,
  189, 191, 213, 236, 264,
  266
Deuker, Christine and Steve,
  109–114
DeWitt, L. G., 23
Dickies 500, 233
Dietl, Richard "Bo," 206
Dixon, Scott, 266
Dorton, Randy, 84, 85
Dover International Speedway,
  36, 39, 87, 95, 136, 178,
  179, 273
Dupri, Jermaine, 217–219
Dupuis, Jody, 170–173
Duvall, Robert, 119, 185, 187

Eagle Raceway, 260
Earnhardt, Dale Jr., 13, 19,
  46, 48, 80, 81, 86, 88, 115,
  123–128, 136, 137, 156,
  162, 163, 166, 169, 171,
  173, 186, 188, 201, 228,
  232, 241, 247, 249, 250,
  275, 281, 284, 290, 294,
  295
Earnhardt, Dale Sr., 9, 13,
  24, 41–46, 48–50, 56–60,
  67–69, 80, 126. 136, 147,
  154, 164–168, 173, 218,
  271, 281, 294, 295
Edwards, Carl, 89, 157, 181,
  182, 201, 218, 227–232,
  237, 297
Egan, Sean, 138
Eichler, Ryan, 79–86
Eldora Speedway, 10
Epton, Juanita, 21, 22

Erickson, Murray, 96–101
Evergreen Speedway, 260

Fernandez, Stefania, 196
Ferrell, Will, 67
Ferrin, Byron, 231, 232
Firecracker 400
Fish, Jamie, 121
Fisher, Sarah, 266
Fittipaldi, Emerson, 90
Fleming, Alec, 171
Flemington Speedway, 59, 265
Flock, Fonte, 37
Ford 400, 115
France
    Annie B., 22
    Betty Jane, 22
    Bill Jr., 9, 205
    Bill Sr., 22, 210, 213
    Brian, 212, 213, 286, 288
Friedman, Russ, 14, 71–79

Gallatin International
    Speedway, 60
Gant, Harry, 253
Geary, Julie, 135, 164–169
Geary, Russ, 164–169
Glauch, Erin, 156
Gordon, Jeff, 9, 19, 73, 80,
    84, 88, 89, 115–122, 126,
    130, 136–138, 140–142,
    161–163, 167, 169, 173,
    186, 255, 256, 260, 281
Green, Marilyn, 271–273
Gregory, Kenny, 87–91
Gregware, Philip and
    Georgia, 106
Grogan, Jon, 171
Gutfield, Greg, 245

Harraka, Paul Sr., 262–264
Harraka, Paulie, 261–269
Harvick, Kevin, 92, 101
Hastings
    Arvil, 119
    Carolyn, 115–122
    Tracy, 115
Hege, Jack, 18–25
Held, Joseph, 109
Helton, Mike, 19, 141
Hendrick, Rick, 50, 53–55,
    84, 85, 184–187, 189–191
Henry, Elizabeth, 138
Hickey, Carol, 140
Hickey, Patrick, 14, 136–142

Hoenstine, Jack, 36–39
Holley, Harold, 155
Homestead-Miami Speedway,
    173, 248, 253
Horner, Jim, 15
Horner, Norma, 14, 15
Hurley, Doug, 14, 143–147
Hussein, Saddam, 57
Hyde, Harry, 185, 188, 191
Hyland, Erica, 51
Hyland, John, 14, 49–55, 274

Indianapolis 500, 84, 132, 231
IndyCar Series, 126
Infineon Raceway, 116, 117
Ingram, Jack, 252
Irelan, Jen, 156, 159
Irvan, Ernie, 106
Irwin, Kenny, 147

Jennings, Peter, 290–293
Joel, Billy, 212
Johnson, Jimmie, 9, 74, 84,
    85, 88, 107, 108, 117, 122,
    126, 178, 191, 237, 254,
    275, 281
Johnson, Junior, 33, 216, 218,
    253

Kahne, Kasey, 9, 84, 88, 171,
    196
Kansas Speedway, 231
Kavka, Christine, 161–163
Kelley, Winston, 112
Kenseth, Kelley, 133
Kenseth, Matt, 9, 89, 129–133
Kent, Debbie, 151, 152
Kent, Kevin, 148–153
Keselowski, Brad, 201–203
Kidman, Nicole, 189
Knaus, Chad, 74, 117, 178,
    237
Knighton, Lily, 171
Knoxville Raceway, 260
Kramer, Mindy, 131, 133
Krupinski, Marty, 83
Kulwicki, Alan, 145

Labonte, Bobby, 32, 181
Leslie-Pelecky, Diandra, 14,
    233–239
LeTarte, Steve, 117
Loder, Quinton, 171
Logano, Joey, 101, 143, 145,
    146, 195
Love, Tim, 180–182

Lowe's Motor Speedway, 49,
    194, 195, 197, 198, 203,
    208, 210, 244
Lowry, Pat, 203

MacNicol
    Bruce, 66, 69, 70
    Chris, 64–70
    Tonya, 66, 67, 70
MacRenolds, Larry, 44
Marlin, Coo Coo, 37
Martin
    Dianne, 206
    George, 204–208
    Mark, 9, 73, 80, 167, 218,
        224, 228
    Teresa, 208
Martinsville Speedway, 23, 32,
    87, 187
Mauldin, Lightning, 214–216
Mauldin, Michael, 214–219
McMurray, Jamie, 72, 75, 77,
    92, 101, 265
Melo, Marty, 208
Meyers, Jimmy, 21
Michigan International
    Speedway, 84, 129, 131,
    133, 149, 155, 158, 291
Miller, Booker and Juanita,
    43, 44, 46, 48
Miller, Wessa, 42–48
Miyata, Tava and Wayne,
    222–226
Monahan, Pete, 156
Montoya, Juan Pablo,
    180–182
Murphy, Ron, 14

NASCAR
    Busch Series, 185
    Camping World Truck
        Series, 117, 207, 237,
        261, 267, 296
    Grand National Division,
        28, 99
    Nationwide Series, 84, 88,
        129, 145, 201, 207,
        252, 268, 296
    Nextel Cup Series, 138
    Sprint All-Star Race, 88
    Sprint Cup Series, 10, 18,
        33, 41, 75, 79, 84, 85,
        92, 95, 98–100, 106,
        117, 141, 144, 145,
        153, 158, 161, 172,
        178, 186, 190, 207,

225, 227, 233–235,
248, 252, 264–267,
271, 291, 294, 296
Whelen All-American
Series, 258, 260, 264
Winston Cup, 253
Nashville Superspeedway, 88
Nave, Kristin, 138
Nemechek, Joe, 65, 68
New Hampshire Motor
Speedway, 172, 179
Newman
Krissie, 111, 113
Paul, 184, 185
Ryan, 9, 109–114, 208
North Wilkesboro Speedway,
23, 33

Obama, Barrack, 57, 253, 269

Paltrow, Gwyneth, 178
Palumbo, Monica, 272–274
Panch, Marvin, 37
Parks, Raymond, 19, 24
Parks, Violet, 19
Parrott, Brad and Todd, 155
Parsons, Benny, 68, 187
Patrick, Danica, 259, 260
Pearson, David, 10, 33, 252
Pepsi 400, 165
Petty
Adam, 147
Kyle, 189, 247
Lee, 19, 28, 216
Richard, 10, 26–29, 33–35,
37, 38, 41, 58, 80, 93,
98, 209, 212, 216, 218,
248, 250–252, 275, 285
Phoenix International Raceway,
204, 207
Pocono Raceway, 11, 13, 39,
81, 82, 87, 88, 91, 173, 179,
187, 202, 245, 281
Poole, David, 46–48
Poole, Katy, 46
Pressley, Robert, 252
Printup, Michael, 160
Punch, Jerry, 184, 187, 188, 190

Quaid, Randy, 185

Ragan, David, 194, 196
Ray, Rachael, 176–178
Reagan, Ronald, 93
Reda, Craig, 136, 154–160
Reda, Jackie, 154, 156–160

Reutimann, David, 207
Rhodes, Anne Marie, 270–275
Richmond International
Raceway, 28, 29, 30–32,
34, 71, 74, 75, 78, 87, 95,
105–108
Richmond, Tim, 23, 187, 188
Robbins, Barbie, 123–128
Roberts, Fireball, 23, 37, 217
Rockingham Raceway, 23, 33
Ross, Diana, 217, 218
Rountree, Al, 116
Roush, Jack, 201
Roy, Spencer and Stephanie,
104–108
Rudd, Ricky, 261, 266, 267, 268
Russ Friedman 400, 71–73

Sacks, Greg, 186, 187, 190
Sadler, Elliot, 101, 115, 119,
120, 238
Santiago, Lenny, 160
Sather, Natalie, 255–260
Sather, Tessa, 258, 259
Sawyer, Elton, 268
Sawyer, Paul, 30
Schecter, Thomas, 266
Schultz, Rusty, 173
Schulz, Bill, 245
Scott, Tony, 187, 189–191
Scott, Wendell Jr., 257
Shandwick, Weber, 83
Sicking, Dean, 235
Sills, Jimmie, 98
Simpson, Bill, 266
Simpson, Don, 191
Smith, Dean, 250
Smith, Shawn, 14
Southern 500, 33
Spencer, Jimmy, 155
Spraker Racing, 207
Stafford Motor Speedway, 59
Starr, David, 155
Steward, Sandy, 228, 232
Stewart, Tony, 9, 10, 19, 24,
74, 84, 88, 89, 98, 101,
104–108, 113, 129–133,
141, 144–146, 157, 166,
168, 228, 240, 242–245,
274, 283
Striley, Joe, 13

Talladega Superspeedway, 39,
57, 60, 66, 69, 87, 128, 148,
150, 151, 153, 179, 182,
250, 281, 291, 294

Tebow, Tim, 19
Texas Motor Speedway, 53,
144, 146, 176, 177, 179,
180, 233, 282
Thomas, Ronnie, 38
Towne, Robert, 186–188
Tri-County Motor Speedway,
217
Truex, Martin Jr., 83, 211
Turner, Curtis, 23–25, 37

Vandebosch, Ingrid, 116
Vickers, Brian, 73, 236, 239,
242, 265
Volusia Speedway, 186

Wall Township Speedway, 59
Wallace, George, 23
Wallace, Rusty, 32, 69, 186,
190, 191, 254
Wallace, Steve, 247
Waltrip, Darrell, 31, 32, 80, 272
Waltrip, Michael, 24, 92, 96,
98–101, 136, 207, 208, 247
Watkins Glen International,
79, 82, 87, 89, 90, 143, 144,
160, 186, 282
Weatherly, Joe, 37, 38
Wheldon, Dan, 266
Williams, Brian, 56–61, 189
Williams, Douglas, 58–60
Willmott, April, 74, 77, 78
Willow Springs Raceway, 184
Winston 500, 60
Wiseman, Shannon, 275
Woodward Dream Cruise, 84
World 600, 31, 216
Wright
Anne and Susan, 31
Jerry, 28, 31
Karen, 27
Mike, 13–35

Yarborough, Cale, 209, 231,
252, 253
Yarbrough, LeeRoy, 37

Zipadelli, Greg, 143–146, 243
Zipadelli, Nanette, 144, 145
Zucker, Gillian, 128